POPE FRANCIS

The Gospel of Luke

D0841677

The Gospel of Luke

A Spiritual and Pastoral Reading

Foreword by Sandra M. Schneiders, IHM

ORBIS BOOKS

Maryknoll, New York 10545

Founded in 1970, Orbis Books endeavors to publish works that enlighten the mind, nourish the spirit, and challenge the conscience. The publishing arm of the Maryknoll Fathers and Brothers, Orbis seeks to explore the global dimensions of the Christian faith and mission, to invite dialogue with diverse cultures and religious traditions, and to serve the cause of reconciliation and peace. The books published reflect the views of their authors and do not represent the official position of the Maryknoll Society. To learn more about Maryknoll and Orbis Books, please visit our website at www.maryknollsociety.org.

Library of Congress Cataloging-in-Publication Data

Names: Francis, Pope, 1936- author.
Title: The Gospel of Luke : a spiritual and pastoral reading / Pope Francis.
Description: English edition. | Maryknoll, New York : Orbis Books, [2021] | "Edited and adapted from the original Italian publication: Luca: Il Vangelo del Padre misericordioso © 2019 by Libreria Editrice Vaticana, Citta del Vaticano and Edizioni San Paolo s.r.l., Cinisello Balsamo (Milano)." | Includes bibliographical references and index. | Summary: "The Gospel of Luke is a pastoral commentary on the Gospel by Pope Francis, drawn from his homilies, writings, and speeches since he was elected pope" —Provided by publisher.
Identifiers: LCCN 2021005410 (print) | LCCN 2021005411 (ebook) | ISBN 9781626984325 (trade paperback) | ISBN 9781608338955 (epub)
Subjects: LCSH: Bible. Luke—Commentaries.
Classification: LCC BS2595.53 .F73 2021 (print) | LCC BS2595.53 (ebook) | DDC 226.4/07—dc23
LC record available at https://lccn.loc.gov/2021005410

Contents

CONTENTS

Foreword

by Sandra M. Schneiders, IHM

Since shortly after the completion of the New Testament around the turn of the first Christian century there have been people, scholars as well as lay readers, who have desired to "harmonize" the Gospels, that is, to create a single document incorporating, hopefully in a non-contradictory but complementary way, the three Synoptic (i.e., "similar view") Gospels of Matthew, Mark, and Luke, to create a single "Jesus story." (John's Gospel is so distinctive that it tended to be seen as a kind of "backbone" or outline for the desired "harmonized" narrative with attention paid to certain places where John resembles more closely the Synoptics, e.g., in the chronology of the Passion.)

Although a number of "synopses" or parallel presentations of the Gospels have been produced and serve important functions in the study of the New Testament, the project of producing a single "harmonized Gospel" has never been successfully realized nor the project itself officially approved by the Church and, we can safely say, never will be. Scholars use "synopses" or "harmonies" which place the three (or four) Gospels in their integrity in parallel columns so that they can see where the Gospels "agree" or are even verbally identical, and where they "disagree" in wording and vary in chronology, even in substance. This supplies important information not only about the historical facts referenced in the texts but about the concerns of the different evangelists as well as their respective communities at the time of the writing of the individual Gospels.

These "comparisons" also bear witness to the richness of the Jesus material, which overflows the boundaries of a single text, a richness that is well captured by the three volumes in this series which present the three Synoptic Gospels through the eyes, heart, and preaching of Pope Francis. While there are apparent and even significant variations having to do with time, place, actions, words of Jesus and others, theological "slants" on various aspects of Jesus's ministry, and so on, there is substantial consistency in what the three Gospels present as the life and teaching of Jesus. So why has the "Synoptic project" of turning the four accounts (or at least the three Synoptic Gospels) into one basic, fully consistent story never actually been realized?

There is a very good reason, which these three volumes of Pope Francis's teaching and preaching on the first three Gospels demonstrates, and it has to do with God's mode of revelation rather than with literary or theological problems with the texts, much less internal contradictions in Jesus's teaching or modeling of human life in God. It is not because Jesus lived or offered an inconsistent or even self-contradictory example or message. Nor is it that one or another of the evangelists had a more accurate source of Jesus-material for the writing of his (or her?) Gospel. Rather, it is because Jesus—truly human as he was truly divine— was, as all humans to some degree are, a rich and highly complex character. And he was experienced, as all well-developed humans are, differently by his diverse contemporaries and interlocutors. No one biography or interpretive study, even of ordinary but especially of extraordinary, human beings, can capture all the richness, all the nuance, of the persons presented and all the complexity of their actions and relationships. So, the reader who is fascinated by such a character will want to read several biographies and even fictionalized historical accounts and third-person interpretations of the person in question.

But the Gospels are an even more complicated phenomenon. They are not "biographies" in the usual sense of the word (although they do truthfully, albeit selectively, recount the life and work of Jesus) but theological/spiritual inspired *interpretations* of Jesus as Son of God incarnate and of his once-for-all universal salvific work. The Church has preserved the four canonical accounts because individually they provide different, but essential, interpretations of that saving enterprise. Both their diversity and their complementarity are important for the formation of our picture of and relationship to Jesus who lived historically among his contemporaries but lives also, sacramentally and spiritually, among his disciples down through the ages since the Resurrection. Reading the Gospels is not about studying a figure of the past, like Saint Teresa of Avila or Saint Francis of Assisi. It is a way of encountering the living Person, Jesus, who is present to us in Word and Sacrament as he was to his contemporaries in the flesh. Francis's reflections on Jesus's message, as presented in the various Gospels, teaches his readers how to "hear" the Gospels, not as discordant but as marvelously rich and variegated.

In recent times, scholars have become aware that there is another dimension of the "Synoptic" question that may be even more interesting, if not more important, for contemporary readers than the historical question of how the diverse Gospels are related to each other in giving us a rounded and in-depth picture of Jesus's person, ministry, and message. This Orbis series, collecting the dispersed discourses of Pope Francis based on each of the three Synoptic Gospels as they are incorporated into the liturgy and other occasions of preaching and teaching throughout the Church year, is a prime instance of this other fascinating feature of the variegated New Testament witness to Jesus. The Gospels present not only the one *mission and ministry of Jesus*, his actions and teaching in all their diversity and unity, but the one *person, Jesus,* in three very distinctive ways.

Without creating three "Jesuses," the evangelists give us three "takes" on the human incarnation of God in Jesus of Nazareth. The three volumes of this collection, each devoted to Pope Francis's preaching on one of the Synoptic Gospels, give us the pope's personal grasp of these three "Jesus portraits" that, not surprisingly, give us a fascinating and inspiring insight into how Jesus has been assimilated by and into the life and teaching of this charismatic pope. Reading these volumes of Francis's meditations and preaching on the three Synoptic Gospels offers us a deep insight into who Jesus is for Pope Francis. What dimensions, aspects, concerns of the scriptural Jesus have spoken most deeply to Francis, shaped the person, the pastor, the leader that he has become and now is for the universal Church, and whom God has chosen to lead the People of God at this particular juncture in world history? I would venture a guess, on the basis of these selections, that Luke may be this Pope's "favorite" Gospel.

I suggest—although it cannot be more than a heuristic hypothesis—that one of the fascinating characteristics of this pope, and an important key to his originality in relation to his immediate predecessors and to his continuity with Pope John XXIII, the instigator and architect of Vatican II, is that, more pointedly than his immediate predecessors, Francis seems to have internalized and perhaps privileges, in a certain way, the Lukan portrait of Jesus. (Most serious readers of the New Testament probably have a "favorite Jesus" among the gospel portraits, whether they are aware of it or not, which brings Francis close to us in our own spiritual journeys.) Let me make a few suggestions about reading Francis's reflections on Luke that readers of this volume might find helpful in relation to their own meditation on the three volumes of this collection. Together they raise a question for the reader: Which synoptic portrait of Jesus resonates most profoundly in my own spirituality?

The evangelist "Luke" (we do not know who this writer was or if his/her name was "Luke") is thought by most commentators to have been not a Jew by birth but a Gentile convert to Christianity, writing later than Matthew and Mark, thus toward the end of the first Christian century (between 70 and 90 CE?). Luke's intended audience seems to be not only born Jews, but perhaps especially Gentiles interested in or converted to Judaism or directly to Christianity; in other words, to people either knowledgeable of God's history with the Jewish people or open to seeing the pattern of this history of promise and fulfillment as Luke presents it.

The sophisticated Greek of Luke's text, the literary quality of Luke's composition, the highly developed and self-consistent theology in this Gospel, and the stated purpose and evident structure of the text to achieve that purpose, suggest that the author was an educated writer (and even "researcher" to use a modern concept) addressing an educated audience who could be presumed to be familiar with the Hebrew Scriptures and history. In this respect, Luke can have a particular appeal to today's Gospel readers who are often, themselves, not professional theologians or religious specialists but who are educated and experienced people seeking guidance amid complicated, diverse, and multifaceted lives.

The cosmopolitan and literary background and tone of Luke's Gospel would account for a number of the most interesting features of this Gospel, for example, Luke's emphasis on the continuity of God's plan of salvation realized in the pattern of promise and fulfillment in human history; Luke's interest in the socially "marginalized" such as the poor, women, foreigners, and the sinful or diseased outcast; and Luke's privileging of the "upset" of human evaluations of negativities—poverty, slavery, discrimination, exclusion, suffering—by a God who chooses to exalt the lowly, free the imprisoned, include the outcast, welcome the strayed, heal the afflicted, and transfigure suffering seen not as God's punishment of the guilty but as a privileged locus of God's sharing and healing, in Jesus, of our human condition.

What Francis highlights so powerfully in his preaching on this Gospel is the theme, so dear to Luke, of God's mercy, God's indefatigable quest for the lost, God's unmerited and even rejected welcome of the strayed and the stubborn, and, above all, God's endless tenderness in embracing the broken, the wounded, the rebellious, the ignorant, the resistant. If we had nothing but Francis's homilies on Luke 15—the mercy parables—we would have a marvelous insight into this pope's image of the infinitely merciful God who is to be the model for all Christians but most especially of anyone called, in the Church, to lead and shepherd God's people.

Luke, among the Gospels, is perhaps the most intentionally "historical" of the four, but history, for Luke, is not just "what happens in time." It is the locus of the appearance of the Holy in time and space, that is, of divine revelation. God reveals Godself most completely in history in the action of the Holy Spirit through God's chosen one, Jesus. The oft-highlighted pattern of "promise and fulfillment" under the powerful action of the Holy Spirit both foretold and interpreted in prophecy is thematic in Luke's overtly theologized treatment of the historical Jesus in his earthly career. And prophecy appears, therefore, not as a kind of fortune-telling (or even future-telling) but as a sensitive insight into the divine plan of salvation that is working itself out in the twists and turns of human experience filled with suffering and salvation. Luke's Gospel has been called the "Gospel of the Holy Spirit" because of its emphasis on history as not simply the "stage" on which the human drama is played out but as the very expression of God's salvific plan and action in the world, that is, of the action of the Spirit of God in human affairs.

Although there is a wide variety of unique features of, and striking theological and spiritual motifs in, Luke's Gospel that could supply much food for meditation and discussion, I highlight a few themes, or motifs, or patterns in this Gospel that might offer some insight into the sometimes surprising (and for some people puzzling or even upsetting) words and actions of Pope Francis. In some ways, Francis's sometimes startling behavior and challenging preaching reminds the attentive observer of the Lukan Jesus. I mention here just a few "franciscan moments," hoping to entice the reader to revisit in these pages Francis's sometimes jolting, but deeply evangelical, takes on contemporary life in the Church and in the world. When our customary "pious ears" are tempted to take offense at Francis's interpretations, we might find ourselves in the company of Jesus's "pious hearers" as presented in the Gospel of Luke!

One of Jesus's primary means of teaching, especially in the Synoptic Gospels, is the use of parables, that is, of "likely (or loaded) stories," in which the reader identifies with one or another of the characters and then finds him or herself on the "short end" of the interpretive stick when the real meaning of the story emerges. For example, in Luke's world (as in ours?), wealth is often a sign, if not of overt divine favor, at least of the worth or merit of the industrious and talented rich in comparison with the poor who could have/should have made a better life for themselves if they had been as hard-working, pious, energetic, ingratiating, or even cunning as their richer neighbors. But Luke's Jesus seems to prefer, even assign greater favor in God's eyes to, the poor, both the materially poor and the spiritually wanting.

At the beginning of the Gospel, Mary's "Magnificat" sings of her true greatness that is rooted in her lowliness, her weakness, her hunger, which are met by the exaltation, the mercy, the gratuitous generosity of God, even to calling her to be *mother* of God's own Son.

In parables like that of the rich man and Lazarus, we witness the reversal of fates when the despised poor man, Lazarus, ends up in the bosom of Abraham while the esteemed and self-satisfied rich man finds himself consumed in the flames of eternal suffering.

Another story, found only in Luke, is that of the grasping tax-collector, Zacchaeus, whose eagerness to "see Jesus" leads to Jesus's acceptance of Zacchaeus's hospitality, even incurring "impurity" by his association with the Lawbreaker, and the latter's resultant conversion from dishonesty and greed to justice and generosity. The same pattern is seen in the story of the "unworthy publican" in the temple whose self-abasing humility finds forgiveness and favor with the God who has little time for the self-promoting Pharisee calling God's attention to his "remarkable" virtues.

Perhaps the most striking and touching articulation of this theme is the story of the so-called "prodigal son," who finds in the welcoming and forgiving arms of the truly "Prodigal Father" the real meaning of God's astounding preferential mercy toward sinners.

In Luke's Gospel, Jesus eats with sinners, welcomes non-Jews, touches "unclean" lepers, allows the unclean to touch him, and refuses to condemn the lawbreakers. And his contemporaries (like some of Francis's official "keepers" or unofficial critics) are scandalized at Jesus's upsetting of good religious and social order. As we read in this volume, some of Francis's homilies and talks, and even more disconcertingly, perhaps, watch his public behavior, we cannot fail to hear the socially and religiously disruptive Jesus who put people before laws and customs without disqualifying or nullifying the latter. For us, Francis raises some of the questions of Jesus's Lukan critics: If the law comes from God, how can it be part of God's plan that people who are lawbreakers be preferred at times to the law itself or found equally acceptable to God as those whose behavior, in their own estimation and that of objective observers, is irreproachable—and *who* (in the Temple of Jesus's time or the Vatican of our own) is competent to decide when and how such is the case?

Another closely related characteristic of Jesus in Luke's Gospel that throws an unsettling light on some of our religiously based proclivities is what some have called, His "status-inversions." Jesus, in Luke, is not only deliberately inclusive, choosing, for example, to share table fellowship with social and religious undesirables, but to present a Samaritan (a heretic!) as the moral superior of a pious and law-observant Jewish "cleric," who passes the mugged stranger on the other side of the street; a poor person as dearer to God than a self-promoting rich man in a society that saw riches as a sign of divine approval; a Gentile or Samaritan more true to Torah than an irreproachably law-abiding, even office-holding, Jew. (The problems with these rich people or "Jews" is not that they are rich or that they are Jews, but that they saw their God-given wealth and Jewish chosenness as a title of superiority rather than a free gift of God.) But Jesus, on his own initiative, eats with sinners, touches lepers, exalts the lowly, and associates with women, children, and foreigners. When we listen to Francis asking, "Who am I to judge?" in what seems like an open-and-shut case of immorality, or preaching acceptance of, outreach to, and friendship with—even an effort to learn from—non-Christians rather than promoting efforts to convert them, drinking from a cup offered him by an unvetted stranger in the crowd in St. Peter's piazza, washing the feet of convicted criminals in a prison rather than of fellow clerics in a basilica, it is hard not to hear Luke's Gospel playing in the background.

An extraordinary feature of Jesus's inclusiveness and status-inversion, one especially important for our times, is the role in his life, as presented in Luke's Gospel, of women. In Jesus's patriarchal society, women fared less well even than in our own. But from the shift of the reader's attention from Jesus's human father and patriarchal lineage (as we find it in Matthew's Gospel) to his virgin Mother to whom alone his birth is announced and who, independently of male consultation or permission, advice, or intervention, accepts the role of parent of the Messiah, we witness, in Luke, a thematic treatment of women as adult religious subjects, independently related to and cherished by God who does not seek male approbation for God's choices nor require women to do so in responding to God.

There are other characteristics of Luke's Gospel that make it especially thought-provoking and challenging for contemporary Christian readers, but these salient "Lukan" features which emerge in Francis's teaching and example suffice, I hope, to invite (and entice) readers to find in this volume of his Luke-based preaching and writing a characteristic of this pope that is both consoling and challenging. Like his Master and Mentor, Pope Francis has a knack for unsettling the self-satisfied and righteous (who we all are, at times, and far too often) and including and consoling the alienated and oppressed, those judged and found wanting in society and/or Church and among whom we all find ourselves more often than we like to admit. In the best of cases, Francis, like Jesus, makes us aware that each of us is both sinner and cherished child of God, and that Jesus's liberating message is intended not just for "them" (whoever appears in the text) but for us. If there is one message that Francis stresses in his commentaries on the Gospel of Luke, it is that God's pre-eminent characteristic in relation to humans is not justice or power but infinite and indefatigable tenderness and mercy that waits as long as it takes to welcome us into God's parental embrace.

Sandra M. Schneiders, IHM, STD
Professor Emerita of New Testament and Spirituality
Jesuit School of Theology of
Santa Clara University
Berkeley, California

Introduction

DISCOVERING THE MERCIFUL FATHER

by Gianfranco Venturi, SDB

This volume, dedicated to the Gospel of Luke, follows the method already adopted in *The Gospel of Matthew* (2019), the gospel of fulfillment, and *The Gospel of Mark* (2020), the gospel of the secret revealed. This latest volume collects the pope's homilies, reflections, and addresses on Luke's Gospel, the gospel of the merciful Father.

The purpose of this book is primarily for personal enrichment as you meet Jesus in the Gospel of Luke, the one who is the revealer of the merciful Father, and discover, through his word and his gestures, the immense mercy of God.

Therefore, these pages are not intended so much for study, or even for preaching, but for those who want to be guided by Pope Francis, a master of prayerful silence, to enter into a simple and lively intimacy with the one who is the Word "full of grace and truth" (John 1:14), the Word made flesh, the revealer of the heavenly Father's mercy, and become like him too—in word and in concrete deeds —merciful toward every person, without exclusion.

As with the aforementioned volumes, this book does not represent an exegetical or systematic reading of the Gospel of Luke, nor is it a progressive *lectio divina* of passages from the Gospel itself; rather it is a collection of wide and various reflections and meditations of Pope Francis—a Jesuit, superior, pastor, bishop and, today, pope—based on sacred scripture. These written or oral fragments, produced for various occasions, are arranged here following the succession of the chapters of the Gospel of Luke. Together, they provide the reader with Pope Francis's insights or reflections on these texts.

Consequently, we have a commentary with different tones, in which the Word resounds as a light that illuminates personal, ecclesial, and social situations, allowing us to discover the merciful Father and, consequently, inviting us to be "merciful like the heavenly Father," as testified to in Jesus's many gestures of closeness and compassion.

The Gospel of Luke

There are various distinctive threads and emphases running through the Gospel of Luke; that of the merciful Father is primary. From the very first verses, Luke attests that he made "careful research on every circumstance, from the very beginning" (1:2) about what Jesus said and did and wants to introduce each Theophilus (lover of God) to the mystery of God, the merciful Father. As he moves from fragment to fragment through the Gospel of Luke, Pope Francis guides today's "Theophiles" toward this mystery of God's mercy revealed in the words and actions of Jesus of Nazareth.

The Gospel opens with two songs to the God who throughout history has given us signs of his "tenderness and mercy." Zachariah, a priest of the ancient covenant, sings to the God who "granted mercy to the fathers," faithful to the oath made; the last of the prophets prophesied that "because of the tender mercy of our God ... the rising sun will come to us from heaven to shine on those living in darkness and in the shadow of death, to guide our feet into the path of peace" (1:67–79).

Mary, "full of grace," opens the period of the new covenant and magnifies the holiness of God, whose "mercy is for those who fear him from generation to generation" (1:46–55).

Throughout the Gospel, we encounter Jesus's words and actions that reveal the merciful Father who "makes his sun rise on the good and the bad." At the heart of the Gospel, chapter 15, Jesus reveals the love of the Father through his words and actions to the point of giving his entire self.

We can briefly recall the words and actions of this mercy: stop, see (gaze), approach (closeness, proximity), have compassion, care, listen, call, touch, free, heal, resurrect, forgive... What emerges from these pages is the rich mercy of God through the actions and words of Jesus.

Through reflecting on the various passages, we can sense that Pope Francis makes use of a dynamic—never rigid and always creative—which he sums up in three verbs: listen, discern, and live (4:16–21).

Listening to the Word

In leafing through this volume, some readers may ask why various passages or verses appear numerous times. The reason is that each reflection presents Pope Francis's particular way of listening to the word on a given day and in a specific situation in which the word resounds and lives again.... By observing this rule, we can never be rigid, because the situations are different—the same biblical passages or verses always carry an originality, a novelty; they testify to the "hand-in-hand" encounter between the word and the situations in which it is announced, the different ways in which the incarnate Word becomes present through actions.

For example, read and compare the many texts relating to the parable of the Good Samaritan (cf. 10:25–37). The same passage is proclaimed in several situations with different listeners: at the Angelus on Sunday, at the Wednesday audiences, to those who work for mercy, to the popular movements of California, for World Peace Day... to the newly ordained bishops, to the Community of Sant'Egidio.... In each reflection on the same passage, the particular circumstances open the word to new understandings: only in contact with the "people," with concrete situations, is it possible to discover and see the relevance of the word and how it is to be fulfilled in the "present," which is the event of God's mercy today.

All this is possible if—as Pope Francis teaches us—we prepare ourselves "for a profound listening to his word and life," we "pay attention to the details of our daily lives and learn to read events with the eyes of faith, keeping ourselves open to the surprises of the Spirit" (cf. 4:16–21).

Listening with the Heart of the Poor

For Pope Francis, "those who understand the word of God best are the poor, because they do not provide a barrier to this word, which is like a double-edged sword that reaches the heart. And the poorer in spirit we become, the better we understand it." The person who has a full heart is like the rich young man who was unable to listen "because his heart was occupied by riches" (cf. 18:18–23). Only a poor Church knows how to listen and is capable of giving all, like the widow who knows how to wait as "the poor widow of her Lord" (21:1–4). We can listen to the word of God only with an open and poor heart.

Discerning the Word

Listening to the word always in relation to the concrete situations of individuals or groups allows us to know how to discern how God acts, what he asks of us, and how we are to live our everyday life. Reflecting on the passage where Jesus and his disciples approach the funeral procession of the only child of the widow of Nain allows Pope Francis to outline the "development" of the "compassion" that arises from the encounter with suffering and to envisage then a "culture of encounter," which is the fruit of this meeting (cf. 7:11–17). The word allows us to "discern events in the light of the promise of God and helps people to see signs of dawn in the darkness of history."

Listening to the word allows us to discern the signs of the time. Pope Francis urges us: "Do not let yourself be deceived by false messiahs; do not let yourself to be paralyzed by fear." We are "to live the period of waiting as a time of witness and perseverance" (cf. 12:54–56; 21:5–11).

Discernment is born in the heart and mind through prayer, when we put "persons and situations in contact with the divine word spoken by the Spirit." It is in this intimacy that choices and behaviors, both personal and ecclesial, are shaped and made firm. "Only in the silence of prayer can one hear the voice of God, perceive the traces of his language, access his truth" (cf. 12:54–56).

"An essential condition for progressing in discernment is to educate ourselves in God's patience and in his times, which are never ours." He does not "let the fire fall upon the infidels" (cf. 9:53–54), nor does he allow the zealous to "pluck the weeds from the field." Every day, it is up to us to welcome from God the hope that preserves us from every abstraction, because it is hope that allows us to discover the grace hidden in the present without losing sight of the long-suffering of his plan of love that goes beyond us.

Living the Word

Discernment leads to living the word heard today, to fulfilling it, to translating it into concrete gestures—it is "the newness of the present hour, which will excite many and stiffen others." After Mary's discernment in the dialogue with the angel Gabriel, she pronounces her "Yes": "Here am I, the servant of the Lord; let it be with me according to your word" (1:38): thus begins a time of fulfillment, of joy that makes you leap for joy (cf. 1:45).

Today, God "comes to meet us daily, in homes, in the suburbs. ... Keep looking for allies, keep looking for men and women capable of believing, capable of remembering, of feeling part of his people to cooperate with the creativity of the Spirit. God continues to walk our neighborhoods and our streets. He goes everywhere in search of hearts capable of listening to his invitation and of making him become flesh, here and now" (cf. 1:26–38), seeking to invite guests to the kingdom's banquet (14:16–24).

For Pope Francis, the word proclaimed cannot remain without a sequel: it opens and indicates paths to follow, expanded horizons. It does not ignore the difficulties of "fulfilling" the word but calls for courage, trusting in the power of the Spirit, who makes every event fruitful. This is why Pope Francis nearly always ends his reflections by suggesting questions or ideas for an examination of conscience, which become further indications of how the word listened to can be fulfilled in our today.

To Be Merciful Like the Father

Listening to the word, the testimony of Jesus, traces the path of mercy and urges all of us to follow it without delay, to be merciful like the Father, to forgive (cf. 6:27–38), and to accept the mandate to evangelize with the word and with our lives (cf. 24:44–49).

Translated and adapted from the original introduction
by Gianfranco Venturi, SDB

1

Announcement

In this gospel passage we notice a contrast between the promises of the angel and Mary's response. This contrast is manifested in the form and content of the words spoken by the two protagonists. The angel says to Mary: "Do not be afraid, Mary, for you have found favor with God. And now, you will conceive in your womb and bear a son, and you will name him Jesus. He will be great and will be called the Son of the Most High, and the Lord God will give to him the throne of his ancestor David. He will reign over the house of Jacob forever" (vv. 30–33). It is a long statement, and it opens unprecedented possibilities. The child that will be born to this humble girl from Nazareth will be called Son of the Most High. It is not possible to conceive of a higher dignity than this. After Mary, seeking an explanation, asks her question, the angel's revelation becomes even more detailed and surprising.

Mary's reply to this is a short sentence that does not speak of glory. It does not speak of privilege but only of willingness and service: "Here am I, the servant of the Lord; let it be with me according to your word" (v. 38). The content is also different. Presented with the prospect of becoming the mother of the Messiah, Mary does not exalt herself but rather remains modest and expresses her acceptance of the Lord's plan. Mary does not boast. She is humble and modest. She always remains the same.

This contrast is meaningful. It makes us understand that Mary is truly humble and does not try to be noticed. She recognizes that she is small before God and that she is happy to be so. At the same time, she is aware that the fulfillment of God's plan depends on her response, and that therefore she is being called to accept it with her whole being.

In this circumstance, Mary's behavior corresponds perfectly to that of the Son of God when he comes into the world. He wants to become the Servant of the Lord, to put himself at the service of humanity to fulfill the Father's plan. Mary says: "Here am I, the servant of the Lord"; and the Son of God upon entering the world says: "Behold, I have come to do your will, O God" (Heb 10:7). Mary's attitude fully mirrors the statement of the Son of God who also becomes the son of Mary. Thus, the Madonna shows that she is in perfect accord with God's plan. Furthermore, she reveals herself as a disciple of his Son, and in the *Magnificat*, she will be able to proclaim that God has "lifted up the lowly" (Luke 1:52), because with her humble and generous response she has obtained great joy and also great glory.

As we admire our Mother for this response to God's call to mission, we ask her to help each of us to welcome God's plan into our lives with sincere humility and brave generosity.

Full of Grace (1:28)[2]

Today we are contemplating the beauty of Mary Immaculate. The gospel, which recounts the episode of the Annunciation, helps us to understand what we are celebrating, above all through the angel's greeting. He addresses Mary with a phrase that is not easy to translate, which means "filled with grace," "created by grace," "full of grace" (cf. Luke 1:28). Before calling her "Mary," he calls her full of grace, thus revealing the new name that God has given her, a name that is mor fitting than the name given to her by her parents. We too call her by this name in each Hail Mary.

What does "full of grace" mean? That Mary is filled with the presence of God. And if she is entirely inhabited by God, there is no room within her for sin. It is an extraordinary thing, because everything in the world, regrettably, is contaminated by evil. Each of us, looking within ourselves, sees dark sides. Even the greatest saints were sinners, and in reality all things—even the most beautiful things—are corroded by evil: everything, except Mary. She is the one "evergreen oasis" of humanity, the only one uncontaminated, created immaculate so as to fully welcome— with her "yes"—God come into the world, and thus to begin a new history.

Each time we acknowledge her as full of grace, we give her the greatest compliment, the same one God gave her. It is a beautiful compliment to give to a woman, to tell her, politely, that she looks youthful. In a certain sense, whenever we say "full of grace" to Mary, we are telling her this too, at the highest level. In fact, we recognize her as forever youthful, because she never aged through sin. There is only one thing that makes us age, grow old interiorly: not time, but sin. Sin ages, because it hardens the heart. It closes it, renders it inert, withers it. But she, being full of grace, is without sin. So she is always youthful; she is "younger than sin" and is "our youngest little sister."[3]

The Church today calls Mary "all fair," *tota pulchra*. Just as her youth does not lie in time, her beauty does not consist in her outward appearance. Mary, as today's gospel reading shows us, does not stand out in appearance. Coming from a simple family, she lived humbly in Nazareth, a village practically unknown. And she herself wasn't well-known: even when the angel visited her, no one knew of it; there were no reporters there that day. Nor did Our Lady have a comfortable life. She had worries and fears. She was "greatly troubled" (v. 29), the gospel says, and when the angel "departed from her" (v. 38), her troubles mounted.

However, being full of grace, she lived a beautiful life. What was her secret? We learn what it was by looking again at the scene of the Annunciation. In many paintings Mary is depicted as seated before the angel with a small book in her hand. This book is the scriptures. Mary was accustomed to listening to God and interacting with him. The Word of God was her secret: close to her heart, it then became flesh in her womb. By dwelling with God, in dialogue with him in every circumstance, Mary made her life beautiful. What makes life beautiful is not appearances, not what is fleeting, but a heart directed toward God. Today, let us look joyfully at her, full of grace. Let us ask her to help us to remain youthful by saying "no" to sin, and to live a beautiful life by saying "yes" to God.

Don't Be Afraid (1:30)[4]

Let us try to listen to the voice of God who inspires courage and bestows the grace needed to respond to his call: "Do not be afraid, Mary, for you have found favor with God" (Luke 1:30). These are the words addressed by God's messenger, the archangel Gabriel, to Mary, an ordinary girl from a small village in Galilee.

Mary's Disturbance

As is understandable, the sudden appearance of the angel and his mysterious greeting: "Hail, favored one! The Lord is with you" (Luke 1:28), strongly disturbed Mary, who was surprised by this first revelation of her identity and her vocation, which as yet had been unknown to her. Mary, like others in the sacred scriptures, trembles before the mystery of God's call, who in a moment places before her the immensity of his own plan and makes her feel all her smallness as a humble creature. The angel, seeing into the depths of her heart, says: "Do not be afraid!" God also reads our inmost heart. He knows well the challenges we must confront in life, especially when we are faced with the fundamental choices that determine who we will be and what we will do in this world. It is the "shudder" that we feel when faced with decisions about our future, our state of life, our vocation. In these moments we are troubled and seized by so many fears.

And you, young people, what are your fears? What worries you most deeply? An "underlying" fear that many of you have is that of not being loved, well-liked, or accepted for who you are. Today, there are many young people who feel the need to be different from who they really are in an attempt to adapt to an often artificial and unattainable standard. They continuously "Photoshop" their images, hiding behind masks and false identities, almost becoming fake selves. Many are obsessed by receiving as many "likes" as possible. Multiple fears and uncertainties emerge from this sense of inadequacy. Others fear that they will not be able to find emotional security and that they will remain alone. Many, faced with uncertainties regarding work, fear not being able to find a satisfactory professional position, not being able to fulfill their dreams. A large number of young people today, both believers and non-believers, are full of fear. Indeed, those who have accepted the gift of faith and seriously seek to find their vocation are not exempt from fears. Some think: Perhaps God is asking or will ask too much of me; perhaps, by following the road he has marked out for me, I will not be truly happy, or I will not be able to do what he asks of me. Others think: If I follow the path that God shows me, who can guarantee that I will be able to stay the course? Will I become discouraged? Will I lose my enthusiasm? Will I be able to persevere for the rest of my life?

In moments when doubts and fears flood our hearts, discernment becomes necessary. It allows us to bring order to the confusion of our thoughts and feelings, to act in a just and prudent way. In this process, the first step in overcoming fears is to identify them clearly, so as not to find ourselves wasting time and energy by being gripped by empty and faceless ghosts. And so, I invite all of you to look within yourselves and to "name" your fears. Ask yourselves: What upsets me? What do I fear most in this specific moment of my life today? What blocks me and prevents me from moving forward? Why do I lack the courage to make the important choices I need to make?

Do not be afraid to face your fears honestly, to recognize them for what they are, and to come to terms with them. The Bible does not ignore the human experience of fear nor its many causes: Abraham was afraid (cf. Gen 12:10ff); Jacob was afraid (cf. Gen 31:31; 32:7); and so were Moses (cf. Exod 2:14; 17:4), Peter (cf. Matt 26:69ff), and the apostles (cf. Mark 4:38–40; Matt 26:56). Jesus himself, albeit in a different way, experienced fear and anguish (cf. Matt 26:37; Luke 22:44).

Discernment is indispensable when searching for one's vocation in life. More often than not, our vocation is not obvious or evident at first but rather is something we come to understand gradually. Discernment, in this case, should not be seen as an individual effort at introspection, with the aim of better understanding our interior make-up so as to become stronger and acquire some balance. In such instances, the person can grow stronger but is still confined to the limited horizon of his or her possibilities and perspectives. Vocation, however, is a call from above, and discernment in this context principally means opening ourselves to the Other who calls. Prayerful silence is therefore required in order to hear the voice of God that resounds within our conscience. God knocks at the door of our hearts, as he did with Mary. He longs to establish friendship with us through prayer, to speak with us through the sacred scriptures, to offer us mercy in the sacrament of reconciliation, and to be one with us in the Eucharist.

"Let it be" Signifies Hope (1:38)[5]

Let us contemplate the one who knew and loved Jesus like no other creature. The gospel reading that we heard reveals the fundamental way Mary expressed her love for Jesus: by doing the will of God. "For whoever does the will of my Father in heaven is my brother and sister and mother" (Matt 12:50). With these words Jesus leaves us with an important message: the will of God is the supreme law that establishes true belonging to him. That is how Mary established a bond of kinship with Jesus even before giving birth to him. She became both disciple and mother to the Son at the moment she received the words of the angel and said: "Here am I, the servant of the Lord; let it be with me according to your word" (Luke 1:38). This "let it be" is not only acceptance but also a trustful openness to the future. This "let it be" is hope!

Bringing the Presence of God (1:39)[6]

Like Mary, never tire of "going out," of going in haste to en-counter and bring others the presence of God (cf. Luke 1:39). She brings the presence of God because she is in profound commun-ion with him. "Blessed is she who believed" (Luke 1:45), Eliza-beth says to her. Mary is the icon of faith. Only in faith does one bear Jesus rather than oneself. As we strive to follow the path of the works of mercy, we are called to renew ourselves in faith. To bring the Lord's presence to those who suffer in body and spirit, we must cultivate the faith, a faith that is born of listening to the word of God and seeking profound communion with Jesus.

The Visitation (1:39–45)[7]

In the gospel mystery of the Visitation, we can see an icon of all Christian volunteer work. Let me present you with three atti-tudes shown by Mary as an aid to interpreting the experience of these days and as an inspiration for your future commitment to service. These three attitudes are listening, deciding, and acting.

First, listening. Mary sets out after hearing the word of the angel: "Your relative Elizabeth in her old age has also conceived a son." (Luke 1:36). Mary knows how to listen to God. It is not sim-ply about hearing, but about listening attentively and responsibly.

The second attitude of Mary is deciding. Mary listens and reflects, but she also knows how to take a step forward: she is decisive. This was the case with the fundamental decision of her life: "Here am I, the servant of the Lord; let it be with me according to your word" (Luke 1:38).

Finally, acting. Mary set out on her journey and "went with haste" (Luke 1:39). Despite the hardships and the criticisms she may have heard, she didn't hesitate or delay, but "went with haste," because she had the strength of God's Word within her. Her way of acting was full of charity, full of love: this is the mark of God.

In volunteer work too, every act of service we provide, even the simplest, is important. Ultimately, service is an expression of openness to the presence of Jesus. It is the experience of love from on high that set us on our way and fills us with joy. World Youth Day volunteers are not only a "workers" but also evangelizers, because the Church exists and serves to evangelize.

Once Mary had finished assisting Elizabeth, she went back home to Nazareth. Quietly and with no fuss, she left in the same way that she came. You too, dear volunteers, will not see all the fruits of your work here in Krakow.... Your brothers and sisters whom you served will bear those fruits in their lives and rejoice in them. That is the "gratuitousness" of love! Yet God knows your dedication, your commitment, and your generosity. You can be sure that he will not fail to repay you for everything you have done for this Church of the young. I commend you to God and to the word of his grace (cf. Acts 20:32). I entrust you to Mary, our Mother—the model of all Christian volunteer service. And I ask you, please, to remember to pray for me.

MAGNIFICAT (1:39–56)[8]

Today, the solemnity of the Assumption of the Blessed Virgin Mary, the gospel reading introduces us to the young woman of

Nazareth who, having received the angel's message, leaves in haste to be closer to Elizabeth in the final months of her miraculous pregnancy. Arriving at Elizabeth's home, Mary hears her utter the words that have come to form the "Hail Mary" prayer: "Blessed are you among women, and blessed is the fruit of your womb" (Luke 1:42). In fact, the greatest gift Mary brings to Elizabeth—and to the whole world—is Jesus, who already lives within her; and he lives not only through faith and through expectation, as in many women of the Old Testament; from the Virgin, Jesus took on human flesh for his mission of salvation.

In the home of Elizabeth and her husband Zechariah, where sadness once reigned for lack of children, there is now the joy of a child on the way, a child who will become the great John the Baptist, the precursor of the Messiah. And when Mary arrives, joy overflows in their hearts, because the invisible but real presence of Jesus fills everything with meaning: life, family, the salvation of the people. Everything!

This joy is expressed in Mary's words in the marvelous prayer that the Gospel of Luke has conveyed to us and which, from the first Latin word, is called *Magnificat*. It is a song of praise to God who works great things through humble people, unknown to the world, as is Mary herself, as is her spouse Joseph, and as is the place where they live, Nazareth; the great things God has done with humble people, the great things the Lord does in the world with the humble, because humility is like an open space that leaves room for God. The humble are powerful because they are humble, not because they are strong. And this is the greatness of the humble and of humility. I would like to ask you—and also myself (but do not answer out loud—each of us can respond in our heart): "How is my humility?"

The *Magnificat* praises the merciful and faithful God who accomplishes his plan of salvation through the little ones and the poor, through those who have faith in him, who trust in his word as did Mary. Here is the exclamation of Elizabeth: "Blessed is she who believed" (Luke 1:45). In that house, the coming of Jesus through Mary created not only a climate of joy and fraternal communion, but also a climate of faith that leads to hope, prayer, and praise.

We would like to have all of this happen today in our homes too. Celebrating Mary most holy assumed into heaven, we would once again wish her to bring to us, to our families, to our communities, this immense gift, this unique grace that we must always seek first and above all the other graces that we also long for in our hearts: the grace that is Jesus Christ!

By bearing Jesus, Our Lady also brings us a new joy full of meaning; she brings us a new ability to traverse with faith the most painful and difficult moments; she brings us the capacity to be merciful, to forgive each other, to understand each other, and to support each other.

Mary is the model of virtue and of faith. Today, in contemplating her Assumption into heaven, the final fulfillment of her earthly journey, we thank her because she always precedes us on the pilgrimage of life and faith. She is the first disciple. And we ask her to support us, that we may have a strong, joyful, and merciful faith. May she help us to be saints, to meet with her, one day, in heaven.

GREAT ASTONISHMENT (1:40)[9]

The gospel highlights the figure of Mary. We see her when, just after having conceived in faith the Son of God, she makes the long trip from Nazareth, in Galilee, to the hill country of Judah, to visit and help her cousin, Elizabeth. The angel Gabriel had revealed to her that her elderly relative, who did not have children, was in her sixth month of pregnancy (cf. Luke 1:26–36). That is why Our Lady, who carried within her a gift and an even greater mystery, goes to see Elizabeth and stays with her for three months. In the meeting between these two women — one old and the other young — it is the young one, Mary, who offers the first greeting. The gospel says: "she entered the house of Zechariah and greeted Elizabeth" (Luke 1:40). After this greeting, Elizabeth feels enveloped in great *astonishment*—don't forget this word, astonishment. Elizabeth feels enveloped in great astonishment that is echoed in these words: "And why has this happened to me, that the mother of my Lord comes to me" (v. 43). And they embrace and kiss each other, joyfully, these two women. The elderly woman and the young one, both pregnant.

To celebrate Christmas in a fruitful manner, we are called to pause in "places" of astonishment. And what are these places of astonishment in everyday life? There are three.

The first place is the *other*, in whom we recognize a brother or sister, because since the birth of Jesus, every face is marked with a semblance of the Son of God. This is so above all when it is the face of the poor, because God entered the world poor, and it was to the poor, in the first place, that he allowed himself to draw near.

Another place of astonishment—the second place in which, if we look with faith, we actually feel astonishment—is history. So many times we think we see it the right way, and instead we risk reading it backwards. It happens, for example, when history seems to us to be determined by the market economy, regulated by finance and business, dominated by the powers that be. The God of Christmas is instead a God who "shuffles the cards"— and he likes doing so! As Mary sings in the *Magnificat*, it is the Lord who puts down the mighty from their thrones and exalts the lowly, who fills the hungry with good things and sends the rich away empty (cf. Luke 1:52–53). This is the second type of astonishment, astonishment in history.

The third place of astonishment is the *Church*. To look on her with the astonishment of faith means not limiting oneself to consider her only as a religious institution, which she is, but to feel her as a mother who, despite her blemishes and wrinkles—we have so many of them!—allows the features of the beloved bride purified by Christ the Lord to shine through. A Church that is able to recognize the many signs of faithful love that God continuously sends her. A Church for which the Lord Jesus will never be a possession to be jealously protected; those who do this err. The Lord Jesus will always be the One who comes to meet her and for whom she waits with trust and joy, giving voice to the hope of the world. She is the Church that calls to the Lord, "Come Lord Jesus," the Mother Church that always has her doors open wide, her arms open to welcome everyone. Moreover, Mother Church goes out from her own doors to seek with a mother's smile all those who are far away and bring them to the mercy of God. This is the astonishment of Christmas.

At Christmas, God gives us all of himself by giving his Only Son, who is all his joy. It is only with the heart of Mary, the humble and poor daughter of Zion, who became the Mother of the Son of the Most High, that it is possible to rejoice and be glad for the great gift of God and for his unpredictable surprise. May she help us to perceive the astonishment in these three wonders— the other, history, and the Church—through the birth of Jesus, the gift of gifts, the undeserved gift who brings us salvation. The encounter with Jesus will also enable us to feel this great astonishment. We cannot experience it, however, we cannot encounter Jesus, if we do not encounter him in others, in history, and in the Church.

"BLESSED IS SHE WHO BELIEVED" (1:44–45)[10]

"Blessed is she who believed" (v. 45). With these words Elizabeth anointed Mary's presence in her house. Words that were born of her womb, that came from within; words that managed to echo all she experienced with her cousin's visit: "When the voice of your greeting came to my ears, the babe in my womb leaped for joy. And blessed is she who believed."

God visits us in a woman's womb by moving the womb of another woman with a song of blessing and praise, with a song of joy. The gospel scene bears all the dynamism of God's visit: when God comes to encounter us, he moves us inwardly; he sets in motion what we are until our whole life is transformed into praise and blessing. When God visits us, he leaves us restless, with the healthy restlessness of those who feel they have been called to proclaim that he lives and is among his people. This is what we see in Mary, the first disciple and missionary, the new Ark of the Covenant who, far from remaining in the reserved space of our temples, goes out to visit and accompany the gestation of John with her presence. She also did so in 1531: she hastened to Tepeyac to serve and accompany the people who were gestating in pain, becoming their Mother and that of all peoples.

With Elizabeth, today we too wish to anoint and greet her by saying: "Blessed is she who believed" and continues to believe in the "fulfillment of what was spoken to her from the Lord" (v. 45). Mary is thus the icon of the disciple, of the believing and prayerful woman who is able to accompany and encourage our faith and our hope in the various stages through which we must pass. In Mary, we have the faithful reflection "not [of] a poetically sweetened faith, but [of] a strong faith above all in a time in which the sweet enchantments of things are broken and there are conflicting contradictions everywhere."[11]

Certainly we must learn from that strong and helpful faith which characterizes our Mother, learn from that faith that is able to enter our history so as to be salt and light in our lives and in our society.

The society we are building for our children is increasingly marked by signs of division and of fragmentation, casting many aside, especially those who find it difficult to obtain the minimum necessary to lead a dignified life. It is a society that likes to boast of its scientific and technological advances, but that has become blind and insensitive to the thousands of faces who have fallen behind on the path, excluded from the blinding pride of the few; a society that ends up creating a culture of disappointment, disenchantment, and frustration in so many of our brothers and sisters, and even anguish in so many others who find it difficult to remain on the path.

It would seem that, without realizing it, we have become used to living in a "society of distrust" with all that this entails for our present and especially for our future, distrust that grad-ually generates states of apathy and dispersion.

Faced with all these situations, we all must say with Eliza-beth: "Blessed is she who believed" and learn from that strong and helpful faith that characterized and characterizes our Mother.

JUSTICE AND TENDERNESS (1:53)[12]

There is a Marian "style" to the Church's work of evangelization. Whenever we look to Mary, we come to believe once again in the revolutionary nature of love and tenderness. In her, we see that humility and tenderness are not virtues of the weak but of the strong who need not treat others poorly in order to feel important themselves.

Contemplating Mary, we realize that she who praised God for "bringing down the mighty from their thrones" and "sending the rich away empty" (Luke 1:52–53) is also the one who brings an openhearted warmth to our pursuit of justice. She is also the one who carefully "treasures all these words and ponders them in her heart" (Luke 2:19). Mary is able to recognize the traces of God's Spirit in events great and small. She constantly contem-plates the mystery of God in our world, in human history, and in our daily lives. She is the woman of prayer and work in Nazareth, and she is also Our Lady of Help, who sets out from her town "with haste" (Luke 1:39) to be of service to others. This interplay of justice and tenderness, of contemplation and concern for others, is what makes the ecclesial community look to Mary as a model of evangelization. We implore her maternal interces-sion that the Church may become a home for many peoples, a mother for all peoples, and that the way may be opened to the birth of a new world. It is the Risen Christ who tells us, with a power that fills us with confidence and unshakeable hope: "See, I am making all things new" (Rev 21:5).

14

BUILDING ON MEMORY (1:68, 72)[13]

We might wonder: What is the Lord asking us to build *today* in our lives, and even more important, upon what is he calling us to build our lives? In seeking to answer to this question, I would like to suggest that a stable foundation upon which we can tirelessly build and rebuild the Christian life is *memory*.

One grace we can implore is that of being able to remember: to recall what the Lord has done in and for us, and to remind ourselves that, as today's gospel passage says, he has not forgotten us but "remembered" us (Luke 1:72). God has chosen us, loved us, called us, and forgiven us. Great things have happened in our personal love story with him, and these things must be treasured in our minds and hearts. Yet there is another memory we need to preserve: it is the memory of a people. Peoples, like individuals, have a memory. Your own people's memory is ancient and precious. Your voices echo those of past sages and saints; your words evoke those who created your alphabet in order to proclaim God's word; your songs blend the afflictions and the joys of your history. As you ponder these things, you can clearly recognize God's presence. He has not abandoned you. Even in the face of tremendous adversity, we can say in the words of today's gospel that the Lord has visited your people (cf. Luke 1:68). He has remembered your faithfulness to the gospel, the first fruits of your faith, and all those who testified, even at the price of their blood, that God's love is more precious than life itself (cf. Ps 63:4). It is good to recall with gratitude how the Christian faith became your people's life breath and the heart of their historical memory.

2

The Birth of Jesus

THE JOY OF THE GOSPEL (2:7–20)[1]

"The people who walked in darkness have seen a great light" (Isa 9:1). This prophecy of Isaiah never ceases to touch us, especially when we hear it proclaimed in the liturgy of Christmas night. This is not simply an emotional or sentimental matter. It moves us because it states the deep reality of what we are: a people who walk, and all around us—and within us as well—there is darkness and light. In this night, as the spirit of darkness enfolds the world, there takes place anew the event that always amazes and surprises us: the people who walk see a great light— a light that makes us reflect on this mystery: the mystery of *walking* and *seeing*.

Walking...
This word makes us reflect on the course of history, that long journey which is the history of salvation, starting with Abraham, our father in faith, whom the Lord called one day to set out, to go forth from his country toward the land which he would show him. From that time on, our identity as believers has been that of a people making its pilgrim way toward the promised land. This

history has always been accompanied by the Lord! He is ever faithful to his covenant and to his promises because he is faithful; "God is light, and in him there is no darkness at all" (1 John 1:5). Yet on the part of the people there are times of both light and darkness, fidelity and infidelity, obedience and rebellion; times of being a pilgrim people and times of being a people adrift.

In our personal history, too, there are both bright and dark moments, lights and shadows. If we love God and our brothers and sisters, we walk in the light; but if our heart is closed, if we are dominated by pride, deceit, and self-seeking, then darkness falls within us and around us. "Whoever hates another believer" —writes the apostle John—"is in the darkness, walks in the darkness, and does not know the way to go, because the darkness has brought on blindness" (1 John 2:11). We are a people who walk, but as a pilgrim people who do not want to go astray.

... and Seeing

On this night, like a burst of brilliant light, there rings out the proclamation of the apostle Paul: "For the grace of God has appeared, bringing salvation to all" (Tit 2:11).

The grace which was revealed in our world is Jesus, born of the Virgin Mary, true man and true God. He has entered our history; he has shared our journey. He came to free us from darkness and to grant us light. In him was revealed the grace, the mercy, and the tender love of the Father: Jesus is Love incarnate. He is not simply a teacher of wisdom, he is not an ideal for which we strive while knowing that we are hopelessly distant from it. He is the meaning of life and history who has pitched his tent among us.

The shepherds were the first to see this "tent," to receive the news of Jesus's birth. They were the first because they were among the last, the outcast. And they were the first because they were awake, keeping watch in the night, guarding their flocks. The pilgrim is bound by duty to keep watch, and the shepherds did just that. Together with them, let us pause before the Child, let us pause in silence. Together with them, let us thank the Lord for having given Jesus to us, and with them let us raise from the depths of our hearts the praises of his fidelity: We bless you, Lord God most high, who lowered yourself for our sake. You are immense, and you made yourself small; you are rich, and you made yourself poor; you are all-powerful, and you made yourself vulnerable.

On this night let us share the joy of the gospel: God loves us. He so loves us that he gave us his Son to be our brother, to be light in our darkness. To us the Lord repeats: "Do not be afraid!" (Luke 2:10). As the angels said to the shepherds: "Do not be afraid!" And I also repeat to all of you: Do not be afraid! Our Father is patient, he loves us, he gives us Jesus to guide us on the way which leads to the promised land. Jesus is the light who brightens the darkness. He is mercy: our Father always forgives us. He is our peace.

THE TRUE SPIRIT OF CHRISTMAS (2:9)[2]

"The grace of God has appeared, bringing salvation to all" (Tit 2:11). The words of the apostle Paul reveal the mystery of this holy night: the grace of God has appeared, his free gift. In the child given to us, the love of God is made visible.

It is a night of glory—that glory proclaimed by the angels in Bethlehem and by us as well, all over the world. It is a *night of joy*, because henceforth and forever, the infinite and eternal God is *God with us*. He is not far off. We need not search for him in the heavens or in mystical notions. He is close at hand. He became man and he will never withdraw from our humanity, which he has made his own. It is a *night of light*. The light prophesied by Isaiah (cf. Isa 9:1), which was to shine on those who walked in a land of darkness, has appeared and enveloped the shepherds of Bethlehem (cf. Luke 2:9).

Discovering and Contemplating the Sign
The shepherds discover simply that "a child has been born to us" (Isa 9:5). They realize that all this glory, all this joy, all this light,

converges on a single point, the sign that the angel indicated to them: "You will find a child wrapped in bands of cloth and lying in a manger" (Luke 2:12). This is the enduring sign for all who would find Jesus, not just then but also today. If we want to celebrate Christmas authentically, we need to contemplate this sign: the frail simplicity of a tiny newborn child, the meekness with which he is placed in a manger, the tender affection with which he is wrapped in his swaddling clothes. That is where God is.

With this sign, the gospel reveals a paradox. It speaks of the emperor, the governor, the high and mighty of those times, yet God does not make himself present there. He appears not in the splendor of a royal palace but in the poverty of a stable; not in pomp and show but in simplicity of life; not in power but in astonishing smallness. In order to meet him, we need to go where he is. We need to bow down, to humble ourselves, to make ourselves small. The newborn child challenges us. He calls us to leave behind fleeting illusions and to turn to what is essential, to renounce our insatiable cravings, to abandon our endless yearning for things we will never have. We do well to leave such things behind in order to discover in the simplicity of the divine child peace, joy, and the luminous meaning of life.

Let us allow the child in the manger to challenge us, but let us also be challenged by all those children in today's world who are lying not in a crib, caressed with affection by their mothers and fathers, but in squalid "mangers that devour dignity." Children who hide underground to escape bombardment, on the streets of large cities, in the hold of a boat overladen with immigrants. Let us allow ourselves to be challenged by those children who are not allowed to be born, by those who cry because no one relieves their hunger, by those who hold in their hands not toys but weapons.

The mystery of Christmas, which is light and joy, challenges and unsettles us because it is at once a mystery of hope and of sadness. It has a taste of sadness, inasmuch as love is not accepted and life is discarded. Such was the case with Joseph and Mary, who were met with closed doors and placed Jesus in a manger, "because there was no place for them in the inn" (v. 7). Jesus was born rejected by some and regarded by many others with indifference. Today, too, that same indifference can exist whenever Christmas becomes a holiday with ourselves at the center rather than Jesus; when the lights of shop windows push the light of God into the shadows; when we are enthused about gifts but indifferent to our neighbors in need. This worldliness has kidnapped Christmas; we need to liberate it!

A Taste of Hope

Yet Christmas has above all a taste of hope because, for all the darkness in our lives, God's light shines forth. His gentle light does not frighten us. God, who is in love with us, draws us to himself with his tenderness by being born poor and frail in our midst, as one of us. He is born in Bethlehem, which means "house of bread." In this way, he seems to tell us that he is born as bread for us; he enters our life to give us his life; he comes into our world to give us his love. He does not come to devour or to lord it over us, but instead to feed and serve us. There is a straight line between the manger and the cross where Jesus will become bread that is broken. It is the straight line of love that gives and saves, the love that brings light to our lives and peace to our hearts.

That night, the shepherds understood this. They were among the marginalized people of those times. Yet no one is marginalized in the sight of God, and that Christmas they themselves were the guests. People who felt sure of themselves, self-sufficient, were at home with their possessions. It was the shepherds who "set out with haste" (cf. Luke 2:16). Tonight, may we too be challenged and called by Jesus. Let us approach him with trust, starting from all those things that make us feel marginalized, from our limitations and our sins. Let us be touched by the tenderness that saves. Let us draw close to God who draws close to us. Let us pause to gaze upon the crib and relive in our imagination the birth of Jesus: light and peace, dire poverty and rejection. With the shepherds, let us enter into the real Christmas, bringing to

Jesus all that we are, our alienation, our unhealed wounds, our sins. Then, in Jesus, we will enjoy the taste of the true spirit of Christmas: the beauty of being loved by God. With Mary and Joseph, let us pause before the manger, before Jesus who is born as bread for our life. Contemplating his humble and infinite love, let us simply tell him: Thank you. "Thank you because you have done all this for me."

GOD'S BLESSING (2:10)[3]

On the first day of the year, the liturgy celebrates the Holy Mother of God, Mary, the Virgin of Nazareth, who gave birth to Jesus, the Savior. That child is *God's blessing* to each man and woman, to the great human family, and to the whole world. Jesus did not take away the evil of the world, but he defeated it at its root. His salvation is not a magical but rather a "patient" salvation, that is, it requires the patience of love, which takes on inequity and removes its power. The patience of love. Love makes us patient. Often we lose our patience; I do too. This is why by contemplating the nativity scene with the eyes of faith, we see the world renewed, freed from the dominion of evil, and placed under the royal power of Christ, the child who lies in the manger.

This is why today the Mother of God blesses us. And how does Our Lady bless us? By showing us her Son. She takes him in her arms and she shows him to us, and thus, she blesses us. She blesses the entire Church; she blesses the whole world. As the angels sang in Bethlehem, Jesus is a "great joy for all the people"; he is the Glory of God and peace for mankind (cf. Luke 2:10). And this is the reason why Saint Pope Paul VI wished to dedicate the first day of the year to peace—it is the World Day of Peace—to prayer, to becoming conscious of and responsible for peace. The message for this year is that peace is a journey of hope, a journey that moves forward through dialogue, reconciliation, and ecological conversion.

Therefore, let us fix our gaze on the Mother and the Son whom she shows us. At the beginning of the year, let us allow ourselves to be blessed by Our Lady with her Son.

On the first page of the calendar of the new year that the Lord has given us, the Church places, as a splendid illumination, the liturgical solemnity of Mary, the most holy Mother of God. On this first day of the solar year, we fix our gaze on her, to resume, under her maternal protection, the journey along the paths of time.

Today's gospel leads us back to the stable of Bethlehem. The shepherds arrive in haste and find Mary, Joseph, and the baby, and they make known the message given to them by the angels, namely, that that infant is the Savior. All are astonished, while "Mary treasured all these words and pondered them in her heart" (v. 19). The Virgin helps us understand how the event of Christmas is to be welcomed: not superficially but in the heart. She shows us the true way to receive God's gift: to keep it in our heart and ponder it. It is an invitation offered to each of us to pray, contemplating and enjoying this gift that is Jesus himself.

It is through Mary that the Son of God assumes bodily form. But Mary's *motherhood* is not reduced to this. Thanks to her *faith*, she is also the first disciple of Jesus, and this "expands" her motherhood. It will be Mary's faith that provokes the first miraculous "sign" in Cana, which helps to raise the faith of the disciples. With the same faith, Mary is present at the foot of the cross and receives the apostle John as her son; and finally, after the Resurrection, she becomes the prayerful mother of the Church on which the power of the Holy Spirit descends on the day of Pentecost.

Mary Intercedes
As mother, Mary plays a most important role: she places herself between her Son Jesus and the people in the reality of their sacrifices, in the reality of their poverty and suffering. Mary *inter-*

cedes, as in Cana, conscious that as a mother she can, but realizing also that she must make the Son aware of the needs of the people, especially the weakest and most impoverished. The World Day of Peace, which we are celebrating today, is dedicated precisely to these people: "Migrants and refugees: men and women in search of peace." Once again, I want to be the voice of these brothers and sisters of ours and invoke a future horizon of peace.

MARY, OUR GUARDIAN (2:19)[5]

"Mary treasured all these words and pondered them in her heart!" (Luke 2:19). In these words, Luke describes the attitude with which Mary took in all that they had experienced in those days. Far from trying to understand or master the situation, Mary is the woman who can treasure, that is to say, protect and guard in her heart, the passage of God in the life of his people. Deep within, she had learned to listen to the heartbeat of her Son, and that, in turn, taught her, throughout her life, to discover God's heartbeat in history. She learned how to be a mother, and in that learning process she gave Jesus the beautiful experience of knowing what it is to be a Son. In Mary, the eternal Word not only became flesh, but also learned to recognize the maternal tenderness of God. With Mary, the God-child learned to listen to the yearnings, the troubles, the joys and the hopes of the people of the promise. With Mary, he discovered himself a Son of God's faithful people.

In the Gospels, Mary appears as a woman of few words, with no great speeches or deeds, but with an attentive gaze capable of guarding the life and mission of her Son, and for this reason, of everything that he loves. She was able to watch over the beginnings of the first Christian community, and in this way she learned to be the mother of a multitude. She drew near to the most diverse situations in order to sow hope. She accompanied her children bearing crosses in the silence of their hearts. How many devotions, shrines, and chapels in the most far-off places, how many pictures in our homes, remind us of this great truth? Mary gave us a mother's warmth, the warmth that shelters us amid troubles, the maternal warmth that keeps anything or anyone from extinguishing in the heart of the Church the revolution of tenderness inaugurated by her Son. Where there is a mother, there is tenderness. By her motherhood, Mary shows us that humility and tenderness are not virtues of the weak but of the strong. She teaches us that we do not have to mistreat others in order to feel important (cf. *Evangelii Gaudium*, 288). God's holy people have always acknowledged and hailed her as the holy Mother of God.

THE DAILY SILENCE (2:19, 51)[6]

In the silence of the daily routine, Saint Joseph, together with Mary, share a single common center of attention: Jesus. With commitment and tenderness they accompany and nurture the growth of the Son of God made human for us, reflecting on everything that has happened. In his Gospel, Saint Luke twice emphasizes the attitude of Mary, which is also that of Saint Joseph: she "treasured all these words and pondered them in her heart." To listen to the Lord, we must learn to contemplate, feel his constant presence in our lives, and we must stop and converse with him, give him space in prayer. Each of us, even you boys and girls, young people, so many of you here this morning, should ask yourselves: "How much space do I give to the Lord? Do I stop to talk with him?" Ever since we were children, our parents taught us to start and end the day with a prayer, taught us to feel that the friendship and the love of God accompany us. Let us remember the Lord more in our daily life!

THE CHILD JESUS (2:21–28)[7]

In these days of Christmas, the child Jesus is placed before us. I am certain that in our homes many families still have a nativity scene arranged, continuing this beautiful tradition begun by Saint

Francis of Assisi, a tradition that keeps the mystery of God who became human alive in our hearts.

Devotion to the child Jesus is widespread. Many saints cultivated this devotion in their daily prayers and wished to model their lives after that of the child Jesus. I think, in particular, of Saint Thérèse of Lisieux, who as a Carmelite nun took the name Thérèse of the Child Jesus and the Holy Face. She is also a doctor of the Church who knew how to live and witness to the "spiritual childhood" which unfolds through meditation, as the Virgin Mary taught, on the humility of God who became small for us. This is a great mystery. God is humble! We, who are proud and full of vanity, believe we are something big. We are nothing! He, the Great One, is humble and becomes a child. This is a true mystery. God is humble. This is beautiful!

Contemplating the Child Jesus

There was a time in which, in the divine-human Person of Christ, God was a child, and this must hold a particular significance for our faith. It is true that his death on the cross and his Resurrection are the highest expressions of his redeeming love. However, let us not forget that the whole of his earthly life is revelation and teaching. In the Christmas season, we remember his childhood. To grow in faith, we need to contemplate the child Jesus more often. Certainly, we know almost nothing of this period of his life. We know of the conferring of his name eight days after his birth and his presentation at the temple (cf. Luke 2:21–28); additionally, we know of the visit of the Magi and the ensuing escape to Egypt (cf. Matt 2:1–23). Then, there is a great leap in time to when he is twelve years old and, with Mary and Joseph, he goes on pilgrimage to Jerusalem for Passover. Instead of returning with his parents, he remains in the temple to speak with the doctors of the law.

Consequently, we know little of the child Jesus, but we can learn much about him if we look to the lives of children. It is a beautiful habit that parents and grandparents have, that of watching what children do.

We discover, first of all, that children want our attention. They have to be at the center. Why? Because they are proud? No! Because they need to feel protected. It is important that we, too, place Jesus at the center of our life and know, even if it may seem paradoxical, that it is our responsibility to protect him. He wants to be in our embrace, he wants to be tended to and be able to fix his gaze on ours. Additionally, we must make the child Jesus smile in order to show him our love and our joy that he is with us. His smile is a sign of the love that gives us the assurance of being loved. Children, finally, love to play. Playing with children, however, means abandoning our logic in order to enter theirs. If we want to have fun with them it is necessary to understand what they like and not be selfish by making them do the things that we like. It is a lesson for us. Before Jesus we are called to abandon our pretense of autonomy—and this is the crux of the matter: our pretense of autonomy. We are called to accept instead the true form of liberty, which consists in knowing and serving him whom we have before us. He, the child, is the Son of God who comes to save us. He has come among us to show us the face of the Father abounding in love and mercy. Therefore, let us hold the child Jesus tightly in our arms; let us place ourselves at his service. He is the font of love and serenity. It will be beautiful today, when we get home, to go to the nativity scene and kiss the baby Jesus and say: "Jesus, I want to be humble like you, humble like God," and to ask him for this grace.

BEING ABLE TO DREAM (2:21–38)[8]

In this passage from the Gospel of Luke, we recall Simeon and Anna—two grandparents. What a capacity to dream these two had! And they recounted their entire dream to Saint Joseph, to Our Lady, to the people.... And Anna went about chatting here and there, saying: "It is he! It is he!" as she recounted the dream of her life. And this is what the Lord asks of us today: to be grandparents. To transmit this vitality to young people, because young people are expecting it from us; not to withdraw, but to give of our best. They are waiting for our experience, for our positive dreams so as to carry out the prophecy and the work.

MEETING JESUS TODAY (2:22–40)[9]

Forty days after Christmas, we celebrate the Lord who enters the temple and encounters his people. In the Christian East, this feast is called the "Feast of Encounter." It is the encounter between God, who became a child to bring newness to our world, and an expectant humanity, represented by the elderly man and woman in the temple.

In the temple, there is also an encounter between two couples: the young Mary and Joseph, and the elderly Simeon and Anna. The elderly receive from the young, while the young draw upon the elderly. In the temple, Mary and Joseph find *the roots of their people*. This is important, because God's promise does not come to fulfillment merely in individuals, once for all, but within a community and throughout history. There too, Mary and Joseph find the roots of *their faith*, for faith is not something learned from a book but the art of living with God, learned from the experience of those who have gone before us. The two young people, in meeting the two older people, thus find themselves. And the two older people, nearing the end of their days, receive Jesus, the meaning of their lives. This event fulfils the prophecy of Joel: "Your old men shall dream dreams, and your young men shall see visions" (2:28). In this encounter, the young see their mission and the elderly realize their dreams—all because, at the center of the encounter, is Jesus.

Let us look to our own lives, dear consecrated brothers and sisters. Everything started in an encounter with the Lord. Our journey of consecration was born of an encounter and a call. We need to keep this in mind. And if we remember aright, we will realize that in that encounter we were not alone with Jesus; there was also the people of God, the Church, young and old, just as in today's gospel. It is striking too, that while the young Mary and Joseph faithfully observe the Law—the gospel tells us this four times—and never speak, the elderly Simeon and Anna come running up and prophesy. It seems it should be the other way around. Generally, it is the young who speak enthusiastically about the future, while the elderly protect the past. In the gospel, the very opposite occurs, because when we meet one another in the Lord, God's surprises immediately follow.

For this to occur in the consecrated life, we have to remember that we can never renew our encounter with the Lord without others. We can never leave others behind, never pass over generations, but must accompany one another daily, keeping the Lord always at the center. For if the young are called to open new doors, the elderly hold the keys. An institute remains youthful by going back to its roots, by listening to its older members. There is no future without this encounter between the old and the young. There is no growth without roots and no flowering without new buds. There is never prophecy without memory, or memory without prophecy and constant encounter.

Today's frantic pace leads us to close many doors to encounter, often for fear of others. Only shopping malls and internet connections are always open. Yet that is not how it should be with consecrated life: the brother and the sister given to me by God are a part of my history, gifts to be cherished. May we never look at the screen of our cellphone more than the eyes of our brothers or sisters or focus more on our software than on the Lord. For whenever we put our own projects, methods, and organization at the center, consecrated life stops being attractive; it no longer speaks to others; it no longer flourishes because it forgets its very foundations—its very roots.

The Encounter with Jesus

Consecrated life is born and reborn of an encounter with Jesus as he is—poor, chaste, and obedient. We journey along a double track: on the one hand, God's loving initiative, from which everything starts and to which we must always return; on the other, our own response, which is truly loving when it has no "ifs" or "buts," when it imitates Jesus in his poverty, chastity, and obedience. Whereas the life of this world attempts to take hold of us, the consecrated life turns from fleeting riches to embrace the One who endures forever. The life of this world pursues selfish pleasures and desires; the consecrated life frees our affections of every possession in order to love God and other people fully. Worldly life aims to do whatever we want; consecrated life chooses humble obedience as the greater freedom. And while worldly life soon leaves our hands and hearts empty, life in Jesus fills us with peace to the very end, as in the gospel, where Simeon and Anna come happily to the sunset of their lives with the Lord in their arms and joy in their hearts.

How good it is for us to hold the Lord "in our arms" (cf. Luke 2:28), like Simeon. Not only in our heads and in our hearts, but also "in our hands," in all that we do: in prayer, at work, at the table, on the telephone, at school, with the poor, everywhere. Having the Lord "in our hands" is an antidote to insular mysticism and frenetic activism, since a genuine encounter with Jesus corrects both saccharine piety and frazzled hyperactivity. Savoring the encounter with Jesus is also the remedy for the paralysis of routine, for it opens us up to the daily "surgings" of grace. The secret to fanning the flame of our spiritual life is a willingness to allow ourselves to encounter Jesus and to be encountered by him. Otherwise, we fall into a stifling life, where disgruntlement, bitterness and inevitable disappointments get the better of us. To encounter one another in Jesus as brothers and sisters, young and old, is thus to abandon the barren rhetoric of "the good old days"—a nostalgia that kills the soul—and to silence those who think that "everything is falling apart." If we encounter Jesus and our brothers and sisters in the everyday events of our life, our hearts will no longer be set on the past or the future but will experience the "today of God" in peace with everyone.

At the end of the Gospels, there is another encounter with Jesus that can inspire the consecrated life. It is that of the women before the tomb. They had gone to encounter the dead; their journey seemed pointless. You too are journeying against the current: the life of the world easily rejects poverty, chastity, and obedience. But like those women, keep moving forward, without worrying about whatever heavy stones need to be removed (cf. Mark 16:3). And like those women, be the first to meet the Lord, risen and alive. Cling to him (cf. Matt 28:9), and go off immediately to tell your brothers and sisters, your hearts brimming with joy (cf. v. 8). In this way, you are the Church's perennial dawn. You, dear consecrated brothers and sisters, are the Church's perennial dawn! I ask you to renew this very day your encounter with Jesus, to walk together toward him. And this will give light to your eyes and strength to your steps.

A Time of Preparation (2:41–51)[10]

This gospel passage shows Jesus as an adolescent, when he had returned with his parents to Nazareth after being lost and found in the temple. There we read that "he was obedient to them" (cf. v. 51); he did not disown his family. Luke then adds that Jesus "grew in wisdom, age and grace before God and men" (cf. v. 52). In a word, this was a time of preparation, when Jesus grew in his relationship with the Father and with others. Saint John Paul II explained that he did not only grow physically but that "there was also a spiritual growth in Jesus," because "the fullness of grace in Jesus was in proportion to his age: there was always a fullness, but a fullness which increased as he grew in age."[11]

From what the gospel tells us, we can say that Jesus, in the years of his youth, was "training," being prepared to carry out the Father's plan. His adolescence and his youth set him on the path to that sublime mission.

In his adolescence and youth, Jesus's relationship with the Father was that of the beloved Son. Drawn to the Father, he grew up concerned for his affairs: "Did you not know that I must be about my Father's business?" (v. 49). Still, it must not be thought that Jesus was a withdrawn adolescent or a self-absorbed youth. His relationships were those of a young person who shared fully in the life of his family and his people. He learned his father's trade and then replaced him as a carpenter. At one point in the Gospels he is called "the carpenter's son" (Matt 13:55) and another time simply "the carpenter" (Mark 6:3). This detail shows that he was just another young person of his town, one who related normally to others. No one regarded him as unusual or set apart from others. For this very reason, once Jesus began to preach, people could not imagine where he had gotten this wisdom: "Is this not Joseph's son?" (Luke 4:22).

In fact, "Jesus did not grow up in a narrow and stifling relationship with Mary and Joseph, but readily interacted with the wider family, the relatives of his parents and their friends."[12] Hence we can understand why, on their return from the pilgrimage to Jerusalem, his parents readily thought that, as a twelve-year-old boy (cf. Luke 2:42), he had been wandering freely among the crowd, even though they had not seen him for an entire day: "supposing him to be in the group of travelers, they went a day's journey" (v. 44). Surely, they assumed, Jesus was among them, mingling with the others, joking with other young people, listening to the adults tell stories and sharing the joys and sorrows of the group. Indeed, the Greek word that Luke uses to describe the group—*synodía*—clearly evokes a larger "community on a journey" of which the Holy Family was a part. Thanks to the trust of his parents, Jesus could move freely and learn to journey with others.

OBEDIENCE AND MISSION (2:48–51)[13]

The gospel goes on to remind us that children are not the property of a family but have their own lives to lead. Jesus is a model of obedience to his earthly parents, placing himself under their charge (cf. Luke 2:51), but he also shows that children's life decisions and their Christian vocation may demand a parting for the sake of the kingdom of God (cf. Matt 10:34–37; Luke 9:59–62). Jesus himself, at twelve years of age, tells Mary and Joseph that he has a greater mission to accomplish apart from his earthly family (cf. Luke 2:48–50). In this way, he shows the need for other, deeper bonds, even within the family: "My mother and my brethren are those who hear the word of God and do it" (Luke 8:21). All the same, in the concern he shows for children — whom the societies of the ancient Near East viewed as subjects without particular rights and even as family property — Jesus goes so far as to present them as teachers, on account of their simple trust and spontaneity toward others. "Truly I tell you, unless you change and become like children, you will never enter the kingdom of heaven. Whoever becomes humble like this child is the greatest in the kingdom of heaven" (Matt 18:3–4).

BEING PROPHETIC VOICES (2:52)[14]

The gospel reminds us of our Christian duty to be prophetic voices in the midst of our communities. Joseph listened to the angel of the Lord and responded to God's call to care for Jesus and Mary. In this way, he played his part in God's plan and became a blessing not only for the Holy Family, but for all of humanity. With Mary, Joseph served as a model for the boy Jesus as he grew in wisdom, age, and grace (cf. Luke 2:52). When families bring children into the world, train them in faith and sound values, and teach them to contribute to society, they become a blessing in our world. Families can become a blessing for all of humanity! God's love becomes present and active by the way we love and by the good works that we do. We extend Christ's kingdom in this world. And, in doing this, we prove faithful to the prophetic mission which we received in baptism.

3

Preparing for Public Ministry

THE CRY OF JOHN THE BAPTIST (3:3)[1]

The liturgy places us in the school of John the Baptist, who preached "a baptism of repentance for the forgiveness of sins." Perhaps we ask ourselves, "Why do we have to convert? Conversion is about an atheist who becomes a believer or a sinner who becomes just. But we don't need it. We are already Christians. So we are okay." But this isn't true. In thinking like this, we don't realize that it is precisely because of this presumption — that because we are Christians everyone is good, and we're okay — that we must convert from the supposition that, all things considered, things are fine as they are and we don't need any kind of conversion.

Let us ask ourselves: Is it true that in the various situations and circumstances of life, we have within us the same feelings that Jesus has? Is it true that we feel as Christ feels? For example, when we suffer some wrongdoing or some insult, do we manage to react without animosity and to forgive from the heart those who apologize to us? How difficult it is to forgive! How difficult! "You're going to pay for this!" This phrase comes from within. When we are called to share joys or sorrows, do we know how to weep sincerely with those who weep and rejoice with those who rejoice? When we should express our faith, do we know how to do it with courage and simplicity, without being ashamed of the gospel? We can ask ourselves so many questions like these. We're not all right. We must always convert and have the sentiments that Jesus had.

The voice of the Baptist still cries in the deserts of humanity today, which are closed minds and hardened hearts. And his voice causes us to ask ourselves if we are actually following the right path, living a life according to the gospel. Today, as then, he admonishes us with the words of the prophet Isaiah: "Prepare the way of the Lord!" (v. 4). It is a pressing invitation to open one's heart and receive the salvation that God offers ceaselessly, almost obstinately, because he wants us all to be free from the slavery of sin.

The text of the prophet amplifies this voice, portending that "all flesh shall see the salvation of God" (v. 6). And salvation is offered to everyone, and every people, without exclusion, to each one of us. None of us can say, "I'm a saint; I'm perfect; I'm already saved." No. We must always accept this offer of salvation. This is the reason for the Year of Mercy: to go farther on this journey of salvation, this path that Jesus taught us. God wants all of humankind to be saved through Jesus, the one mediator (cf. 1 Tim 2:4–6).

Therefore, each one of us is called to make Jesus known to those who do not yet know him. But this is not to proselytize. No, it is to open a door. "Woe to me if I do not preach the gospel!" (1 Cor 9:16), Saint Paul declared. If Our Lord Jesus has changed our lives, and he changes it every time we go to him, how can we not feel the passion to make him known to those we encounter at work, at school, in our apartment building, in the hospital, in meeting places? If we look around us, we find people who would be willing to begin—or begin again—a journey of faith were they to encounter Christians in love with Jesus. Shouldn't we and couldn't we be these Christians? I leave you this question: "Am I truly in love with Jesus? Am I convinced that Jesus offers and gives me salvation?" And, if I am in love, I have to make him known! But we must be courageous: lay low the mountains of pride and rivalry; fill in the ravines dug by indifference and apathy; make straight the paths of our laziness and our compromises.

WHAT SHOULD WE DO? (3:10, 12, 14)[2]

In today's gospel reading, there is a question posed three times: "What shall we do?" (Luke 3:10, 12, 14). It is asked of John the Baptist by three categories of people: first, the crowd in general; second, the publicans or tax collectors; and, third, some soldiers. Each group questions the prophet on what must be done to implement the conversion that he is preaching. John's reply to the first group, the crowd, is to share essential goods or basic necessities. Therefore he says: "Whoever has two tunics should share with the person who has none. And whoever has food should do likewise" (v. 11). Then he tells the second group, the tax collectors, to collect no more than the amount owed (cf. v. 13). What does this mean? No taking "bribes." John the Baptist is clear. And he tells the third group, the soldiers, not to extort anything from anyone and to be content with their wages (cf. v. 14). There are three answers to the questions posed by each of the three groups. Three answers for an identical path of repentance, which is manifested in concrete commitments to justice and solidarity. It is the path that Jesus points to in all his preaching, the path of diligent love for neighbor.

From John the Baptist's admonitions, we understand the general tendencies of those who at that time held power in various forms. Things have not changed very much. However, no category of people is excluded from following the path of repentance to obtain salvation, not even the tax collectors, considered sinners by definition: not even they are excluded from salvation.

God does not preclude anyone from the opportunity to be saved. He is, rather, anxious to show mercy, to show it toward everyone, and to welcome each one into the tender embrace of reconciliation and forgiveness.

We feel that this question—"What should we do?"—is also ours. Today's liturgy tells us, in the words of John the Baptist, that it is necessary to repent, to change direction, and to take the path of justice, solidarity, sobriety: these are the essential values of a fully human and genuinely Christian life. Repent! It sums up the message of the Baptist.

The liturgy of this Third Sunday of Advent helps us to rediscover a special dimension of repentance: joy. Whoever repents and approaches the Lord feels joy. The prophet Zephaniah says to us today: "Shout for joy, daughter Zion!" addressing Jerusalem (Zeph 3:14); and the apostle Paul exhorts the Christians of Philippi: "Rejoice in the Lord always" (Phil 4:4). Today, it takes courage to speak of joy, which, above all, requires faith! The world is beset by many problems, and the future is burdened by uncertainties and fears. Yet, Christians are a joyful people, and their joy is not something superficial and ephemeral but deep and stable, because it is a gift from the Lord that fills life. Our joy comes from the certainty that "the Lord is near" (Phil 4:5): he is close with his tenderness, his mercy, his forgiveness, and his love.

May the Virgin Mary help us to strengthen our faith, so that we are able to welcome the God of joy, the God of mercy who always wants to live among his children. May our Mother teach us to share tears with those who weep in order to be able to also share a smile.

THE RESPONSE OF JOHN (3:10)[3]

We too are like the crowds who ask John, "What then should we do" (Luke 3:10). The response of the Baptist is immediate. He invites us to act justly and to look after those who are in need. What

John demands of his interlocutors, however, is what is reflected in the Law.

We, on the other hand, are asked for a more radical commitment. Before the Holy Door that we are called to pass through, we are asked to be instruments of mercy, knowing that we will be judged on this. Those who are baptized know that they have a greater task. Faith in Christ leads to a lifelong journey: to be merciful like the Father. The joy of passing through the Door of Mercy is accompanied by a commitment to welcome and witness to a love that surpasses justice, a love that knows no boundaries. It is for this infinite love that we are responsible, despite our contradictions.

FROM THE BAPTISM OF JOHN TO THE BAPTISM OF JESUS (3:21–22)[4]

The gospel presents Jesus in the waters of the River Jordan at the center of a wondrous divine revelation. Saint Luke writes: "When Jesus also had been baptized and was praying, the heaven was opened, and the Holy Spirit descended upon him in bodily form like a dove. And a voice came from heaven, 'You are my Son, the Beloved; with you I am well pleased'" (Luke 3:21–22). In this way, Jesus is consecrated and manifested by the Father as the Savior Messiah and liberator.

The Work of the Holy Spirit
In this event—attested by all four Gospels—is the passing from the baptism of John the Baptist, symbolized by water, to the baptism of Jesus "with the Holy Spirit and with fire" (Luke 3:16). Indeed, the Holy Spirit is the principal artisan in Christian baptism: it is he who burns and destroys original sin, restoring to the baptized the beauty of divine grace; it is he who frees us from the dominion of darkness, namely sin, and transfers us to the kingdom of light, namely love, truth, and peace: this is the kingdom of light. Let us think about the dignity to which baptism elevates us! "See what love the Father has given us, that we should be

called children of God; and that is what we are" (1 John 3:1), the apostle John exclaims. This splendid reality of being children of God entails the responsibility of following Jesus, the obedient Servant, and reproduces his features in our very selves: namely openness, humility, tenderness. This is not easy, especially when there is so much intolerance, arrogance, and harshness around us. But with the strength we receive from the Holy Spirit, it is possible!

The Holy Spirit, received for the first time on the day of our baptism, opens our heart to the Truth; to all Truth. The Spirit impels our life on the challenging but joyful path of charity and solidarity toward our brothers and sisters. The Spirit gives us the tenderness of divine forgiveness and permeates us with the invincible power of the Father's mercy. Let us not forget that the Holy Spirit is a living and vivifying presence in those who welcome him. He prays in us and fills us with spiritual joy.

Recalling Our Baptism

Today, the feast of the Baptism of Jesus, let us ponder the day of our baptism. All of us were baptized; let us give thanks for this gift. I ask you a question: Which of you knows the date of your baptism? Surely not everyone. Therefore, I encourage you to find out the date, by asking, for example, your parents, your grandparents, your godparents, or going to the parish. It is very important to know it, because it is a date to be celebrated; it is the date of our rebirth as children of God. For this reason, homework for this week is to go and find out the date of your baptism. Celebrating that day means and reaffirms our adherence to Jesus, with the commitment to live as Christians, members of the Church and of a new humanity, in which we are all brothers and sisters.

4

The Good News

THE MISSION OF JESUS (4:16–19)[1]

Jesus, the Father's envoy, comes, as Isaiah stresses, "to bring good news to the oppressed, to bind up the brokenhearted, to proclaim liberty to the captives, and release to the prisoners; to proclaim the year of the Lord's favor" (Isa 61:1–2).

These words, which Jesus will speak in his discourse at the synagogue in Nazareth (cf. Luke 4:16–19), clarify that his mission in the world consists in the liberation from sin and from the personal and social slavery that it produces. He has come to the earth to restore the dignity and freedom of the children of God to all humanity—which only he can communicate—and thereby to give joy.

THE THREE ASPECTS OF MISSION (4:16–21)[2]

Even in these troubled times, the mystery of the Incarnation reminds us that God continually comes to encounter us. He is God-with-us, who walks along the often dusty paths of our lives.

He knows our anxious longing for love, and he calls us to joy. In the diversity and the uniqueness of each and every vocation—personal and ecclesial—there is a need to listen, discern, and live this word that calls to us from on high and, while enabling us to develop our talents, makes us instruments of salvation in the world and guides us to full happiness.

These three aspects—*listening, discerning,* and *living*—were also present at beginning of Jesus's own mission, when, after his time of prayer and struggle in the desert, he visited his synagogue in Nazareth. There he listened to the word, discerned the content of the mission entrusted to him by the Father, and proclaimed that he had come to accomplish it "today" (cf. Luke 4:16–21).

Listening

The Lord's call—let it be said at the outset—is not as clear-cut as any of those things we can hear, see, or touch in our daily experience. God comes silently and discreetly, without imposing on our freedom. Thus it can happen that his voice is drowned out by the many worries and concerns that fill our minds and hearts.

We need, therefore, to learn how to listen carefully to his word and the story of his life, but also to be attentive to the details of our own daily lives in order to learn how to view things with the eyes of faith and to keep ourselves open to the surprises of the Spirit.

We will never discover the special, personal calling that God has in mind for us if we remain enclosed in ourselves, in our usual way of doing things, in the apathy of those who fritter away their lives in their own little world. We would lose the chance to dream big and to play our part in the unique and original story that God wants to write with us.

Jesus, too, was called and sent. That is why he needed to recollect himself in silence. He listened to and read the word in the synagogue, and with the light and strength of the Holy Spirit he revealed its full meaning with reference to his own person and the history of the people of Israel.

Nowadays, listening is becoming more and more difficult, immersed as we are in a society full of noise, overstimulated and bombarded by information. The outer noise that sometimes prevails in our cities and our neighborhoods is often accompanied by our interior dispersion and confusion. This prevents us from pausing and enjoying the taste of contemplation, reflecting serenely on the events of our lives, going about our work with confidence in God's loving plan, and making a fruitful discernment.

Discerning

When Jesus reads the passage of the prophet Isaiah in the synagogue in Nazareth, he discerns the content of his mission and presents it to those who await the Messiah: "The Spirit of the Lord is upon me, because he has anointed me to bring good news to the poor. He has sent me to proclaim release to the captives and recovery of sight to the blind, to let the oppressed go free, to proclaim the year of the Lord's favor" (Luke 4:18–19).

In the same way, each of us can discover our own vocation only through spiritual discernment. This is "a process by which a person makes fundamental choices, in dialogue with the Lord and listening to the voice of the Spirit, starting with the choice of one's state in life."[3]

Thus, we come to discover that *Christian vocation always has a prophetic dimension*. The scriptures tell us that the prophets were sent to the people in situations of great material insecurity and of spiritual and moral crisis to address, in God's name, a message of conversion, hope, and consolation. Like a whirlwind, the prophet unsettles the false tranquility of consciences that have forgotten the word of the Lord. He discerns events in the light of God's promise and enables people to glimpse the signs of dawn amid the dark shadows of history.

Today, too, we have great need of discernment and of prophecy. We have to resist the temptations of ideology and negativity and to discover, in our relationship with the Lord, the places, the means and the situations through which he calls us.

Every Christian ought to grow in the ability to "read within" his or her life, and to understand where and to what he or she is being called by the Lord in order to carry on his mission.

Living

Finally, Jesus announces the newness of the present hour, which will enthuse many and harden the heart of others. The fullness of time has come, and he is the Messiah proclaimed by Isaiah and anointed to liberate prisoners, to restore sight to the blind, and to proclaim the merciful love of God to every creature. Indeed, Jesus says that "today this scripture has been fulfilled in your hearing" (Luke 4:21).

The joy of the gospel, which opens us to encountering God and our brothers and sisters, does not abide our slowness and our sloth. It will not fill our hearts if we keep standing by the window with the excuse of waiting for the right time, without accepting this very day the risk of making a decision. Vocation is today! The Christian mission is now! Each of us is called—whether to the lay life in marriage, to the priestly life in the ordained ministry, or to a life of special consecration—to become a witness of the Lord, here and now.

This "today" that Jesus proclaimed assures us that God continues to "come down" to save our human family and to make us sharers in his mission. The Lord continues to call others to live with him and to follow him in a relationship of particular closeness. He continues to call others to serve him directly. If he lets us realize that he is calling us to consecrate ourselves totally to his kingdom, then we should have no fear! It is beautiful, and a great grace, to be completely and forever consecrated to God and the service of our brothers and sisters.

Today, the Lord continues to call others to follow him. We should not wait to be perfect to respond with our generous "yes," nor be fearful of our limitations and sins, but instead open our hearts to the voice of the Lord. To listen to that voice, to discern our personal mission in the Church and the world, and at last to live it in the today that God gives us.

May Mary Most Holy, who as a young woman living in obscurity heard, accepted, and experienced the Word of God made flesh, protect us and accompany us always as we continue on our journey.

THE GOOD NEWS (4:18)[4]

"The Spirit of the Lord is upon me, because he has anointed me to preach good news to the poor. He has sent me to proclaim release to the captives and recovery of sight to the blind, to let the oppressed go free" (Luke 4:18). Jesus, anointed by the Spirit, brings *good news* to the poor. Everything he proclaims, and we priests too proclaim, is *good news*, news full of the joy of the gospel—the joy of those anointed in their sins with the oil of forgiveness and anointed in their charism with the oil of mission, to anoint others in turn.

Like Jesus, the priest makes the message joyful with his entire person. When he preaches—briefly, if possible!—he does so with the joy that touches people's hearts with that same word with which the Lord has touched his own heart in prayer. Like every other missionary disciple, the priest makes the message joyful through his whole being. For, as we all know, it is in the little things that joy is best seen and shared: when by taking one small step we make God's mercy overflow in situations of desolation; when we decide to pick up the phone and arrange to see someone; when we patiently allow others to take up our time...

The phrase "*good news*" might appear as just another way of saying "the gospel." Yet those words point to something essential: the joy of the gospel. The gospel is good news because it is, in essence, a message of joy.

The *good news* is the precious pearl of which we read in the gospel. It is not a thing but a mission. This is evident to anyone who has experienced the "delightful and comforting joy of evangelizing" (*Evangelii Gaudium*, 10).

The *good news* is born of anointing. Jesus's first "great priestly anointing" took place, by the power of the Holy Spirit, in the womb of Mary. The good news of the Annunciation inspired the Virgin Mother to sing her *Magnificat*. It filled the heart of Joseph, her spouse, with sacred silence, and it made John leap for joy in the womb of his mother Elizabeth.

In today's gospel passage, Jesus returns to Nazareth and the joy of the Spirit renews that anointing in the little synagogue of that town: the Spirit descends and is poured out upon him, anointing him "with the oil of gladness" (cf. Ps 45:7).

Good news. A single word—gospel—that, even as it is spoken, becomes truth, brimming with joy and mercy. We should never attempt to separate these three graces of the gospel: its *truth*, which is non-negotiable; its *mercy*, which is unconditional and offered to all sinners; and its *joy*, which is personal and open to everyone. Truth, mercy, and joy: these three go together.

The truth of the *good news* can never be merely abstract, incapable of taking concrete shape in people's lives because they feel more comfortable seeing it printed in books.

The mercy of the *good news* can never be a false commiseration, one that leaves sinners in their misery without holding out a hand to lift them up and help them take a step in the direction of change.

This message can never be gloomy or indifferent, for it expresses a joy that is completely personal. It is "the joy of the Father, who desires that none of his little ones be lost" (*Evangelii Gaudium*, 237). It is the joy of Jesus, who sees that the poor have the good news preached to them, and that the little ones, in turn, go out to preach the message (cf. *Evangelii Gaudium*, 5).

The joys of the gospel are special joys. I say "joys" in the plural, for they are many and varied, depending on how the Spirit chooses to communicate them to every person in every age and in every culture. They need to be poured into new wineskins, the ones the Lord speaks of in expressing the newness of his message.

I would like to share with you, dear priests, dear brothers, three images or icons of those new wineskins in which the *good news* is kept fresh—for we have to keep it fresh—never turning sour but rather pouring forth in abundance.

The Water Jars at Cana

A first icon of the *good news* would be the stone water jars at the wedding feast of Cana (cf. John 2:6). In one way, they clearly reflect that perfect vessel which is Our Lady herself, the Virgin Mary. The gospel tells us that the servants "filled them up to the brim" (John 2:7). I can imagine one of those servants looking to Mary to see if what he had poured was enough, and Mary signaling to add one more pailful. Mary is the new wineskin brimming with contagious joy. Without her, dear priests, we cannot move forward in our priesthood! She is "the handmaid of the Father who sings his praises" (*Evangelii Gaudium*, 286), Our Lady of Prompt Succor, who, after conceiving in her immaculate womb the Word of life, goes out to visit and assist her cousin Elizabeth. Her "contagious fullness" helps us overcome the temptation of fear, the temptation to keep ourselves from being filled to the brim and even overflowing, the temptation to a faint-heartedness that holds us back from going forth to fill others with joy. This cannot be, for "the joy of the gospel fills the hearts and lives of all who encounter Jesus" (*Evangelii Gaudium*, 1).

The Samaritan Woman's Jug

A second icon of the *good news* that I would like to share with you today is the jug with its wooden ladle that the Samaritan woman carried on her head in the midday sun (cf. John 4:5–30). It speaks to us of something crucial: the importance of concrete situations. The Lord, the Source of Living Water, had no means of drawing the water to quench his thirst. So the Samaritan woman drew the water with her jug, and with her ladle she quenched the Lord's thirst. She sated it even more by concretely confessing her sins. By mercifully shaking the vessel of that Samaritan women's soul, the Holy Spirit overflowed upon all the people of that small town, who asked the Lord to stay with them.

The Lord gave us another new vessel or wineskin full of this "inclusive concreteness" in that Samaritan soul who was Mother Teresa of Calcutta. He called to her and told her: "I am thirsty." He said: "My child, come, take me to the hovels of the poor. Come, be my light. I cannot do this alone. They do not know me, and that is why they do not love me. Bring me to them." Mother Teresa, starting with one concrete person, thanks to her smile and her way of touching their wounds, brought the good news to all. We do this in the way we touch wounds with our hands, our priestly way of caressing the sick and those who have lost hope. The priest must be a man of tender love. Concreteness and tenderness!

The Lord's Pierced Heart

The third icon of the *good news* is the fathomless vessel of the Lord's pierced heart: his utter meekness, humility, and poverty, which draw all people to himself. From him we have to learn that announcing a great joy to the poor can be done only in a respectful, humble, and even humbling way. Concrete, tender, and humble: in this way our evangelization will be joyful. Evangelization cannot be presumptuous, nor can the integrity of the truth be rigid, because truth became flesh, it became tenderness; it became a child, it became a man and, on the cross, it became sin (cf. 2 Cor 5:21). The Spirit proclaims and teaches "the whole truth" (cf. John 16:3), and he is not afraid to do this one step at a time. The Spirit tells us in every situation what we need to say to our enemies (cf. Matt 10:19), and at those times he illumines our every small step forward. This meekness and integrity give joy to the poor, revives sinners, and grants relief to those oppressed by the devil.

Dear priests, as we contemplate and drink from these three new wineskins, may the *good news* find in us that "contagious fullness" that Our Lady radiates with her whole being, the "inclusive concreteness" of the story of the Samaritan woman, and the "utter meekness" whereby the Holy Spirit ceaselessly wells up and flows forth from the pierced heart of Jesus, our Lord.

EVANGELIZING THE POOR (4:18)[5]

Let us imagine that we too enter the synagogue of Nazareth, the village where Jesus has grown up and lived until he is about thirty years old. What happens is an important event, which delineates Jesus's mission. He stands up to read the sacred scripture. He opens the scroll of the prophet Isaiah and takes up the passage where it is written: "The Spirit of the Lord is upon me, because he has anointed me to bring good news to the poor" (Luke 4:18). Then, after a moment of silence filled with expectation by everyone, he says, in the midst of their general amazement: "Today this scripture has been fulfilled in your hearing" (v. 21).

Evangelizing the poor is Jesus's mission. According to what he says, this is also the mission of the Church and of every person baptized in the Church. Being a Christian is the same thing as being a missionary. Proclaiming the gospel with one's word, and before that, with one's life, is the primary aim of the Christian community and of each of its members. It is noted here that Jesus addresses the *good news* to all, excluding no one, indeed, favoring those who are distant, the suffering, the sick, and those cast out by society.

Let us ask ourselves: What does it mean to evangelize the poor? First, it means drawing close to them, having the joy of serving them, of freeing them from their oppression, and all of this in the name of and with the Spirit of Christ, because he is the gospel of God, he is the mercy of God, he is the liberation of God, he is the One who became poor so as to enrich us with his poverty. The text of Isaiah, reinforced with little adaptations introduced by Jesus, indicates that the messianic announcement of the kingdom of God come among us is addressed in a preferential way to the marginalized, to captives, to the oppressed.

In Jesus's time, these people probably were not at the center of the community of faith.

Let us ask ourselves, today, in our parish communities, in our associations, in our movements, are we faithful to Christ's plan?

Is the priority evangelizing the poor, bringing them the joyful good news? Indeed, it does not only involve providing social assistance, much less political activity. It involves offering the strength of the gospel of God who converts hearts, heals wounds, and transforms human and social relationships according to the logic of love. The poor are indeed at the center of the gospel.

A HYMN OF HOPE (4:18–19)[6]

Simeon's canticle is the hymn of the believer, who at the end of his days can exclaim: "Hope does not disappoint us" (cf. Rm 5:5). God never deceives us. Simeon and Anna, in their old age, were capable of a new fruitfulness, and they testify to this in song. Life is worth living in hope because the Lord keeps his promise. Jesus himself will later explain this promise in the synagogue of Nazareth: the sick, the prisoners, those who are alone, the poor, the elderly, and the sinners are all invited to take up this same hymn of hope. Jesus is with them; Jesus is with us (cf. Luke 4:18–19).

THE TEMPTATION TO NEGOTIATE WITH GOD (4:21–30)[7]

This passage of Luke the evangelist is not simply the account of an argument between compatriots arising from envy and jealousy, as sometimes happens even in our neighborhoods, but it highlights a temptation to which a religious man is always exposed—all of us are exposed—and from which it is important to distance ourselves. What is this temptation? It is the temptation to consider religion as a human investment and, consequently, to *negotiate* with God, seeking one's own interest. Instead, true religion entails accepting the revelation of a God who is Father and who cares for each of his creatures, even the smallest and most insignificant in our eyes. Jesus's prophetic ministry consists precisely in declaring that no human condition can constitute a reason for exclusion from the Father's heart, and that the only privilege in the eyes of God is that of not having privileges, of not having godparents, of being abandoned in his hands.

"Today this scripture has been fulfilled in your hearing" (Luke 4:21). The "today" proclaimed by Christ applies to every age. It echoes for us too in this square, reminding us of the relevance and necessity of the salvation Jesus brought to humanity. God comes to meet the men and women of all times and places in their real-life situations. He also comes to meet us. It is always God who takes the first step. He comes to visit us with his mercy, to lift us up from the dust of our sins. He comes to extend a hand to us, to enable us to return from the abyss into which our pride made us fall. And he invites us to receive the comforting truth of the gospel and to walk on the paths of good. He always comes to find us, to look for us.

Let us return to the synagogue. Surely that day, in the synagogue of Nazareth, Mary, his mother, was also there. We can imagine her heart beating, a small foreboding of what she will suffer under the cross, seeing Jesus there in the synagogue, first admired, then challenged, then insulted, threatened with death. In her heart, filled with faith, she kept everything. May she help us to convert from a god of miracles to the miracle of God, who is Jesus Christ.

THE OLD WOMEN AND THE THEOLOGIAN (4:31–37)[8]

Many times we find, among our faithful, simple old women who perhaps didn't finish elementary school, but who speak about things better than a theologian does, because they have the Spirit of Christ. Saint Paul, who despite his effective preaching had no particular academic qualifications—he had not taken courses in human wisdom at the Lateran or Gregorian Pontifical Universities —spoke to satisfy the Spirit of God.

In this gospel passage, the word "authority" appears twice. The people "were astonished by Jesus' teaching, for his word was spoken with authority." And then again, at the very end of the passage, the gospel tells us that "they were all amazed and said to one another: 'What is this word? For with authority and power he commands.'" The people were astonished because when Jesus spoke, when he preached, he had authority that the other preachers, the legal experts who were teaching the people, didn't have.

The question to ask yourself is: What is this authority of Jesus, this new thing that astounded the people? What is this gift, different from the legal experts' manner of speaking and teaching? The answer is definitive. This authority is precisely the unique and special identity of Jesus. Indeed, Jesus was not a common preacher. Jesus was not one who taught the Law like all the others: he did so in a different way, in a new way, because he had the strength of the Holy Spirit.

In the liturgy, we read that passage in which Jesus presents himself, visits his synagogue, and speaks of himself in the words of the prophet Isaiah: "The Spirit of the Lord is upon me, because he has anointed me to bring good news." This, too, confirms that Jesus's authority comes precisely from this special anointing of the Holy Spirit. Jesus is anointed, the first Anointed One, the true Anointed One. And this anointing gives authority to Jesus.

Here, then, the freedom of Jesus is the very anointing of the Holy Spirit. And we can ask ourselves what our identity as Christians is. In the First Letter to the Corinthians (2:10–16), Saint Paul explains that "we impart this in words not taught by human wisdom." And therefore, Paul's preaching does not emanate from human wisdom, because his words were taught to him by the Holy Spirit. In fact, he preached with the anointing of the Spirit, expressing spiritual matters of the Spirit in spiritual terms.

However, the unspiritual man does not receive the gifts of the Spirit of God . . . and he is not able to understand them because they are spiritually discerned. Thus, if we Christians do not understand the gifts of the Spirit, if we do not bear and we do not offer testimony, we do not have identity.

The spiritual man judges all things but is himself to be judged by no one. Indeed, who has known the mind of the Lord? But now we have the mind of Christ, that is, the Spirit of Christ.

And this is the Christian identity: not having the spirit of the world, that manner of thinking, that manner of judging.

The Authority of the Spirit

Ultimately, what gives authority, what gives identity is the Holy Spirit—the anointing of the Holy Spirit. This is why people don't love those preachers, those legal experts, because they spoke truthfully about theology, but they didn't reach the heart. They didn't give freedom; they weren't capable of identifying with the people because they were not anointed by the Holy Spirit. However, the authority of Jesus—and the authority of the Christian— comes from this very capacity to understand the gifts of the Spirit, to speak the language of the Spirit. It comes from this anointing of the Holy Spirit.

Lord, give us the Christian identity that you have. Give us your Spirit; give us your way of thinking, of feeling, of speaking. Lord, grant us the anointing of the Holy Spirit.

THE KINGDOM AND ITS CHALLENGES (4:43)[9]

Reading the scriptures also makes it clear that the gospel is not merely about our personal relationship with God. Nor should our loving response to God be seen simply as an accumulation of small personal gestures to individuals in need, a kind of "charity à la carte," or a series of acts aimed solely at easing our conscience. The gospel is about the kingdom of God (cf. Luke 4:43); it is about loving God who reigns in our world. To the extent that he reigns within us, the life of society will be a setting for universal fraternity, justice, peace, and dignity. Both Christian preaching and life, then, are meant to have an impact on society. We are seeking God's kingdom: "Strive first for the kingdom of God and his righteousness, and all these things will be given to you as well" (Matt 6:33). Jesus's mission is to inaugurate the kingdom of his Father; he commands his disciples to proclaim the good news that "the kingdom of heaven is at hand" (Matt 10:7).

5

The Mission of the Disciples

THE CALL OF SAINT PETER (5:1–11)[1]

In today's gospel passage, Luke's narrative offers us the call of Saint Peter. His name—as we know—was Simon, and he was a fisherman. On the shore of the Sea of Galilee, Jesus sees him as he is arranging his nets, along with other fishermen. He finds him exhausted and discouraged, because that night they had caught nothing. And Jesus surprises him with an unexpected gesture: he gets into his boat and asks him to put out a short distance from the land because he wants to speak to the people from there—there were many people. So Jesus sits down in Simon's boat and teaches the crowd gathered along the shore. But his words re-open even Simon's heart to trust. Then, with another surprising "move." Jesus says to him: "Put out into the deep and let down your nets for a catch" (v. 4).

Simon responds with an objection: "Master, we have worked all night long but have caught nothing." And, as an expert fisherman, he could have added: "If we didn't catch anything during the night, we aren't going to catch anything during the day." However, inspired by Jesus's presence and enlightened by his word, he says: "Yet if you say so, I will let down the nets" (v. 5).

It is the response of faith, which we too are called to give; it is the attitude of willingness that the Lord asks of all his disciples, especially those who are tasked with responsibilities in the Church. And Peter's trustful obedience creates a remarkable result: "When they had done this, they caught so many fish that their nets were beginning to break" (v. 6).

It is a miraculous catch, a sign of the power of Jesus's word: when we place ourselves generously in his service, he accomplishes great things in us. This is what he does in each of us: he asks us to welcome him on the boat of our life, to set out anew with him, and to sail a new sea, one that proves to be full of surprises. His call to go out into the open sea of the humanity of our time, to be witnesses to goodness and mercy, gives new meaning to our existence, which is often at risk of collapsing in upon itself. At times we may be surprised and uncertain before the call that the Divine Master addresses to us, and we may be tempted to reject it because of our inadequacy. Peter too, after this incredible catch, said to Jesus: "Go away from me, Lord, for I am a sinful man!" (v. 8). This humble prayer is beautiful: "Go away from me, Lord, for I am a sinful man." But he says it on his knees before the One whom by this point he recognizes as "Lord." And Jesus encourages him by saying: "Do not be afraid; from now on you will be catching people" (v. 10). God—if we trust in him—frees us from our sin and opens a new horizon before us: to cooperate in his mission.

The greatest miracle that Jesus accomplished for Simon and the other tired and discouraged fishermen was not so much the net full of fish as having helped them not to fall victim to disappointment and discouragement in the face of failure. He prepared them to become proclaimers of and witnesses to his word and the kingdom of God. And the disciples' response was immediate and unreserved: "When they had brought their boats to shore, they left everything and followed him" (v. 11).

May the Blessed Virgin, model of prompt adherence to God's will, help us to feel the allure of the Lord's call and make us willing to cooperate with him to spread his word of salvation everywhere.

Artisans of Peace, Promoters of Life (5:1–11)[2]

The gospel writer tells us that the calling of the first disciples happened along the shore of Lake Gennesaret, where the people came together to hear a voice capable of guiding and illuminating them. It was also the place where fishermen used to bring their tiring days to an end, where they looked for sustenance in order to live a dignified and happy life, one not lacking the basic necessities. It is the only time in the entire Gospel of Luke that Jesus preaches near the Sea of Galilee. On the open sea their hopes for a bountiful catch had been turned into frustration with what seemed to be pointless and wasted efforts. According to an ancient Christian interpretation, the sea also represents the vastness where all peoples live; because of its turmoil and darkness, it evokes everything that threatens human existence and that has the power to destroy it.

We use related expressions to define *crowds*: a human tide, a sea of people. That day, Jesus had the sea behind him, and in front of him a crowd that followed him because they knew how deeply moved he was by human suffering . . . and they knew of his impartial, profound, and true words. Everyone came to hear him. The word of Jesus has something special that leaves no one indifferent. His word has the power to convert hearts, to change plans and projects. It is a word demonstrated in action, not academic findings or cold agreements removed from people's pain. His word applies both to the safety of the shore and the fragility of the sea.

This beloved city, Bogotá, and this beautiful country, Colombia, convey many of the human scenarios presented by the gospel. Here too crowds come together, longing for a word of life to enlighten all their efforts, and to indicate the nature and beauty of human existence. These crowds of men and women, the young and the old, dwell in a land of unimaginable fertility, which could provide for everyone. But here, as in other places, there is a thick darkness that threatens and destroys life: the darkness of injustice and social inequality; the corrupting darkness of personal and group interests that selfishly consume what is destined for the good of all without any accountability; the darkness of disrespect for human life which daily destroys the lives of many innocent people, whose blood cries out to heaven; the darkness of thirst for vengeance and the hatred that stains the hands of those who would right wrongs on their own authority; the darkness of those who become numb to the pain of so many victims. Jesus scatters and destroys all this darkness with the command he gives to Peter in the boat: "Put out into the deep water" (v. 4).

But the command to cast out nets is not directed only to Simon Peter. He was directed to put out into the deep, like those in your homeland who first recognized what is most urgent, like those who took the initiative for peace, for life. Casting out the nets involves responsibility. In Bogotá and in Colombia a vast community journeys forward, called to conversion in a healthy net that gathers everyone into unity, working for the defense and care of human life, especially when it is most fragile and vulnerable: in a mother's womb, in infancy, in old age, in conditions of defenselessness and in situations of social marginalization. Great multitudes of people in Bogotá and in Colombia can also become truly vibrant, just, and fraternal communities, if they hear and welcome the word of God. From these evangelized multitudes will arise many men and women transformed into disciples who with a truly free heart follow Jesus, men and women capable of loving life in all its phases of respecting and promoting it.

Like the apostles, we need to call out to one another, to signal each other, like fishermen, to see each other again as brothers and sisters, companions on the way, partners in this common cause which is the homeland. Bogotá and Colombia are at the same time the shore, the lake, the open sea, the city through which Jesus has passed and passes, to offer his presence and his fruitful word, to call us out of darkness and bring us to light and to life. He calls everyone, so that no one is left to the mercy of the storms; to go into the boat of every family, for families are the sanctuaries of life; to make space for the common good above any selfish or personal interests; to carry the most fragile and promote their rights.

Peter experiences his smallness. He experiences the immensity of the word and the power of Jesus. Peter knows his weakness, his ups and downs, as we all know our own, and as is also known in the history of violence and division of your people—a history that has not always found us sharing the boat through the storm, the misfortunes. But in the same way as he did with Simon, Jesus invites us to put out into the deep. He encourages us to take shared risks, to not fear taking risks together, to leave behind our selfishness and to follow him; to give up our fears, which do not come from God and which paralyze us and prevent us becoming artisans of peace, promoters of life. Put out into the deep, Jesus tells us. The disciples signaled one another to meet in the boat. Let it also be so for this people.

You Will Be Catching People (5:5, 10)[3]

All family life is a "shepherding" in mercy. Each of us, by our love and care, leaves a mark on the life of others. With Paul, we can say: "You yourselves are our letter, written on our hearts...not with ink but with the Spirit of the living God" (2 Cor 3:2–3). Each of us "will be a fisher of people" (Luke 5:10) who in Jesus's name "casts the nets" (cf. Luke 5:5) to others, or a farmer who tills the fresh soil of those whom he or she loves, seeking to bring out the best in them. Marital fruitfulness involves helping others, for "to love anybody is to expect from him something which can neither be defined nor foreseen; it is at the same time in some way to make it possible for him to fulfil this expectation."[4] This is itself a way to worship God, who has sown so much good in others in the hope that we will help make it grow.

Rekindle the Memory of His Call (5:11)[5]

Let us gratefully rekindle the memory of his call, which is stronger than any resistance and weariness on our part. As we continue this celebration of the Eucharist, the center of our lives, let us thank the Lord for having entered through our closed doors with his mercy, for calling us, like Thomas, by name, and for giving us the grace to continue writing his gospel of love.

MERCY PURIFIES THE HEART (5:12–16)[6]

"Lord, if you choose, you can make me clean" (Luke 5:12) is the request that we heard addressed to Jesus by a leper. This man did not ask only to be healed, but to be "made clean," that is, wholly restored, in body and in heart. Indeed, leprosy was considered a form of a curse from God, of profound uncleanliness. A leper had to stay away from everyone; he could not enter the temple or attend any divine service. Far from God and far from men, lepers lived a sad life!

Despite this, that leper who approached Jesus did not resign himself to the disease or to the regulations that had made him an excluded man. To reach Jesus, he was not afraid to break the law and enter the city—something he should not have done, because this was prohibited. When he found Jesus, the man "bowed with his face to the ground and begged him, 'Lord, if you choose, you can make me clean'" (v. 12). All that was done and said by this man, who was considered unclean, was an expression of his faith! He recognized Jesus's power: he was certain that Jesus had the power to heal him and that all depended on his will. This faith was the force that allowed him to break every convention and seek the encounter with Jesus and, kneeling before him, call him "Lord."

The supplication of the leper demonstrates that when we present ourselves to Jesus, it is not necessary to make long speeches. A few words are enough, provided that they are accompanied by complete trust in his omnipotence and in his goodness. Entrusting ourselves to God's will in fact means submitting ourselves to his infinite mercy. I will even share with you a personal confidence. In the evening, before going to bed, I say this short prayer: "Lord, if you will, you can make me clean!" And I pray five "Our Fathers" — one for each of Jesus's wounds, because Jesus has cleansed us with his wounds. If I do this, you can do it too in your home. You can say: "Lord, if you choose, you can make me clean!" and think about Jesus's wounds and say an "Our Father" for each of them. Jesus always hears us.

Jesus is deeply struck by this man. The Gospel of Mark emphasizes that, "moved with pity, he stretched out his hand and touched him, and said to him, 'I will; be clean'" (Mark 1:41). Jesus's gesture accompanies his words and renders the teaching more explicit. Contrary to the regulations of the Law of Moses, which prohibited a leper from drawing near (cf. Lev 13:45–46), Jesus extends his hand and even touches him. How often do we encounter a poor person who comes to meet us? We can also be generous, we can have compassion, but usually we do not touch him. We offer him coins, we toss them, but we avoid touching his hand. And we forget that that person is the Body of Christ! Jesus teaches us not to be afraid to touch the poor and the excluded, because he is in them. Touching the poor, touching the excluded can cleanse us from hypocrisy and make us distressed over their condition. So many people think that it would be better if refugees stayed in their land, but they suffer so much there. They are our refugees, but so many consider them excluded. Please, they are our brothers! A Christian excludes no one, gives a place to everyone, allows everyone to come.

After healing the leper, Jesus commands him not to speak of this to anyone but tells him: "Go and show yourself to the priest, and, as Moses commanded, make an offering for your cleansing, for a testimony to them" (v. 14). What Jesus says demonstrates at least three things. First: the grace that acts in us does not seek sensationalism. Usually it moves with discretion and without glamour. To treat our wounds and guide us on the path of holiness grace patiently models our heart on the heart of the Lord, so that we can gradually assume his thoughts and feelings. Second: by having the priest officially verify the healing and by conducting an expiatory sacrifice, the leper is readmitted to the community of believers and to social life. His reintegration completes the healing. As he himself had asked, now he is completely made clean. And third: by presenting himself to the priests, the leper bears witness to them of Jesus and his messianic authority. The power of compassion with which Jesus healed the leper led this man's faith to open itself to the mission. He was excluded, and now he is one of us.

Let us consider ourselves, our afflictions.... We each have our own. Let us think sincerely. How often do we cover them with the hypocrisy of "good manners"? And precisely then, it is necessary to be alone, to kneel before God and pray: "Lord, if you choose, you can make me clean!" Do it, do it before going to bed, every evening. Now together let us say this beautiful prayer: "Lord, if you choose, you can make me clean!"

THE HEALING OF THE PARALYTIC (5:17–26)[7]

The Book of Isaiah (35:1–10) speaks to us of renewal: the wilderness rejoices and blossoms so they will see the glory of the Lord. Therefore, the wilderness will blossom, and that which was desert, that which was ugly, that which was rejected, will be filled with flowers: it will be renewed. Thus, the prophecy of Isaiah foretells the coming of the Savior: it is the change from ugly to beautiful, from evil to good. Moreover, this will give us joy, will help us because of the foretold healings: "Then the eyes of the blind shall be opened, and the ears of the deaf unstopped; then shall the lame leap" (vv. 5–6) and even in the desert "a highway shall be there, and it shall be called the Holy Way" (v. 8). It will be a path that his people may follow. These words illustrate a change for the better, which is why the people waited for the Messiah, waited for him whom the prophet Isaiah had announced.

Indeed, Jesus came, Jesus healed, Jesus taught, and Jesus showed the people a path of change, and for this reason the people followed him. He was not followed because he was "today's news": he was followed because the message of Jesus reached the heart. The Bible says that he spoke with authority, not as the doctors of the law spoke, and the people understood. Furthermore, the people saw that Jesus healed, and they followed him also for this reason: many sick were brought to him because he restored their health. This is all recounted in the day's gospel passage (Luke 5:17–26).

Nonetheless, what Jesus did was not just a change from ugly to beautiful, from evil to good: Jesus transformed. Indeed, it was not a matter of making beautiful, not a problem of cosmetics, of makeup. In reality, the Lord changed everything from within. He effected change through a re-creation: God created the world; humankind fell into sin; Jesus came to re-create the world.

The message of the gospel passage is clear: before healing that man, Jesus forgave his sins. The Lord goes there, to the re-creation; he re-creates the man from a sinner into an upright person; he re-creates him as an upright person. In essence, he makes him new, he renews him, and this scandalizes. Therefore, the doctors of the law begin to question, to murmur: "Who is this who is speaking blasphemies? Who can forgive sins but God alone?"

Jesus "scandalized" because he is able to make us—us sinners —into new persons. Magdalene realized this when she went to him, weeping and washing his feet with her tears, drying them with her hair. She realized that here was the healer of her scourge. She was a healthy woman. She had her health, but she had a wound within her : she was a sinner. She realized that this man could heal not only the body but also the wound of the soul; he could re-create her. It takes great faith to recognize this. To understand such faith, we have prayed to the Lord today in the collect prayer, that he might help us prepare ourselves with great faith for Christmas.

Great faith is required for the healing of the soul, for existential healing, the re-creation that Jesus brings. It isn't easy. "All things are possible to him who believes," Jesus had said to the father of that [possessed] child after the Transfiguration. "I believe, Lord, but help my unbelief," said the poor man. This, because he too understood that there was something more.

The Courage to Let Yourself Be Re-created
To be transformed is the grace of health that Jesus brings. Often, when we think about this, we say: "But, I can't take it!" because to begin a new life, to allow myself to be transformed, to allow myself to be re-created by Jesus is very difficult. The prophet Isaiah said: "Strengthen the weak hands, and make firm the feeble knees. Say to those whose hearts are fearful, 'Be strong, do not fear! Here is your God'" (35:3–4).

This is why "courage" is the word of God: "Courage, allow yourselves to be re-created." Not only to be healed, but to be re-created: to have our hearts be re-created. We are all sinners, but we need to look at the root of our sin. The Lord goes down beneath it and re-creates it. And that bitter root will blossom: it will blossom with works of justice, and you will be a new man, a new woman.

The temptation is that of not allowing oneself to be re-created by the Lord, whereby we limit ourselves to recognizing that "Yes, yes, I have sins," but "I go, I confess, two little words, and then I continue in the same way." In other words, with just two brushstrokes of paint, we believe that that's the end of the story. On the contrary, we need to recognize our sins, with a name and a surname: I did this, this, this, and I am ashamed in my heart. Then I can open my heart, "Lord, the only one I have, re-create me, re-create me!" Only in this way will we have the courage to go with true faith toward Christmas, without ever hiding the gravity of our sins.

A great saint, a biblical scholar, had too strong a character with many impulses toward anger. He asked forgiveness from the Lord, always doing many penances. And he offered to the Lord many sacrifices. That saint, speaking with the Lord, said: "Are you content, Lord?"—"No!"—"But I have given you everything!"—"No, something is lacking." So the poor man did another penance, said another prayer, engaged in another vigil: "I gave you this, Lord, okay?"—"No, something is lacking"—"But what is lacking, Lord?"—"Your sins are lacking, give me your sins!"

This is precisely what the Lord asks of us today: "Courage, give me your sins, and I will make you a new man, a new woman." Lord, give us the grace to believe this.

JESUS CALLS LEVI (5:27–32)[8]

I am always a bit afraid to use certain common expressions in our ecclesial language. "Vocational pastoral ministry" could bring to mind one of the many areas of the Church's action, an office of the Curia, or perhaps the development of a project. I am not saying these things aren't important, but there is much more. Vocational pastoral ministry is an encounter with the Lord! When we welcome Christ, we experience a decisive connection that brings light to our existence, pulls us out of the angst of our little world, and transforms us into disciples in love with our Master.

You know—I have said it at other times—that I have chosen this motto *"Miserando atque eligendo,"* remembering the early years when I felt the strong call of Lord. It did not happen after a conference or because of a nice theory, but because I experienced Christ's merciful gaze upon me. This is how it happened. I'm telling you the truth. So, it is nice that you have come here, from many parts of the world, to reflect on this theme—but please, it must not end here with a nice conference! Vocational pastoral ministry is learning the style of Jesus who passes through the places of daily life, stops without being hurried, and, by looking at our brothers with mercy, leads them to encounter God the Father.

The evangelists often stress a particular aspect of Jesus's mission: He went out in the streets and began to walk (cf. Luke 9:51), "travelling through cities and villages" (cf. Luke 9:35), and he encountered the sufferings and hopes of the people. He is "God with us," who lives in the homes of his children and does not fear mingling with the crowds in our cities, becoming the leaven of newness where people struggle for a different life. In the case of Matthew's vocation, we find the same detail: first Jesus goes out again to pray, then he sees Levi sitting at the tax office, and finally he calls him (cf. Luke 5:27). Let us ponder these three verbs, which indicate the dynamism of all vocational pastoral ministry: go out, see, and call.

To go out. Vocational pastoral ministry needs a Church in motion, able to expand her borders, measuring them not on the narrow-mindedness of human calculations nor the fear of making mistakes, but on the broad measure of the merciful heart of God. There cannot be a fruitful sowing of vocations if we simply remain closed within the convenient pastoral criterion of "we have always done it this way," without "being bold and creative in this task of rethinking the goals, structures, style and method of evangelization in our respective communities."[9] We have to learn to go out from our rigidness that makes us incapable of communicating the joy of the gospel, out from the standardized formulas that often prove to be anachronistic, out from the preconceived analyses that slot the lives of people into cold categories—go out from all of this.

To see. When he goes into the streets, Jesus stops and meets the gaze of the other, without rushing. This is what makes his call attractive and fascinating. Unfortunately, today haste and the stimuli to which we are subjected often do not leave space for that interior silence in which the Lord's call echoes.

At times this can happen in our communities, when pastors and pastoral workers who are hurried, overly preoccupied with things to do, risk falling into an empty organizational activism that leaves them unable to stop and meet people. The gospel, however, shows us that vocation begins with a look of mercy that settles upon an individual.

It is that term: *"miserando,"* which expresses the embrace of the eyes and of the heart at the same time. This is how Jesus looked at Matthew. Finally, this "publican" did not feel a look of contempt or judgment upon him but felt instead that he was looked at with love. Jesus challenged people's prejudices and labels. He created an open space in which Matthew was able to reexamine his life and embark on a new path.

It is a look of discernment that accompanies people, without taking over their conscience and without pretending to control the grace of God. Finally, it is an attentive and watchful look, and is thus continuously called on to purify itself.

To call. This is the typical verb of the Christian vocation. Jesus does not make long speeches, he does not provide a program to adhere to, he does not proselytize, nor does he offer prepackaged answers. In speaking to Matthew, he merely says: "Follow me!" In this way, he stirs in Matthew the appeal of discovering a new destination, of opening his life toward a "place" that goes beyond the little desk where he is seated. Jesus's desire is to put people on a path, to move them from lethal sedentariness, to break the illusion that you can live happily by remaining comfortably seated among your own certainties.

NEW WINES IN NEW WINESKINS (5:33–39)[10]

The scribes and Pharisees wanted to trap Jesus. Reminding him that John and his disciples fast, they ask him: "You are such friends with John and your disciples are friends, who seem to be just, why don't you do the same?" (cf. v. 33). To which Jesus replies, speaking of two things: a feast and newness.

Jesus primarily tells us about a feast, a wedding feast, and says that we are in a time of feasting! There is something new here, there is a feast! Something has happened and something is renewed, made new. And it is curious that Jesus, at the end, uses the image of wine such that it is impossible not to connect this wedding feast to the new wine of Cana. Basically, everything is a symbol that speaks of newness, above all when Jesus says: "No one puts new wine into old wineskins." Thus, for new wine, new wineskins. This is the newness of the gospel. What does the gospel bring us? Joy and newness.

However, these doctors of the law were locked up in their commandments, in their rules. Saint Paul, speaking about them, often tells us that before faith came—that is, Jesus—we were all held as prisoners under the law. Yet this law was not cruel: held as prisoners, waiting for faith to come, that faith which would be revealed in Jesus himself.

The people had the Law that had been given by Moses as well as so many of these customs and little laws that the experts and theologians had decreed. Thus, the law held them as prisoners. And they were waiting for freedom, for the definitive freedom that God would give to his people through his Son.

Saint Paul tells us: "When the fullness of time had come, God sent his Son, born of a woman, born under the law in order to redeem" (Gal 4:4–5). The newness of the gospel is for redemption from the law. One of you may say: "But Father, don't Christians have laws?" Yes! Jesus said: "I have come not to abolish but to fulfill" (Matt 5:17). And the fullness of the law, for example can be found in the Beatitudes, the law of love, total love, as he, Jesus, has loved us.

When Jesus reproaches these people, these doctors of the law, he admonishes them for not having safeguarded the people with the law, but for having made them slaves of so many little laws, of so many little things that they had to do—and do without the freedom that he brought us with the new law, the law that he sanctioned with his blood.

This, then, is the newness of the gospel, which is a feast, a joy; it is freedom. It is that very redemption that the whole of humanity was waiting for when they were held by the law, but as prisoners. And this is also what Jesus meant to tell us: "Jesus, what do we do now?" The answer is: "To what is new, newness; to new wine, new wineskins." Therefore, one need not fear making changes according to the law of the gospel, which is a law of faith. Saint Paul makes a good distinction: sons of law and sons of faith. To new wine, new wineskins. This is why the Church asks us, all of us, for a few changes. She asks us to leave aside fleeting structures; they aren't necessary! And get new wineskins, those of the gospel.

To the question posed by the Pharisees and scribes, Jesus basically responded: "We cannot fast as you do during a feast. Days will come when the bridegroom is taken away." And in saying this he was thinking of his passion, he was thinking of the times of the passion of so many Christians, where they will encounter the cross.

The fact remains, however, that the gospel is newness, the gospel is a feast. And one can fully live the gospel only with a joyous and a renewed heart. Lord give us the grace of this observance of the law: to observe the law—the law which Jesus brought to fulfillment—in the commandment of love, in the commandments which come through the Beatitudes, those commandments of the renewed law of the newness of the gospel. Lord, give us the grace of not being prisoners. Give us the grace of joy and of the freedom that brings us the newness of the gospel.

LEAVE THE OLD WINESKINS (5:37–39)[11]

I encourage you to be attentive to the different forms of marginalization that exist on the geographical and existential peripheries. Do not be afraid to *"leave the old wineskins,"* and to face the transformation of structures, where this can be beneficial to a service which is more evangelical and coherent with your original charism. Structures, in some cases, give false protection and restrain the vitality of charity and service to the kingdom of God. I want to repeat this: structures, in certain cases, give false protection and restrain the vitality of charity and service to the kingdom of God. But at the basis of these processes there is always the joyful experience of the encounter with Christ and of consecration to him; there is the joyful demand of the primacy of God and of placing nothing before him and before "matters" of the Spirit; there is the gift of manifesting his mercy and his tenderness in fraternal life and in mission.

6

The Way of Jesus

On the Sabbath, Jesus heals a man whose right hand is withered. However, Jesus's preaching and manner of acting are not appreciated by the doctors of the law. For this reason, the scribes and Pharisees watch him to see what he will do: they spy on him because they have bad intentions in their hearts. And so, after Jesus opens a dialogue and asks whether it is lawful to do good or to do harm on the Sabbath, they do not speak. They remain silent. Luke recounts that, after the miracle was performed by the Lord, they were beside themselves with fury—and here the gospel uses a truly "strong" expression—they discussed with one another what they might do to Jesus.

In short, they began arguing over how to kill the Lord. This scene is repeated many times in the gospel. These doctors of the law do not say, "We don't agree, let's talk." Instead, they are furious and, unable to control their fury, they begin persecuting Jesus, unto death.

There can be no Christianity without persecution. We remember the last of the Beatitudes: when they bring you to the synagogues, persecute you, insult you: this is the fate of a Christian. Moreover, today, in light of the fact that this is happening throughout the world, with the complicit silence of so many authorities that could stop it, we are faced with this Christian fate: to take the very path of Jesus.

In particular, today I would like to recall one of the many great persecutions, that of the Armenian people... the first nation that converted to Christianity, the first, persecuted simply for the fact of being Christian.

Today, the gospel tells us where this story began with Jesus. What they did to Jesus, historically, has been done to his body, which is the Church. Today... as brother bishops, dear brother Patriarch and all of you, Armenian bishops and faithful and priests, I would like to embrace you and remember this persecution that you have suffered, and remember your saints, so many saints who have died of hunger and from the cold, from torture, and in the desert, for being Christians.

The Way of the Cross

The mystery of God that is in Christ brings the cross: the cross of persecution, the cross of hatred, the cross which comes from the fury of these men, the doctors of the law. But who causes the fury? We all know: the father of evil.

May the Lord make us feel today in the body of the Church the love of our martyrs and also our martyrial vocation. We do not know what will happen here. We don't know! But should this persecution happen here one day, may the Lord give us the grace of testimonial courage that all of these Christian martyrs had—especially the Christians of the Armenian people.

CATHOLIC ... BUT NOT TOO CATHOLIC (6:12–19)[2]

On the feast day of the apostles Saints Simon and Jude the Church invites us to reflect on *how and what the Church is*. In the Letter to the Ephesians, the first thing that Paul tells us is that we are neither strangers nor sojourners, we are not passing through, in this city that is the Church, but we are fellow citizens (cf. 2:19–22).

Thus, the Lord calls us to his Church with the rights of citizens: we are not passing through, we are rooted there. Our life is there.

And Paul makes an icon of the building of the temple, describing it as "built upon the foundation of the apostles and prophets, with Christ Jesus himself as the cornerstone." This is exactly what the Church is, for we are built upon the pillars of the apostles: the cornerstone, the foundation, is Christ Jesus himself, and we are inside.

We are also able to see this same vision of the Church developed further in the gospel passage (6:12–19), which tells how Jesus chose the apostles. The evangelist says that Jesus went into the hills to pray. And then he called these twelve. He chose them. Jesus came down with them from the hills and found on a level place, waiting for him, "a great crowd of his disciples," whom he would send out and a great multitude of people who sought to touch him in order to be healed.

In other words, Jesus prays, Jesus calls, Jesus chooses, Jesus sends out his disciples, Jesus heals the crowd. And within this temple, Jesus, who is the cornerstone, does all this work; it is he who leads the Church forward in this way. Just as Paul writes, this Church is "built upon the foundation of the apostles and prophets, with Christ Jesus himself as the cornerstone." This is confirmed by the gospel passage, which tells us that the Lord chose from them twelve: all sinners. Judas wasn't the most sinful—I don't know who was the most sinful—but poor Judas is that one who closed himself to love and this is why he became a traitor. The fact remains that all of the apostles fled at the difficult moment of the Passion, and they left Jesus alone: all are sinners. Nevertheless, Jesus himself chose them.

Thus, Jesus creates the Church through his prayer, through the selection of the apostles, through the choice of the disciples whom he then sends out, and through the encounter with the people. Jesus is never separated from the people: He is always in the midst of the crowd who seek to touch him, "for power came out from him and healed all of them," as Luke highlights in his Gospel.

We are citizens, fellow citizens of this Church. For this reason, if we do not enter this temple and become part of this construction so that the Holy Spirit may dwell in us, we are not in the Church. Instead, we are watching from the threshold, perhaps saying: "How beautiful, yes, this is beautiful!" Consequently, we end up being Christians who go no farther than the "reception desk" of the Church. They are there, at the threshold, with the attitude of one who thinks: *Well yes, I'm Catholic, but not too Catholic!*

How to Build the Church Today

Perhaps the most beautiful thing one can say about how the Church is built is the first and last word of the gospel passage: "Jesus prays." He went out to the mountain to pray; and he spent the night in prayer to God" (v. 12). Jesus prays and Jesus heals, specifically because "power came out of him and healed them all." Precisely within this framework—Jesus prays and Jesus heals—there is all that one can say about the Church. Jesus who prays for his own, for the pillars, for the disciples, for his people; and Jesus who heals, who accommodates the people, who bestows health of soul and body.

We remember Jesus's dialogue with Peter, *the pillar.* The Lord chose him in that moment and reassured him, telling him: "I have prayed for you that your own faith may not fail" (Luke 22:32). It is Jesus who prays for Peter. This dialogue ends after Peter denies Jesus. And therefore, the Lord asks him, by the Sea of Tiberias: "Simon son of John, do you love me more than these?" (John 21:15).

This dialogue shows Jesus who prays and Jesus who heals Peter's heart, wounded by betrayal. And even so, he makes a pillar of him. This means that Peter's sin doesn't matter to Jesus: He seeks the heart. But to find this heart, and to heal it, he prayed.

The reality of Jesus who prays and Jesus who heals applies even today, for all of us. We cannot comprehend the Church without this Jesus who prays and this Jesus who heals. Holy Spirit, enable us all to understand this Church which has power in Jesus's prayer for us and which is capable of healing us all.

THE PRIVILEGED PLACE OF THE POOR (6:20)[3]

God's heart has a special place for the poor, so much so that he himself "became poor" (2 Cor 8:9). The entire history of our redemption is marked by the presence of the poor. Salvation came to us from the "yes" uttered by a lowly maiden from a small town on the fringes of a great empire. The Savior was born in a manger, in the midst of animals, like children of poor families. He was presented at the temple along with two turtledoves, the offering made by those who could not afford a lamb (cf. Luke 2:24; Lev 5:7). He was raised in a home of ordinary workers and worked with his own hands to earn his bread. When he began to preach the kingdom, crowds of the dispossessed followed him, illustrating his words: "The Spirit of the Lord is upon me, because he has anointed me to preach good news to the poor" (Luke 4:18). He assured those burdened by sorrow and crushed by poverty that God has a special place for them in his heart: "Blessed are you who are poor, for yours is the kingdom of God" (Luke 6:20). He made himself one of them: "I was hungry and you gave me food to eat," and he taught them that mercy toward all of these is the key to heaven (cf. Matt 25:5ff.).

THE NAVIGATOR AND THE FOUR WOES (6:20–26)[4]

We can imagine the context in which Jesus delivered his sermon on the Beatitudes, as Matthew relates in his Gospel (cf. 5:1–12). Jesus, the crowds, and the disciples were on the mountain, and Jesus began to speak and taught the new law, which does not erase the old one, because he himself said that every last iota of the old law must be accomplished. In fact, Jesus perfects the old law, the door to its fullness, and this is the new law, which we call the Beatitudes. They are indeed the Lord's new law for us. In fact, the Beatitudes are the guide for the journey, the itinerary; they are the navigator of the Christian life: it is precisely here, on this road, with the directions of this navigator that we can move forward in our Christian life.

The Beatitudes contain so many beautiful things.

However, I would like to focus on the way the evangelist Luke explains this. Compared to the passage from Matthew, today's liturgy from chapter 6 of Luke's Gospel says the same, but at the end, he adds something else that Jesus said—the four woes. Luke lists the "blessed, blessed, blessed, blessed," but he then adds "woe, woe, woe, woe."

There are precisely four woes. That is to say: "Woe to you that are rich, for you have received your consolation. Woe to you that are full now, for you will be hungry. Woe to you who are laughing now, for you shall mourn and weep. Woe to you, when all men speak well of you, for that is what their ancestors did to the false prophets." These woes illuminate the essence of this page, this guide for the Christian journey.

The first "woe" concerns the *wealthy*. I have said many times that riches are good and that what is bad, what is wrong, is the attachment to riches, woe! It is, in fact, idolatry: when I am attached, then I am idolatrous. It is certainly no coincidence that most idols are made of gold. There are those who feel happy that they are not lacking anything, and they have a satisfied heart, a closed heart, with no horizons: they laugh, they are satiated, and they have no appetite for anything. Then there are those who like the praise: they like that everyone speaks well of them and because of this they are calm. But "woe to you," says the Lord: this is the anti-law, it is the wrong navigator.

It is important to note that these are the three steps that lead to perdition, whereas the Beatitudes are the steps that bring you forward in life. The first of the three steps that lead to perdition is, in fact, *attachment to riches*, feeling that there is nothing that you need. The second is *vanity*, desiring that everyone say nice things about me, that everyone speak well of me. I feel important. Too much praise and in the end I believe that I am right, unlike others. Jesus suggested that we think about the parable of the Pharisee and the publican: "I thank you that I am not like other people" (Luke 18:11). When we are consumed by vanity, we can even end up saying—and this happens every day—"Thank you, Lord, because I am such a good Catholic, unlike my neighbor, that neighbor."

The third woe is *pride*, which is laughter that closes the heart. These three steps lead us to perdition because they are the anti-beatitudes: attachment to riches, vanity, and pride.

The Beatitudes, on the contrary, are the guide for the journey that leads us to the kingdom of God. Among all of them, however, there is one that, though I would not say is key, does make us think: "Blessed are the meek": precisely, meekness. Jesus speaks of himself, saying: Learn from me for I am meek of heart, I am humble and meek of heart. Therefore, meekness is a way of being that brings us very close to Jesus, whereas the opposite attitude always brings enmity, war, and many horrible things. Meekness of heart is not the same as foolishness. No, it is another thing; meekness is depth in understanding the greatness of God, and adoration.

The Beatitudes are the ticket, the guide sheet for our life to avoid getting lost and losing ourselves. It would be good for us to read them today. There are not many—it takes five minutes, chapter 5 of Matthew. Read them, at home, for five minutes. It is a good thing to do because the Beatitudes are the way, the guide. We should also think about the four anti-beatitudes listed by the evangelist Luke; those four woes make us take a wrong turn and end up badly.

A Change of Heart (6:24–26)[5]

I would like to ask you for a favor—more than a favor. I should like to give you a mission: a mission that you alone, in your poverty, will be able to carry out. Allow me to explain. Jesus, at times, was very strict and strongly reprimanded people who were not ready to welcome the Father's message. Just as he said the beautiful word "blessed" to the poor, the hungry, those who weep, those who are hated and persecuted, he also said another word that, spoken by him, is frightening! He said: "Woe!" He said it to the rich, the well satisfied, those who laugh now, those who enjoy flattery, and hypocrites. I give you the mission to pray for them, that the Lord may change their hearts. I ask you also to pray for the perpetrators of your poverty, that they may convert! Pray for the many wealthy people who dress in purple and fine linen and celebrate with large banquets, without realizing that there are many people like Lazarus at their door, eager to be fed the leftovers from their table. Pray also for the priests, the Levites, who—upon seeing the man beaten and left for dead—pass him by, looking the other way, because they have no compassion.

To all of these people, and also certainly to others who are linked in a negative way to your poverty and great pain, smile at them from your heart, wish them well, and ask Jesus to convert them. I assure you that, if you do this, there will be great joy in the Church, in your hearts, and also in your beloved France.

Be Merciful Like the Father (6:27–38)[6]

In this passage from Luke, the Lord says: "Be merciful, just as your Father is merciful" (v. 36). It is an invitation to understand others, not to condemn them. The Lord, the Father, is so merciful. He always forgives. He always wants to make peace with us. But if we are not merciful, how can the Lord be merciful us you, since we will be judged by the same standard by which we judge others?

For this reason, if you are a priest and don't feel you are merciful, tell your bishop so that you can be given administrative work, but don't go to the confessional, please! Because a priest who isn't merciful does so much harm in the confessional: he lambastes people! Perhaps one could justify it, saying: "No, father, I am merciful, but I'm a little upset. . . ." Before entering the confessional, go to the doctor who can give a pill for your nerves! But be merciful!

We must be merciful even with ourselves. Instead of complaining—"He did this..."—we should ask ourselves: "What have I done?" After all, who can say that he is a worse sinner than I am? None of us can say this. Only the Lord can. All of us can say, "I am a sinner and I need mercy and I need forgiveness. And this is why I have forbearance for others, I forgive others and I am merciful with others." The Christian way is what Paul teaches to his own in the Letter to the Colossians: "Clothe yourselves with compassion, kindness, humility, meekness, and patience" (Col 3:12).

This, then, is the Christian way. It is not arrogance, it is not condemnation, it is not speaking ill of others. The Christian way is compassion, kindness, lowliness, meekness, and patience. Ultimately, it is the way of Jesus, the way by which Jesus made peace and reconciliation, until the end. Indeed, at the end, in the final moments of life, he managed to hear something that the thief said and responded: "Yes, yes, yes, come with me, dear one, come to Paradise."

Lord, give each of us the grace to be forbearing with others, to forgive, to be merciful, as the Lord is merciful with us, and to act in the Christian way of compassion, kindness, lowliness, meekness, and patience.

GENEROSITY (6:35)[7]

Saint Thomas Aquinas explains that "it is more proper to charity to desire to love than to desire to be loved";[8] indeed, "mothers, who are those who love the most, seek to love more than to be loved."[9] Consequently, love can transcend and overflow the demands of justice, "expecting nothing in return" (Luke 6:35), and the greatest of loves can lead to "laying down one's life" for another (cf. John 15:13). Can such generosity, which enables us to give freely and fully, really be possible? Yes, because it is demanded by the gospel: "You received without payment, give without payment" (Matt 10:8).

BE MERCIFUL TOWARD OTHERS (6:37–38)[10]

With regard to our neighbor the Lord tells us that we must not judge: "Do not judge, and you will not be judged; do not condemn, and you will not be condemned. Forgive, and you will be forgiven" (6:37–38). Of course, each of us he may think: "I never judge, I don't judge."

But if we look at our life, at our attitudes, how many times do our conversations involve judging others, maybe even a little bit? Of course one would say, "This is wrong." But who has made you a judge?

In reality, judging others is bad because the only judge is the Lord. After all, Jesus knows our tendency to judge others and admonishes us because, to the extent that you judge, you will be judged; if you are merciful, God will be merciful with you. So, don't judge.

We can ask ourselves: In our meetings, how many minutes are spent judging others? . . . Be merciful as your Father is merciful. And even more, be generous: "Give and it will be given to you." But what will I be given? "A good measure, pressed down, shaken together, running over, will be put into your lap; for the measure you give will be the measure you get back" (v. 38). And that is the abundance of the generosity of Lord, when we are abundant in our mercy and not in judging.

THE LOGIC OF COMPASSION (6:37)[11]

Looking at our families with the sensitivity with which God looks at them helps us to direct our consciences in the same way as his. The emphasis placed on mercy places reality before us in a realistic way, not, however, with just any realism, but with the realism of God. The analyses we make are important. They are necessary and help us to have a healthy realism. But nothing can compare to gospel realism, which does not stop at describing various situations, problems—much less sins—but which always goes a step further and is able to see an opportunity, a possibility behind every face, every story, every situation. Gospel realism is total concern for the other, for others, and does not create an obstacle out of the ideal and the "ought to be" in encountering others in whatever situations they may be. It is not a matter of proposing the gospel ideal. On the contrary, it invites us to live that realism within history, with all that it entails. This does not mean not being clear about doctrine, but it avoids falling into judgmental attitudes that do not consider the complexity of life.

Gospel realism is practical because it knows that "grain and weeds" grow together, and the best grain—in this life—will always be mixed with a few weeds. I understand those who prefer a more rigorous pastoral care which leaves no room for confusion. I understand them. But I sincerely believe that Jesus wants a Church that is attentive to the goodness which the Holy Spirit sows in the midst of human weakness; a Mother who, while clearly expressing her objective teaching, always does what good she can, even if in the process, her shoes get soiled by the mud of the street; a Church that is able to treat the weak with compassion, avoiding aggravation or unduly harsh or hasty judgments. The gospel, itself, tells us not to judge or condemn (cf. Matt 7:1; Luke 6:37).[12]

MENDING THE HOLES (6:39–42)[13]

When a brother, a sister from the community makes a mistake, how does one correct that person? The Lord has given us advice on how to correct others. But today he repeats what he has said and adds: one must correct him or her, but as a person who sees and not as one who is blind. As the Gospel according to Luke states: "Can a blind person guide a blind person?" (v. 39).

Thus, to correct another person it is necessary to see clearly and to follow several rules of behavior that the Lord himself proposed.

First of all, the advice he gives for correcting a brother we heard the other day; it is to take aside your brother who made the error and speak to him, telling him, "Brother, in this regard, I believe you have not done well." And to take him aside, indeed, means to correct him with *charity*. To act otherwise would be like performing surgery without anesthesia, resulting in a patient's painful death. Charity is like anesthesia, which helps a person to receive the care and to accept the correction. Here, then, is the first step toward a brother: take him aside, gently, lovingly, and speak to him.

Therefore, when one must say something to a sister, to a brother, always speak with charity, without causing wounds in our communities, parishes, institutions, religious communities.

Along with charity, it is necessary to *tell the truth* and never say something that isn't true. In fact, many times in our communities things are said to another person that aren't true: they are libelous. Or, if they are true, they harm the reputation of that person.

In this respect, a way to approach a brother is to say: "I am telling you this because this is what you have done. It is true. It isn't a rumor that I have heard." Rumors wound. They are insults to a person's reputation. They are strikes at a person's heart. And so the truth is always needed, even if at times it doesn't feel good to hear it. In every case, if the truth is told with charity and with love, it is easier to accept. This is why it is necessary to speak the truth with charity: this is how one must speak to others about faults.

Jesus speaks of the third rule, *humility*, in this passage from Luke's Gospel. Correct others without hypocrisy, that is, with humility. If you must correct a tiny flaw, consider that you have so many that are greater. The Lord says this effectively: first take the log out of your own eye, and then you will see clearly to take out the speck from your neighbor's eye. Only in this way will you not be blind and be able to see clearly in order to truly help your brother. Thus, humility is important in order to recognize that I am a greater sinner than my neighbor. Afterwards, I must help him or her to correct the flaw.

If I do not perform brotherly correction with charity, do not perform it in truth, and do not perform it with humility, I become blind. And if I do not see, how can I heal another blind person?

Fraternal correction is an act of healing the body of the Church. It is a compelling image, like mending a hole in the fabric of the Church. However, one must proceed with much sensitivity, like mothers and grandmothers when they mend, and this is the very way that one must perform brotherly correction.

However, if you are not capable of performing fraternal correction with love, with charity, in truth and with humility, you will offend and damage that person's heart. You will create extra wounds and you will become a blind hypocrite, as Jesus says. Indeed, the day's reading from the Gospel of Luke reads: "You hypocrite, first take the log out of your own eye." And while it is necessary to recognize oneself as being a greater sinner than the other, as brothers, however, we are called to help to correct him.

There is a sign which perhaps can help us: when one sees something wrong and feels that he should correct it but experiences a certain pleasure in doing so, then it is time to pay attention, because that is not the Lord's way. Indeed, in the Lord there is always the cross, the difficulty of doing something good. And love and gentleness always come from the Lord.

This whole line of reasoning on fraternal correction demands that we not judge—even if we Christians are tempted to act as scholars, almost as if to move outside the game of sin and of grace, as if we were angels.

This is a temptation that Saint Paul also speaks of in his First Letter to the Corinthians (9:16–19, 22–27): "so that after proclaiming to others I myself should not be disqualified." The apostle, therefore, reminds us that a Christian who, in community, doesn't do things—even brotherly correction—in charity, in truth and with humility, is disqualified because he has not managed to become a mature Christian.

SHARING THE JOY (6:41)[14]

To accompany someone in the search for the essential is beautiful and important, because it enables us to share the joy of savoring the meaning of life. It often happens that we encounter people who linger on superficial, ephemeral, and banal things, sometimes because they have never met anyone who spurs them to seek something else, to appreciate the true treasures. Teaching someone to look to the essential is a crucial help, especially in a time such as ours which seems to have lost its bearings and pursues short-lived satisfaction.

Teaching to discover what the Lord wants from us and how we can respond means taking the path to grow in our own vocation, the path of true joy. This is how Jesus's words to James and John's mother, and then to the whole group of disciples, points the way to avoid falling into envy, ambition, and adulation—temptations that are always lurking even among us Christians. The need for counseling, admonition, and teaching must not make us feel superior to others but obligates us first and foremost to return to ourselves to verify whether we are coherent with what we ask of others.

Let us not forget Jesus's words: "Why do you see the speck in your neighbor's eye, but do not notice the log in your own eye?" (v. 41). Let us ask the Holy Spirit to help us be patient in bearing wrongs, and humble and simple in giving counsel.

7

The Way of Mercy

The figure of the centurion in this gospel passage teaches us that
a man of government must, above all, *love his people*. The Jewish
elders say to Jesus that the centurion deserves what he asks for
because he loves our people. A ruler who does not love cannot
govern. At most, he can only make a bit of order, but he cannot
govern. David disobeys the rules of the census sanctioned by the
Mosaic Law to emphasize the belonging of the life of every man
to the Lord (cf. Exod 30:11–12). David, however, once he understood his sin, went to great lengths to avoid punishment for his
people because, even if he was a sinner, he loved his people.

The ruler must also be humble like the centurion of the
gospel reading, who could have boasted of his power when he
asked Jesus for help, but he was a humble man and said to the
Lord: "Do not trouble yourself, for I am not worthy to have you
come under my roof . . . but only speak the word, and let my servant be healed" (vv. 6, 7). These are the two virtues of a ruler, as
the word God indicates: love for the people and humility.

Therefore, all who take responsibility in government must
ask themselves these two questions: Do I love my people to serve

them better? And am I humble enough to hear the opinions of others in order to choose the best path? If they cannot ask these questions, their governing will not be good.

Jesus Raises the Mother's Son (7:11–15)[2]

I would like to stress the last phrase of this passage in the Gospel of Luke. After Jesus brought the young man, the only son of a widow, back to life, we are told: "Jesus gave him to his mother" (v. 15). And this is our hope! All our loved ones who are gone, the Lord will give back to us and we will be together with them. This hope does not disappoint! Let us remember well this action of Jesus: "And Jesus gave him to his mother." Thus will the Lord do with all our loved ones!

A Culture of Encounter (7:11–17)[3]

The word of God speaks of an encounter. There is an encounter between people, an encounter between people on the street. And this is something unusual. In fact, when we go into the street, every man thinks of himself: he sees, but does not look; he hears, but does not listen; in short, everyone goes their own way. And consequently, people pass by each other, but they do not encounter each other. Encounter is something else entirely, and this is what the gospel reading today proclaims to us: an encounter between a man and a woman, between an only son who is alive and an only son who is dead; between a happy group of people—happy because they have encountered Jesus and followed him—and a group of people who weep as they accompany the woman, who is a widow on her way to bury her only son.

The gospel passage says: "When the Lord saw her, he had compassion on her" (v. 13). This is not the first time the gospel speaks of Christ's compassion. When Jesus saw the crowds on the day of the multiplication of the loaves he was also seized with great compassion, and before the tomb of his friend Lazarus, he wept.

This compassion is not the same as what we normally feel, for example, when we go out into the street and see something sad: "What a shame!" After all, Jesus did not say: "What a poor woman!" On the contrary, he went further. He was seized with compassion. And he drew near and spoke to her saying: "Do not weep." Jesus involves himself with that woman's problem with compassion. "He drew near, he spoke, and he touched." The gospel says that he touched the coffin. Surely, however, when he said, "Do not weep," he touched the widow as well. A caress, because Jesus was moved. And then he performed the miracle, that is, he raised the young man to life.

The Fruitfulness of the Encounter

The only son who is dead resembles Jesus and is transformed into an only son who is alive, like Jesus. And Jesus's action truly shows the tenderness of an encounter, and not only the tenderness, but the fruitfulness of an encounter. The dead man sat up and began to speak, and Jesus returned him to his mother. He did not say: "A miracle has been done." No, he said: "Come, take him, he is yours." That is why every encounter is fruitful. Each encounter returns people and things to their place.

This discourse also reaches out to the people of today who are far too accustomed to a culture of indifference and who therefore need to work and ask for the grace to build a culture of encounter, of this kind of fruitful encounter, an encounter that returns to each person their dignity as children of God, the dignity of living. We are accustomed to indifference whether it be when we see the calamities of this world or when faced with "little things." We limit ourselves to saying: "Oh, what a shame, poor people, they suffer so much," and then we move on. An encounter, however, is different. If I do not look—seeing is not enough; no, look—if I do not stop, if I do not look, if I do not touch, if I do not speak, I cannot create an encounter, and I cannot help to create a culture of encounter.

At seeing the miracle that Jesus performed, the people were seized by fear and they glorified God. And I like to see here, too, the day-to-day encounter between Jesus and his bride, the Church, who awaits his return. And every time Jesus finds pain, a sinner, a person in the street, he looks at them, he speaks to them, and he returns them to his bride. Therefore, this is today's message, and it has to do with Jesus's encounter with his people: the encounter of Jesus who serves, who helps, who is the servant, who lowers himself, who is compassionate with all those in need. And when we say "those in need" let us think not only of the homeless, but also of ourselves, of those of us who are in need— in need of Jesus's words, of his caress—and also of those who are dear to us. So often people eat while watching TV or writing messages on their phones. Each person is indifferent to that encounter. Even right there at the core of society, which is the family, there is no encounter. Let us work for the culture of encounter, in a simple way, as Jesus did.

TO LOOK WITH THE HEART (7:11–17)[4]

Despite being with the disciples in the midst of a large crowd, Jesus had the ability to look at a person, a widow who went to bury her only son. We must keep in mind that in the Old Testament, the poorest were widows, orphans, foreigners, and strangers. In scripture, there are continually exhortations such as: "Take care of the widow, the orphan and the migrant." After all, the widow is alone, the orphan needs care to fit into society, and, with regard to the foreigner, the migrant, reference is continually made to exile in Egypt. It is a real refrain in Deuteronomy, in Leviticus. It is a refrain in the commandments. It seems that these were precisely the poorest, even poorer than slaves: the widow, the orphan, the migrant, and the stranger.

This is the attitude of Jesus, who has the ability to look at detail: there were so many in the crowd, but he looks at them. ... Jesus looks with his heart.

THE MERCY OF JESUS (7:21–22)[5]

At Cana, the distinctive features of Jesus and his mission are clear. He comes to the help of those in difficulty and need. Indeed, in the course of his messianic ministry he would heal many people of illnesses, infirmities, and evil spirits; give sight to the blind; make the lame walk; restore health and dignity to lepers; raise the dead; and proclaim the good news to the poor (cf. Luke 7:21–22). Mary's request at the wedding feast, suggested by the Holy Spirit to her maternal heart, clearly shows not only Jesus's messianic power but also his mercy.

APOSTOLIC COURAGE (7:24–30)[6]

Everyone was attracted by the witness of John the Baptist, the man who was in the desert. Indeed, the Pharisees and the doctors of the law also came to see him, but with an air of detachment. The gospel emphasizes that they too were present, but they were not getting baptized by John—that is, they were not listening with theirs hearts, only with their ears, to judge him—they thwarted God's plan for them. This same behavior can be found in the indifference with which the doctors of the law received the prophets: they listened to the prophets but did not follow them.

Alluding to John, Jesus asked the people: "What did you go out into the wilderness to look at? A reed shaken by the wind? What then did you go out to see? Someone dressed in soft robes? Look, those who put on fine clothing and live in luxury are in royal palaces" (v. 25). Such men are also found "among the bishops." The crowd in Luke's Gospel, however, was seeking a prophet. In fact, they were seeking the last of the prophets, the last of that group of people who began the journey with our father Abraham up until this moment. Thus, here we speak of "the last" prophet, because after him comes the Messiah. And Jesus referred to John as "more than a prophet," a great man. Indeed, Jesus said:

"I tell you, among those born of women, none is greater than John." And it was "this great man" who attracted the people.

Where was John's greatness in preaching to and attracting the people? Above all, it can be found in his faithfulness to his mission. John was a man faithful to what the Lord asked of him. Therefore, he was great because he was faithful. And this faithfulness could also be seen in the way he preached. In fact, John boldly said harsh things to the Pharisees, to the doctors and teachers of the law. He didn't say to them: "Gentlemen, behave yourselves." No. He simply called them a "brood of vipers." John never minced his words. With those who came to him, but never with an open heart, he was always forthright: "Brood of vipers!" This meant that he was risking his life, yes, but he was faithful. He treated King Herod the same way, saying directly to him: "Adulterer! It is not right to live thus, adulterer!"

Of course, if in today's Sunday homily a pastor says: "Among you there are a brood of vipers and many adulterers," his bishop would receive letters of concern: "You're sending us this priest who insults us!" In reality, John insulted people because he was faithful to his vocation and to the truth.

But John's attitude toward the people was completely different. He was very understanding. To those who asked: "What must we do to convert?" he simply replied: "He who has food, share it with the one who has none. Whoever has two cloaks should share with the one who has none." In other words, he began with the least; he behaved like a true shepherd, a great pastor and prophet.

So, to the tax collectors, who were the public sinners because they exploited the people, he simply suggested: "Do not demand more than what is just." He began with a small step and he baptized them. In the same way, he advised the soldiers: "Do not threaten or denounce anyone; be content with your wages, your salary." Simply put, we must be careful not to enter the world of bribes, as happens when a policeman is bribed to overlook a fine.

John, therefore, was concrete, but measured, and to baptize all these sinners, he only asked in return for a minimal step forward, because he knew that with this step, the Lord would do the rest. And they would convert.

This great prophet was a shepherd who understood the situation of the people and helped them move forward with the Lord. But despite being great, strong, sure of his vocation, John also had dark moments and had his doubts. We read of this in the gospel where it is explained that John began to doubt in prison. Indeed, in John's eyes, Jesus was a savior, but not as he had imagined him. And maybe someone whispered in his ear: "He is not a savior! Look, he does not do this, this, this..." And with anguish in prison, the great man, so sure of his vocation, doubted. Moreover, the great can afford to doubt, because they are great.

Jesus's response to John the Baptist was repeated in the synagogue of Nazareth: "Go and tell John what you have seen and heard: the blind receive their sight, the lame walk, lepers are cleansed, and the deaf hear, the dead are raised up, the poor have good news preached to them. And blessed is he who does not take offense at me."

What Jesus did with the least of men, John also did in his preaching, with the soldiers, with the crowds, and with the tax collectors. Nevertheless, in prison he began to doubt. And this, he stressed, is beautiful, namely, that the great can afford to doubt. In fact, they are confident in their vocation, but each time the Lord shows them a new path along the journey, they begin to doubt. And then the questions begin: "But this is not orthodox; this is heretical, this is not the Messiah that I was expecting. ...The devil does this work and some friends also help, right?" Right here is the greatness of John, a great man, the last of that group of believers that began with Abraham. John is the one who preaches repentance, who does not mince words in condemning the proud, who at life's end permits himself to doubt. This is a beautiful example of Christian life.

Let us ask John for the grace of apostolic courage to always say things truthfully—with *pastoral love*. This means receiving people with what little one can give, the first step; and even the grace to doubt. Because it can happen that at life's end, one can ask: "Is everything that I believed in true, or was it just fantasy?" It is the temptation against faith, against the Lord. It is important, then, that the great John, who is the least in the kingdom of heaven—for this he is great—may help us follow in the Lord's footsteps.

CHRISTIAN? YES, BUT... (7:32)[7]

In scripture we meet a discontented people (cf. Num 21:4–9) and criticizing is a way out of their unhappiness. In their discontent, they vented, but they didn't realize that the soul becomes poisoned with this attitude. Thus, the serpents arrive, because, like the venom of serpents, at this moment these people had a poisoned spirit.

Jesus, too, speaks of the same attitude, of this way of not being content, of being dissatisfied (cf. Matt 11:17; Luke 7:32). He says: "How are you to be understood? Are you like those youths in the marketplace: 'We played the flute for you, and you did not dance; we wailed, and you did not weep'?" The problem wasn't salvation but rather liberation, because everyone wanted this. The problem was God's way—they didn't like dancing to God's song; they did not like mourning to God's lamentations. So what did they want? They wanted to act according to their own thoughts, to choose their own path to salvation. But that path didn't lead anywhere.

This is an attitude that we still encounter today. Among Christians, how many are somewhat poisoned by discontentment? We hear: "Yes, truly, God is good. Christians, yes, but..." They are the ones who end up not opening their heart to God's salvation and always asking for conditions; the ones who say: "Yes, yes, yes, I want to be saved," but on the path of their own choosing. This is how the heart becomes poisoned. This is the heart of "lukewarm Christians" who always have something to complain about: "Why has the Lord done this to me?"—"But he saved you, he opened the door for you, he forgave you of so many sins"—"Yes, yes, it's true, but..." Thus, the Israelites in the desert said: "I would like water, bread, but the kind I like, not this worthless food. I loathe it." And we too so often say that we loathe the divine way.

Jesus Heals Us from the Poison

Not accepting the gift of God in his way, that is the sin; that is the venom that poisons the soul. It takes away your joy, it doesn't let you go.

So, how does the Lord resolve this? With the poison itself, with sin itself. In other words, he takes the poison, the sin, upon himself and is lifted up. Thus, this lukewarmness of the soul, this being halfway Christians—"Christians, yes, but...."—becomes healed. The healing comes only by looking to the cross, by looking to God who takes on our sins: "My sin is there." How many Christians in the desert die of their sorrow, of their lamenting, of their not wanting God's way? This is for every Christian to reflect upon: while God saves us and shows us what salvation is like, I am not really able to tolerate a path that I don't like much. This is the selfishness that Jesus rebukes in his generation, that John the Baptist speaks of: "He has a demon." And when the Son of Man came, he was defined as a "glutton" and a "drunkard." And so, who understands you? Me, also, with my spiritual whims before the salvation that God gives me, who understands me?

Let us look at the serpent, the venom there in the Body of Christ, the poison of all the sins of the world, and let us ask for the grace to accept the divine way of salvation; to also accept this food, so wretched that the Hebrews complained about it—the grace, that is, to accept the ways by which the Lord leads me forth. Help us to leave behind this temptation to become "Christians, yes, but..."

THE TEARS OF THE SINNER (7:36–50)[8]

Jesus was the guest of a Pharisee named Simon. He wanted to invite Jesus to his home because he had heard people speak of him as of a great prophet. And while they were seated at the meal, there entered a woman known throughout the city to be a sinner. This woman, without saying a word, threw herself at Jesus's feet and burst into tears; her tears bathed the feet of Jesus, and she dried them with her hair, then kissed them and anointed them with the perfumed oil she had brought with her.

Two figures stand out: Simon, the zealous servant of the law, and the anonymous sinful woman. While the former judges others based on appearances, the latter, through her actions, expresses the sincerity of her heart. Simon, though having invited Jesus, does not want to compromise himself or entangle his life with the Master; the woman, on the contrary, entrusts herself completely to him with love and veneration.

The Pharisee cannot fathom why Jesus would let himself be "contaminated" by sinners. He thinks that if Jesus were a real prophet, he would recognize sinners and keep his distance in order to keep from being soiled, as if they were lepers. This attitude is typical of a certain way of understanding religion, and it is based on the fact that God and sin are radically opposed. The word of God, however, teaches us to distinguish sin from the sinner: one should not have to compromise with sin, but sinners—that is, all of us!—are like the sick who need to be treated. And to heal them, the doctor needs to get close, examine them, and touch them. Naturally, the sick person, in order to be healed, must recognize that he needs the doctor!

Jesus Sides with the Sinner

Between the Pharisee and the sinful woman, Jesus sides with the latter. Jesus, free of the prejudices that hinder the expression of mercy, lets her approach him. He, the Holy One of God, lets her touch him without fear of contamination. Jesus is free, because he is close to God who is the merciful Father. And this closeness to God, the merciful Father, gives Jesus freedom. Furthermore, by entering into a relationship with the sinner, Jesus puts an end to that state of isolation to which the ruthless judgment of the Pharisee and of her fellow citizens—the same people who exploited her—had condemned her: "Your sins are forgiven" (v. 48). The woman can now go "in peace." The Lord sees the sincerity of her faith and conversion; thus, before everyone, he proclaims: "Your faith has saved you" (v. 50).

On one side, there is the lawyer's hypocrisy; on the other, the sincerity, humility, and faith of the woman. We are all sinners, but too often we fall into the temptation of hypocrisy, of believing ourselves to be better than others, and we say: "Just look at your sin." We all need, however, to look at our own sins, our own shortcomings, our own mistakes, and then look to the Lord. This is the lifeline of salvation: the relation between the "I" of the sinner and the Lord. If I feel I am righteous, there is no saving relationship.

At this point, an even greater wonder astounds all those at the table: "Who is this, who even forgives sins?" (v. 49). Jesus does not answer explicitly, but the conversion of the sinner is before the eyes of all, and it shows that from him there emanates the power of the mercy of God, which is able to transform hearts.

The sinful woman teaches us the connection between faith, love, and recognition. "Many sins" have been forgiven her and therefore she has loved much, "but the one to whom little is forgiven loves little" (v. 47). Even Simon himself has to admit that the one who is guiltiest loves more. God has wrapped each and every one of us in the same mystery of mercy, and from his love, which always comes to us first, we learn how to love. As Saint Paul recalls: "in him we have redemption through his blood, the forgiveness of our trespasses, according to his grace that he lavished on us" (Eph 1:7–8). In this passage, "grace" is virtually synonymous with mercy, and we are told that God has "lavished" it upon us, meaning that it far exceeds our expectations, since it brings to fulfillment God's saving plan for each one of us.

Let us recognize the gift of faith. Let us give thanks to the Lord for his love which is so great and unmerited! Let us allow the love of Christ be poured into us. The disciple is drawn to this love and builds on it; and from this love each one of us can be nourished and fed. Thus, from the grateful love that we, in turn, pour out upon our brothers and sisters in our homes, in our families, and in our societies, the mercy of the Lord may be communicated to everyone.

The Living God Is Merciful (7:47)[9]

Jesus allows a woman who was a sinner to approach him during a meal in the house of a Pharisee, scandalizing those present. Not only does he let the woman approach, but he even forgives her sins, saying: "Her sins, which were many, have been forgiven; hence she has shown great love. But the one to whom little is forgiven, loves little" (v. 47). Jesus is the incarnation of the Living God, the one who brings life amid so many deeds of death, amid sin, selfishness, and self-absorption. Jesus accepts, loves, uplifts, encourages, forgives, restores the ability to walk, and gives back life. Throughout the Gospels, we see how Jesus, by his words and actions, brings the transforming life of God. This was the experience of the woman who anointed the feet of the Lord with ointment: she felt understood, loved, and she responded with a gesture of love. She let herself be touched by God's mercy, she obtained forgiveness, and she started a new life. God, the Living One, is merciful. Do you agree? Let's say it together: God, the Living One, is merciful! All together now: God, the Living One, is merciful. Once again: God, the Living One is merciful!

Divine Forgiveness (7:49)[10]

We have heard the reaction of the dining companions of Simon the Pharisee: "Who is this, who even forgives sins?" (v. 49). Jesus has just made a scandalous gesture. A woman of the city, known by all as a sinner, entered Simon's house, stooped at Jesus's feet and anointed them with fragrant oil. All those who were there at the table were whispering: "If Jesus is a prophet, he should not accept such gestures from a woman like that." Those poor women, who served only to be met in secret, even by leaders, or to be stoned. According to the mentality of the time, there must be a clear division between saint and sinner, between pure and impure.

But Jesus's attitude is different. From the beginning of his ministry in Galilee, he approaches lepers, the demon-possessed, all the sick, and all the marginalized people. Conduct of this kind was not at all customary, such that Jesus's compassion for the excluded, the "untouchable," would be one of the things that upsets his contemporaries the most.

Wherever there is a person who suffers, Jesus takes on their burden, and that suffering becomes his own. Jesus does not preach like the stoic philosophers, saying that the condition of suffering must be borne with heroism. Jesus shares human pain and, when he comes across it, that attitude which characterizes Christianity—mercy—bursts forth from his heart. Jesus feels mercy in the face of human suffering. Jesus's heart is merciful. Jesus feels compassion. Literally, Jesus feels his heart tremble. Many times in the gospel we see this type of reaction. Christ's heart embodies and reveals the heart of God, who, wherever there is a man or woman suffering, wishes healing, liberation, and fullness of life for him or her.

This is why Jesus *opens his arms to sinners*. How many people, even today, persist in an ill-chosen life because they have found no one willing to look at them in a different way, with the eyes, or better, with the heart of God—that is, to look at them with hope? Jesus, instead, sees a possibility for resurrection even in those who have made many mistaken choices. Jesus is always there, with an open heart. He throws open the mercy that he has in his heart. He forgives, embraces, understands, and draws near. That is how Jesus is!

At times we forget that for Jesus it is not a matter of easy, low-cost love. The gospels reveal the first negative reactions toward Jesus precisely when he forgives a man's sins (cf. Mark 2:1–12). It is a man who is suffering doubly because he cannot walk and because he feels "inadequate." Jesus understands that the second pain is greater than the first, and so he greets him immediately with a message of liberation: "My son, your sins are forgiven" (v. 5). He frees him from the oppressive feeling of inadequacy. It is then that several scribes—those who believe they are perfect (I think of the many Catholics who believe they are perfect and scorn others...this is sad)—are scandalized by Jesus's words, which sound like blasphemy, because "only God can forgive sins."

We who are accustomed to experiencing the forgiveness of sins, perhaps at too "low" a "cost," must, at times, remind ourselves of the high price of God's love for us. Each of us has cost a great deal: Jesus's life! He would have offered it even for just one of us. Jesus does not go to the cross because he heals the sick, because he preaches charity, because he proclaims the beatitudes. The Son of God goes to the cross, above all, because he forgives sins; because he wants the total, definitive liberation of people's hearts; because he does not accept that the human being exhausts his entire existence with this indelible "tattoo," with the thought of not being able to be welcomed by the merciful heart of God. It is with these sentiments that Jesus goes to encounter sinners, who are all of us.

This is how sinners are forgiven. They are not just comforted on the psychological level, because they are freed from the sense of guilt. Jesus does much more: he offers people who have made mistakes the hope of a new life. "But Lord, I am but a rag"—"Look forward and I will make you a new heart." This is the hope that Jesus gives us. A life marked by love. Matthew, the publican, who is a traitor to his country, an exploiter of the people, becomes an apostle of Christ. Zacchaeus, the rich, corrupt man from Jericho—this man surely had a degree in bribery—is transformed into a benefactor of the poor. The Samaritan woman, who had five husbands and is now living with another, hears the promise of "living water," which can well up within her forever (cf. John 4:14). This is how Jesus changes hearts; he does so with all of us.

It does us good to consider that God did not choose people who never make mistakes as the first dough to shape his Church.

The Church is a people of sinners who feel the mercy and forgiveness of God. Peter understood the truth about himself more from the crowing of the cock than from his impulses of generosity, which swelled his chest, making him feel superior to others.

Brothers and sisters, we are all poor sinners in need of God's mercy, which has the power to transform us and to give us back hope, day after day. And he does! And to the people who understand this fundamental truth, God gives the most beautiful mission in the world, namely, love for brothers and sisters, and the message of a mercy which he does not deny anyone. And this is our hope. Let us go forth with this trust in the forgiveness, in the merciful love of Jesus.

THE LANGUAGE OF LOVE (7:50)[11]

To be open to a genuine encounter with others, *a kind look* is essential. This is incompatible with a negative attitude that readily points out other people's shortcomings while overlooking one's own. A kind look helps us to see beyond our own limitations, to be patient, and to cooperate with others, despite our differences. Loving kindness builds bonds, cultivates relationships, creates new networks of integration, and knits a firm social fabric. In this way, it grows ever stronger, for without a sense of belonging we cannot sustain a commitment to others; we end up seeking our convenience alone and life in common becomes impossible. Antisocial persons think that others exist only for the satisfaction of their own needs. Consequently, there is no room for the gentleness of love and its expression. Those who love are capable of speaking words of comfort, strength, consolation, and encouragement. These were the words that Jesus himself spoke: "Take heart, my son!" (Matt 9:2); "Great is your faith!" (Matt 15:28); "Arise!" (Mark 5:41); "Go in peace" (Luke 7:50); "Be not afraid" (Matt 14:27). These are not words that demean, sadden, anger, or show scorn. In our families, we must learn to imitate Jesus's own gentleness in our way of speaking to one another.

8

Parables and Miracles

THE GIFT OF FORTITUDE (8:4–8)[1]

The Lord always comes to sustain us in our weakness. and he does this by a special gift: the gift of *fortitude*. There is a parable told by Jesus that helps us to grasp the importance of this gift. A *sower* goes out to sow; however, not all of the seed that he sows bears fruit. What falls along the path is eaten by birds; what falls on rocky ground or among brambles springs up but is soon scorched by the sun or choked by thorns; only what falls on good soil is able to grow and bear fruit (cf. Mark 4:3–9; Matt 13:3–9; Luke 8:4–8). As Jesus himself explains to his disciples, this sower represents the Father, who abundantly sows the seed of his word. The seed, however, often meets with the aridity of our heart, and even when received is likely to remain barren. However, through the gift of fortitude, the Holy Spirit liberates the soil of our heart. He frees it from sluggishness, from uncertainty, and from all the fears that can hinder it, so that the Lord's word may be put into practice authentically and with joy. The gift of fortitude is a true help. It gives us strength, and it also frees us from so many obstacles.

GUARD AND CULTIVATE (8:4–15)[2]

Jesus, the Master, teaches the crowds and the small group of his disciples by accommodating himself to their ability to understand. He does this with parables, like that of the sower (cf. Luke 8:4–15). The Lord is always flexible in his way of teaching. He does it in a way that everyone can understand. Jesus does not seek to "play the professor." Instead, he seeks to reach people's hearts, their understanding, and their lives, so that they may bear fruit.

The parable of the sower speaks to us of "cultivating." It speaks of various kinds of soil, ways of sowing and bearing fruit, and how they are all related. Ever since the time of Genesis, God has quietly urged us to "cultivate and care for the earth."

God does not only give us life. He gives us the earth; he gives us all of creation. He does not only give man a partner and endless possibilities. He also gives human beings a task, he gives them a mission. He invites them to be a part of his creative work, and he says: "Cultivate it! I am giving you seeds, soil, water and sun. I am giving you your hands and those of your brothers and sisters. There it is. It is yours." It is a gift, a present, an offering. It is not something that can be bought or acquired. It precedes us and it will be there long after us.

AN HONEST AND GOOD HEART (8:15)[3]

In the parable of the sower, Saint Luke has left us these words of the Lord about the "good soil": "These are the ones who, when they hear the word, hold it fast in an honest and good heart, and bear fruit with patient endurance" (v. 15). In the context of Luke's Gospel, this mention of an honest and good heart that hears and keeps the word is an implicit portrayal of the faith of the Virgin Mary. The evangelist himself speaks of Mary's memory, of how she treasured in her heart all that she had heard and seen, so that the word could bear fruit in her life. The Mother of the Lord is the perfect icon of faith. As Saint Elizabeth would say: "Blessed is she who believed" (Luke 1:45).

THE LIGHT DOES NOT GO IN THE FRIDGE (8:16–18)[4]

This gospel passage is on the theme of the light, of Jesus's advice not to cover the lamp but rather to let the light shine and illuminate, so that those who enter may see the light. This advice is also reiterated in the gospel acclamation of the evangelist Matthew: "Let your light shine before others, so that they may see your good works and give glory to your Father in heaven" (5:16).

From the start, it is important not to fall into misunderstanding, because typically, in daily speech, we say: "But this is a bright person; or this person is not very bright." Indeed, in the gospel, we do not speak about this type of human brightness. ... It is something else. In fact, to cherish the light is to safeguard something that we have received as a gift, and if we are bright, then we are luminous, in the sense of having received the gift of light on the day of baptism. It is precisely for this reason that at the beginning, in the early centuries of the Church, and even still in some Eastern Churches, baptism is called "enlightenment"; and still to this day, when we baptize a child, we give a candle as a sign of light: it is the light that is the gift of God.

Now, the light that Jesus gives at baptism is a true light, a light that comes from within, because it is the light of the Holy Spirit. It is not an artificial light; the light is not manufactured. It is a mild, serene light that does not go out. Therefore, it cannot be covered. And if you cover this light, you become lukewarm or simply Christian in name.

To better understand the nature of this light that Jesus tells us to cherish, and which is given as a gift to everyone, we think of the Transfiguration on Mount Tabor, when Jesus let all of his light be seen. This is the light that we must cherish and not hide.

And we do this in our daily life. Thus, one might ask, "Father, how can this light be hidden? How can one hide the light so that it does not enlighten, and why do people not see the light that comes from good works?" Here once again, it is the liturgy itself that comes to our aid.

In the first reading, taken from the Book of Proverbs (3:27–34), we read about the wise counsel of a father to his children. First and foremost, it reads: "Do not withhold good from those to whom it is due, when it is in your power to do it." This is very simple: If you can do good, do good. On one hand, everyone has the right to receive good, because we are all children of the Father who gives us good. On the other hand, those who do not do good, when they are able to do so, are covering the light, which becomes dark.

Do not say to your neighbor: "Yes, go now, go, go . . . then come by again and I will give it to you tomorrow." If you have what the person is asking for now — and this is a very strong argument made in the Bible — do not make the needy person wait; do not pay his salary the following day. If you take his cloak in pledge, because you have given him a loan, give it to him in the evening, so that he can sleep. Never put off the good. The light is not meant to be kept in the fridge, that is to say, it should not be preserved. The good is to be done today, and if you do not do it today, tomorrow it will not be there. Do not hold the good until tomorrow. And those who think with the logic of "Go now, come by again, I will give it to you tomorrow" are heavily covering the light.

The Book of Proverbs adds another piece of advice: "Do not plan evil against your neighbor who lives trustingly beside you. This is also a reality before our eyes every day. Very often, people trust in one person or another, and that person plots the evil to destroy them, to sully their reputation, to make them fail. It is the little bit of *mafia* that we all have at the ready: one who takes advantage of his neighbor's trust in order to plot evil, he is a *mafioso*, even if he does not actually belong to a criminal organization. This is the *mafia*; it takes advantage of trust. And this covers the light. It darkens you. All *mafia* is dark.

The passage continues: "Do not quarrel with anyone without cause, when no harm has been done to you." This also occurs in everyday life. We like contention, right? Always. We are always looking for a little something to quarrel about. But in the end, we grow weary of contention: one cannot live this way. It is better to let it go, to forgive to the point of pretending not to see things in order to avoid quarrelling constantly.

The wise father in the scripture continues with his advice and says: "Do not envy the violent and do not choose any of their ways; for the perverse are an abomination to the Lord, but the upright are in his confidence." It happens sometimes that we are jealous, that we envy those who have things, who have success, or who are violent. Yet, if we were to consider the history of the violent, of the powerful, we would realize that the same worms will devour us and devour them; the same! In the end, we will all be the same. The fact remains that envying power and being jealous...covers the light. And the scripture goes even further: "The Lord's curse is on the house of the wicked, but he blesses the abode of the righteous." It is then added that the Lord, instead, shows favor "to the humble."

Therefore, listen to this advice concerning everyday life—it does not deal with unusual things—and welcome the invitation to be children of light, and not children of darkness, and to guard the light that was given to you as a gift on the day of baptism. All of us who have received baptism pray that the Holy Spirit will help us not to fall into these bad habits that cover the light, and that he will help us to carry forward the light we received freely, that light of God that does so much good: the light of friendship, the light of meekness, the light of faith, the light of hope, the light of patience, the light of goodness.

THE "FAMILY" OF JESUS (8:19–21)[5]

Jesus himself offered this an amazing opportunity to every person, bringing himself one step closer to us. This is what emerges clearly from this gospel passage, in which we read that Jesus was preaching with a great crowd while his family came to see him.

When he is told that his mother, his relatives, his family are there, Jesus broadens the concept and says: "My mother and my brothers are those who hear the word of God and do it" (v. 21). Here is the "extra step" that Jesus takes. He affirms that his family is larger than the small one in which he came into the world. In this way, he makes us think of us who are his family, that is, those who hear the word of God and put it into practice.

CROSSING TO THE OTHER SIDE OF THE LAKE (8:22)[6]

I wanted to open the first Holy Door of the Jubilee of Mercy there in Bangui, a week in advance, as a sign of faith and hope for that people, and symbolically for all the African peoples most in need of redemption and comfort. Jesus's invitation to the disciples: "Let us go across to the other side of the lake" (v. 22), was the motto for Central Africa. "Cross over to another shore," in the civil sense, means to leave behind war, division, and poverty and to choose peace, reconciliation, and development. But this presumes a "passing" that takes place in the conscience, in the attitudes and intentions of the people. On this level, the contribution of religious communities is crucial. For this reason I met the Evangelical and Muslim communities, sharing prayer and the commitment for peace. With the priests and consecrated people, but also with young people, we shared the joy of feeling that the Risen Lord is with us in the boat, and he guides us to the other shore.

TOUCHING CHRIST WITH THE HEART (8:45–46)[7]

It was only in this way—by taking flesh, by sharing our humanity—that the knowledge proper to love could come to full fruition. For the light of love is born when our hearts are touched and we open ourselves to the interior presence of the beloved, who enables us to recognize his mystery. Thus we can understand why, together with hearing and seeing, Saint John can speak of faith as touch, as he says in his First Letter: "What we have heard, what we have seen with our eyes, what we have looked at and touched with our hands, concerning the word of life" (1 John 1:1). By his taking flesh and coming among us, Jesus has touched us, and through the sacraments, he continues to touch us even today. Transforming our hearts, he unceasingly enables us to acknowledge and acclaim him as the Son of God. In faith, we can touch him and receive the power of his grace. Saint Augustine, commenting on the account of the woman suffering from hemorrhages who touched Jesus and was cured (cf. Luke 8:45–46), says: "To touch him with our hearts: that is what it means to believe."[8] The crowd presses in on Jesus, but they do not reach him with the personal touch of faith, which apprehends the mystery that he is the Son who reveals the Father. Only when we are configured to Jesus do we have the eyes needed to see him.

9

Discipleship

THE REMORSE OF CONSCIENCE (9:7–9)[1]

As we read in this Gospel of Luke, "Herod the ruler heard about all that had taken place, and he was perplexed, because it was said by some that John had been raised from the dead, by some that Elijah had appeared, and by others that one of the ancient prophets had arisen. Herod said, 'John I beheaded; but who is this about whom I hear such things?' And he tried to see him." But Herod's was not a simple curiosity. His problem was something he felt within: a remorse in the soul, a remorse in the heart. You can sense this clearly when he says: "No, it is not John because I had him beheaded." In other words, he is immediately reminded of the crime he committed. Herod carried that guilt inside and tried to see Jesus to reassure himself, for he had that remorse inside.

The way in which Herod solved the problem is significant. Herod wanted to see miracles, but Jesus did not perform a "circus" in front of him. Therefore, instead of saying "Let him go..." and saving him, Herod handed him over to Pilate. The two then "became friends," and Jesus paid the price. What did Herod ultimately do? He covered one crime—his remorse of conscience—with another crime.

His father, Herod the Great, had done the same thing. When the Magi came to tell him about the newborn king of the Jews, Herod, who had great power but had committed many criminal acts, was upset and afraid that his kingdom would be taken away. So he asked the Magi to report back to him what they found, and when he did not hear from them because they did not return to him, he killed the children.

Why did Herod kill the children? The answer, which delves into the psyche and heart of the king of Judea, is found in an ancient Christian hymn that the Church sings on December 28: "You kill children in the flesh because fear is killing your heart." The ruler kills out of fear; to cover up one crime with another. Both father and son, therefore, went on covering up crimes, covering up "the remorse of conscience."

In fact, this is not simply remembering something. It is a plague—a plague that hurts us when we have done evil in our life. But this wound is hidden, not seen; we ourselves don't even see it, because we get used to carrying it and then it anesthetizes itself. It is within us and when it hurts, we feel remorse. At that moment, not only am I aware that I have done harm, but I feel it: I feel it in my heart, I feel it in my body, in my soul, in life. And that is precisely the moment when there is the temptation to cover the pain so as not to feel it anymore.

"Lord, give us the grace to have the courage to accuse ourselves and to tell the truth about our life": say this to yourself and then tell the Lord so that he can forgive you. It is like when a surgeon takes you to the operating room to have surgery: he doesn't just anesthetize you and then do nothing. The doctor opens you, looks for the problem and, when he finds it, he heals it and removes the problem. The same happens with us: we must be open so that the sore can be found and healed, and the remorse of conscience be removed.

GOD'S LOGIC: TO SERVE (9:11–17)[2]

The gospel passage speaks of the miracle of the multiplication of the loaves. I would like to reflect on one aspect of it that never fails to impress me and makes me think. We are on the shore of the Sea of Galilee, and daylight is fading. Jesus is concerned for the people who have spent so many hours with him: there are thousands of them, and they are hungry. What should he do? The disciples also pose the problem and tell Jesus: "Send the crowd away" so that they can go and find provisions in the villages close by. But Jesus says: "You give them something to eat" (v. 13). The disciples are discomfited and respond: "We have no more than five loaves and two fish," as if to say, barely enough for ourselves.

Jesus well knows what to do, but he wishes to involve his disciples, he wants to teach them. The disciples' attitude is the human one that seeks the most realistic solution that does not create too many problems: dismiss the crowd, they say. Let each person organize himself as best he can. Moreover, you have already done so much for them: you have preached, you have healed the sick.... Send the crowd away!

Jesus's outlook is very different. It is dictated by his union with the Father and his compassion for the people, that mercifulness of Jesus for us all. Jesus senses our problems; he senses our weaknesses and our needs. Looking at those five loaves, Jesus thinks: this is Providence! God can make this small amount suffice for everyone. Jesus trusts in the heavenly Father without reserve; he knows that for him everything is possible. And so he tells his disciples to have the people sit down in groups of fifty. This is not merely coincidental, for it means that they are no longer a crowd but have become communities nourished by God's bread. Jesus then takes those loaves and fish, looks up to heaven, recites the blessing—the reference to the Eucharist is clear—breaks the loaves and gives them and the fish to the disciples who distribute them...and the loaves and fish do not run out—they do not run out! This is the miracle: rather than a multiplication, it is a sharing, inspired by faith and prayer. Everyone eats and some is left over. It is the sign of Jesus, the Bread of God for humanity.

The disciples witness the message but fail to understand it. Like the crowd, they are swept up by enthusiasm for what has occurred. Once again, they follow human logic rather than God's, which is that of service, love, and faith. The feast of Corpus Christi asks us to convert to faith in Providence, so that we may share the little we are and have and never withdraw into ourselves. Let us ask our Mother Mary to help us in this conversion, so that we may follow truly and more closely the Jesus whom we adore in the Eucharist. May it be so.

NOTHING WASTED (9:17)[3]

A few days ago, on the feast of Corpus Christi, we read the account of the miracle of the multiplication of the loaves. Jesus fed the multitude with five loaves and two fish. The end of this passage is important: "And all ate and were filled. What was left over was gathered up, twelve baskets of broken pieces (v. 17). Jesus asked the disciples to ensure that nothing was wasted: nothing thrown out! And there is this fact of the twelve baskets: Why twelve? What does it mean? Twelve is the number of the tribes of Israel, and it represents symbolically the whole people. This tells us that when the food was shared fairly, with solidarity, no one was deprived of what he or she needed, every community could meet the needs of its poorest members. Human and environmental ecology go hand in hand.

I would therefore like us all to make the serious commitment to respect and care for creation, to pay attention to every person, to combat the culture of waste and of throwing out so as to foster a culture of solidarity and encounter.

The Compass for Conversion (9:22–25)[4]

Today, the Liturgy of the Word makes us reflect on *three realities that lie before us as conditions for conversion*: the reality of being human—the reality of life; the reality of God; and the reality of the journey. All three are realities of the human experience that the Church, and we too, have before us for this conversion.

The first reality is the reality of being human: you are faced with a choice: "See, I have set before you this day life and good, death and evil" (Deut 30:15–20). We humans are faced with this reality: either it is good; or it is evil.... But if your heart turns away and if you do not listen and if you allow yourself to be drawn in to worshiping other gods, you will walk the path of evil. And we perceive this in our lives: we can always choose either good or evil; this is the reality of human freedom. God made us free. The choice is ours. But the Lord does not leave us on our own. He teaches us, admonishes us: "Be careful, there is good and there is evil." Worshiping God, fulfilling the commandments is the way of goodness; going the other way, the way of idols, false gods—so many false gods—makes a mess of life. And this is a reality: the reality of being human is that we are all faced with good and evil.

Then there is another reality, the second powerful reality: the reality of God. Yes, God is there, but how is God there? God made himself Christ: this is the reality, and it was difficult for the disciples to understand this. "Jesus said to his disciples: 'The Son of man must suffer many things, and be rejected by the elders and chief priests and scribes, and be killed, and on the third day be raised'" (vv. 22–25). Thus, God took up all of human reality, minus the sin: there is no God without Christ. A God "disembodied," without Christ, is not a real God. In fact, the reality of God is God-made-Christ for us, for our salvation, and when we distance ourselves from this, from this reality, and we distance ourselves from the cross of Christ, from the truth of the Lord's wounds, we also distance ourselves from God's love, from his mercy, from salvation, and we follow a distant ideological path to God. This is not God who came to us, who came close to save us, and who died for us.

This is the reality of God: God revealed in Christ. There is no God without Christ. In this regard, I think of a dialogue by a French writer of the last century, a conversation between an agnostic and a believer. The well-meaning agnostic asked the believer: "But how is it possible? For me, the question is: How is it possible that Christ is God? I cannot understand this. How is it possible that Christ is God?" And the believer answered: "For me, this is not a problem, the problem would be if God had not made himself Christ."

Therefore, this is the reality of God: God-made-Christ; God-made-flesh. And this is the foundation of the works of mercy, because the wounds of our brothers are the wounds of Christ; they are the wounds of God, because God made himself Christ. We cannot experience Lent without this second reality. We must convert ourselves not to an abstract God, but to a concrete God who became Christ.

Here, then, is the reality of being human—we are faced with good and evil; we are faced with the reality of God—God-made-Christ. The third reality with which we are faced is the reality of the journey. The question is: How do we go? Which road do we take? "If any man would come after me, let him deny himself and take up his cross and follow me." The reality of the journey is that of Christ: following Christ, doing the will of the Father, as he did, by taking up our daily crosses and denying ourselves in order to follow Christ. This means not doing what I want but what Jesus wants: following Jesus. And Jesus says that on this path we lose our life so as to regain it afterwards. It is a continuous loss of life, the loss of "doing what I want" and the loss of material comforts. It is always being on the path of Jesus, who was in service to others, to the adoration of God: that is the just path.

These, then, are the three realities: "the human reality—of life, of being faced with good and evil; the reality of God—God who made himself Christ, for we cannot worship a God who is not Christ, because this is the reality. There is also the reality of the journey. The only sure way is to follow Christ crucified, the scandal of the cross. And these three realities are a Christian's compass. With these three road signs, which are realities, we will not take the wrong path. "Repent," says the Lord. That is, take seriously these realities of the human experience: the reality of life, the reality of God, and the reality of the journey.

How to Follow the Master (9:23)[5]

On this World Day of the Sick, let us ask Jesus in his mercy, through the intercession of Mary, his mother and ours, to grant to all of us this same readiness to be of service to those in need, and, in particular, our infirm brothers and sisters. At times, this service can be tiring and burdensome, yet we are certain that the Lord will surely turn our human efforts into something divine. We, too, can be the hands, arms, and hearts that help God to perform his miracles, so often hidden. We, too, whether healthy or sick, can offer up our toil and sufferings like the water that filled the jars at the wedding feast of Cana and was turned into the finest wine. In quietly helping those who suffer, as in illness itself, we take our daily cross upon our shoulders and follow the Master (cf. Luke 9:23). Even though the experience of suffering will always remain a mystery, Jesus helps us to reveal its meaning.

Losing Your Life (9:24)[6]

In this gospel passage resound some of Jesus's most incisive words: "For those who want to save their life will lose it, and those who lose their life for my sake will save it" (v. 24).

This is a synthesis of Christ's message, and it is expressed very effectively in a paradox, which shows us his way of speaking —almost lets us hear his voice.... But what does it mean "to lose one's life for the sake of Jesus"? This can happen in two ways:

explicitly by confessing the faith, or implicitly by defending the truth. Martyrs are the greatest example of losing one's life for Christ. Over two thousand years, a vast host of men and women have sacrificed their lives to remain faithful to Jesus Christ and his gospel. And today, in many parts of the world, there are many, many—more than in the first centuries—so many martyrs, who give up their lives for Christ, who are brought to death because they do not deny Jesus Christ. This is our Church. Today, we have more martyrs than in the first centuries! However, there is also daily martyrdom, which may not entail death but is still a "loss of life" for Christ, by doing one's duty with love, according to the logic of Jesus, the logic of gift, the logic of sacrifice. Let us consider: How many fathers and mothers put their faith into practice every day by offering up their own lives in a concrete way for the good of their family? Think about this! How many priests, brothers, and sisters carry out their service generously for the kingdom of God? How many young people renounce their own interests in order to dedicate themselves to children, the disabled, the elderly ... ? They are martyrs too! Daily martyrs; martyrs of everyday life!

And then there are many people—Christians and non-Christians alike—who "lose their lives" for truth. Christ said, "I am the truth." Therefore, whoever serves the truth serves Christ. One of those who gave his life for the truth was John the Baptist. Tomorrow, June 24, is his great feast, the solemnity of his birth. John was chosen by God to prepare the way for Jesus, and he revealed him to the people of Israel as the Messiah, the Lamb of God who takes away the sin of the world (cf. John 1:29). John consecrated himself entirely to God and to his envoy, Jesus. But, in the end, what happened? He died for the sake of the truth when he denounced the adultery of King Herod and Herodias. How many people pay dearly for their commitment to truth, upright people who are not afraid to go against the current? How many just men prefer to go against the current, so as not to deny the voice of conscience, the voice of truth? And we, we must not be afraid! Among you are many young people. To you young people, I say:

Do not be afraid to go against the current when they want to rob us of hope, when they propose rotten values, values like food gone bad—and when food has gone bad, it harms us; these values harm us. We must go against the current! And you, young people, are the first: go against the tide and have the daring to move precisely against the current. Go forward, be brave, and go against the tide! And be proud of doing so.

THE TRANSFIGURATION (9:28–36)[7]

I invite you to be educators, spiritual guides, and catechists for those who are at your home, who take part in your communities, and who approach the Eucharist. Take them by the hand and lead them to Mount Tabor (cf. Luke 9:28–36), guiding them to the knowledge of the mystery they profess, to the splendor of the divine face hidden in the word which perhaps they are used to hearing without perceiving its power. For those who already walk with you, find places and prepare tents in which the Risen Christ can reveal his splendor. Spare no energy to accompany them on the climb. Do not let them resign themselves to the plain. Gently and carefully remove the wax that slowly collects in their ears, preventing them from hearing God who attests: "This is my Son, the Beloved; with him I am well pleased" (cf. Matt 17:5).

LISTEN TO HIM (9:35)[8]

"It is good for us to be here!" Peter cries out after seeing the Lord Jesus transfigured in glory. Are we able to repeat these words with him? I think the answer is yes, because here today, it is good for all of us to be together around Jesus! It is he who welcomes us and who is present in our midst here in Rio. In the gospel we have heard God the Father say: "This is my Son, the Beloved; listen to him!" (Luke 9:35). If it is Jesus who welcomes us, we too want to welcome him and listen to his words. It is precisely through the welcome we give to Jesus Christ, the Word made flesh, that the Holy Spirit transforms us, lights up our way to the future, and enables us joyfully to advance along that way with wings of hope (cf. *Lumen Fidei*, 7).

UNITY (9:46)[9]

Divisions among Christians, while they wound the Church, wound Christ, and divided, we cause a wound to Christ; the Church is indeed the body of which Christ is the head. We know well how much Jesus wanted his disciples to remain united in his love. It suffices to consider his words, written in the Gospel according to John, in Jesus's prayer to the Father when his passion was imminent: "Holy Father, protect them in your name that you have given me, so that they may be one, as we are one" (John 17:11). This unity was already threatened while Jesus was still among them. In fact, in the gospel it is recorded that the apostles argued among themselves about who was the greatest, the most important (cf. Luke 9:46). The Lord, however, emphatically insisted on unity in the name of the Father, allowing us to understand how much more credible our proclamation and our witness will be if we are first able to live in communion and to love each other. That is what his apostles, with the grace of the Holy Spirit, would then deeply understand and take to heart, so much so that Saint Paul would reach the point of imploring the community of Corinth with these words: "I appeal to you, brothers and sisters, in the name of our Lord Jesus Christ, that all of you be in agreement and that there be no divisions among you, but that you be united in the same mind and the same purpose" (1 Cor 1:10).

JOURNEY TO JERUSALEM (9:51–56)[10]

This gospel passage depicts Our Lord in Gethsemane in the moments leading up to his passion and notes that, faced with his cross, Jesus did two things: he made the resolute decision to undertake his journey, and he announced to his disciples that he was determined to accept the will of the Father until the end. Only once did he allow himself to ask the Father to remove this cross. Jesus is obedient to what the Father wants; he is resolute and obedient and nothing else.

The Lord's journey was not only an example of a journey of suffering and dying on the cross, but also of a journey of patience. Faced with what was to come, he communicated to his disciples that the time was drawing closer. However, as many gospel accounts describe, the disciples did not understand what he said or did not want to understand because they were afraid. Luke, in his Gospel, recounts that the Samaritans did not want to receive Jesus in a village. And the reaction of James and John is strong: "Lord, do you want us to command fire to come down from heaven and consume them?" (v. 56.). Jesus turned and rebuked them. Indeed, at times they concealed the truth; they spoke about their own concerns which were wholly removed from what Jesus was saying or, as we can read in today's gospel, they searched for distractions so as not to think about what was awaiting the Lord.

The disciples' attitude led them not to question and not to understand. Perhaps they believed that it was better not to ask about this. Thus, when Jesus said to them that he must go to Jerusalem, where "the Son of Man must undergo great suffering ... and be killed" (cf. Luke 9:21; Matt 16:21), the disciples did not understand; they were busy "carving up the cake" of the future kingdom of God. They were ashamed because they had been speaking of who among them was the greatest. Meanwhile, Jesus was all alone. He was unaccompanied. No one understood the mystery, the loneliness of Jesus on his journey toward Jerusalem: alone! It was like this until the very end. The gospel tells us that he was accompanied by only one angel to comfort him in the Garden of Gethsemane.

Listening with the Heart (9:51–61)[11]

This gospel passage shows a very important step in Christ's life: the moment when, as Saint Luke writes: "He [Jesus] set his face to go to Jerusalem" (v. 51). Jerusalem is the final destination where Jesus, at his last Passover, must die and rise again and thus bring his mission of salvation to fulfillment.

From that moment, after that "firm decision" Jesus aimed straight for his goal and, in addition, said clearly to the people he met who asked to follow him what the conditions were: to have no permanent dwelling place; to know how to be detached from human affection; and not to give in to nostalgia for the past.

Jesus, however, also told his disciples to go before him on the way to Jerusalem and to announce his arrival, but not to demand anything: if the disciples did not find a readiness to welcome him, they should keep going, they should move on. Jesus never demands, Jesus is humble, Jesus invites. If you want to, come. This is the humility of Jesus; he is always inviting but never demanding.

All of this gives us food for thought. It tells us, for example, of the importance that the conscience had for Jesus too: listening with his heart to the Father's voice and following it. Jesus, in his earthly existence, was not as it were "remote-controlled": he was the incarnate Word, the Son of God made man, and at a certain point he made the firm decision to go up to Jerusalem for the last time. It was a decision taken in his conscience, but not alone: together with the Father, in full union with him! He made his decision out of obedience to the Father and in profound and intimate listening to his will. For this reason, his decision was firm, because it was made together with the Father. Jesus found the strength and light for his journey in the Father. And Jesus was free, he took the decision freely. Jesus wants us to be Christians, freely as he was, with the freedom that comes from dialogue with the Father, from dialogue with God. Jesus does not want selfish Christians who follow their own ego, who do not talk to God.

Nor does he want weak Christians, who have no will of their own—"remote-controlled" Christians incapable of creativity, who always seek to connect with the will of someone else and are not free. Jesus wants us to be free. And where is this freedom created? It is created in dialogue with God in the person's own conscience. If a Christian is unable to speak with God, if he cannot hear God in his own conscience, he is not free. He is not free.

This is why we must learn to listen to our conscience more. But be careful! This does not mean following my own ego, doing what interests me, what suits me, what I like.... It is not this! The conscience is the interior place for listening to the truth, to goodness, for listening to God. It is the inner place of my relationship with him, the One who speaks to my heart and helps me to discern, to understand the way I must take and, once the decision is made, to go forward, to stay faithful.

LEARNING THE PATIENCE OF GOD (9:53–54)[12]

An essential condition for progressing in discernment is to educate ourselves in the patience of God and his times, which are never our own. He does not "bid fire upon the infidels" (cf. Luke 9:53–54), nor does he permit zealots to "pull the weeds from the field" that they see growing there (cf. Matt 13:27–29). It is up to us every day to welcome from God the hope that preserves us from all abstraction, because it enables us to discover the hidden grace in the present without losing sight of the forbearance of his design of love that transcends us.

THE FIRE OF LOVE (9:54)[13]

In the gospel, Jesus announces: "I came to bring fire to the earth, and how I wish it were already kindled!" (Luke 12:49). By imitating the divine Master, you too are called to bring fire into the world. But there is a bad fire and a good fire, holy fire. Luke the evangelist tells us that once, while he was walking toward Jerusalem, Jesus sent ahead of him messengers who entered a village of Samaritans who didn't want to welcome him. Then his two disciples, the brothers James and John, said: "Do you want us to command fire to come down from heaven and consume them?" (v. 54). But Jesus turned and scolded them and then went on to another village. This is the wrong fire. God does not like it. In the Bible, God is compared to fire, but it is a fire of love, that conquers people's hearts—not one of violence—a fire that respects the freedom and the times of each person.

The good fire is the fire of Jesus, of him who baptizes in the name of the Holy Spirit and fire: "I came to bring fire to the earth" (Luke 12:49). It is the fire of charity that purifies the hearts and that flares up on the cross of Christ. It is the fire of the Holy Spirit descended with power at Pentecost. It is fire that separates gold from other metals. In other words, it helps to us to distinguish what has worth eternally from what has little value. As Jesus says, "Everyone will be salted with fire" (Mark 9:49). It is the fire of trials and difficulties that temper, it is the fire that makes us strong and wise. It is also the fire of fraternal charity.

10

The Christian Life

LAMBS AMONG WOLVES (10:1–9)[1]

The day's prayer calls on "all people to welcome God's word and become holy people loyal to God." If it is necessary to "receive the word," then there is a need for sowers of the word, missionaries, true heralds, like Saints Cyril and Methodius, patrons of Europe, who were skillful heralds who had spread the word of God and were even able to do so in the language of the people so that they could understand it.

The day's liturgical readings are also about missionary work, with Jesus sending forth his disciples (cf. Luke 10:1–9), and Paul and Barnabas also being sent out (cf. Acts 13:46–49). What traits should be found in the personality of an emissary, an emissary charged with proclaiming the word of God?

Firstly, it is said that Paul and Barnabas spoke with *frankness*. God's word, therefore, must be transmitted with frankness, that is, openly, and with strength and courage. These characteristics can be found in the translation of the Greek word, *parresia*, used by Paul in the Bible. This means that the word of God cannot be brought as a proposal—"if you like"—or as a good philosophical or moral idea—"you can live like this." Rather, it needs to be introduced with frankness, with strength so that the word may penetrate down to the bone.

The person without courage—spiritual courage, heartfelt courage—who is not in love with Jesus, from whom courage comes, might say something interesting, something ethical, something that will do good, philanthropic good. However, God's word will not be found in him and therefore, he will be unable to form the people of God because only God's word proclaimed with this frankness, with this courage, is capable of forming God's people.

The second characteristic required of the Lord's emissaries is found in the scripture passage in which Jesus says, "The harvest is plentiful, but the laborers are few; therefore ask the Lord of the harvest to send out laborers into his harvest" (v. 2). The word of God must be proclaimed through *prayer*, and this should be done "always." In fact, without prayer, you may offer a good conference, good education, good, very good, but it is not God's word. Indeed, only from a heart in prayer can God's word come forth. Prayer is therefore necessary so that the Lord may accompany the sowing of the word, and the Lord may water the seed so that it may sprout.

Finally, a third trait emerges from the gospel which is interesting. It is reads: "See, I am sending you out like lambs into the midst of wolves." What does this mean? The true preacher is one who knows he is weak, who knows he cannot defend himself from himself. The emissary, in the midst of wolves, could object and ask, "But Lord, so they might eat me?" And the answer is, "Go! This is the way." There is a most profound reflection by John Chrysostom: "If you do not go out as a lamb but go as a wolf among wolves, the Lord will not protect you; defend yourself on your own." Thus, when the preacher believes he is too intelligent or when one who has the responsibility of proclaiming the word of God tries to be sly and thinks, "I can get along with these people," then it will end badly, or he will end up negotiating God's word with those who are powerful and arrogant.

The Church has a mission. This is the way the word of God should be proclaimed, and this is how great missionaries are, the ones who proclaim the word, not as their own but with the courage and frankness that come from God. They do not feel they are great; they pray. Indeed, the great missionaries who have sowed and have helped the Church grow in the world were brave and humble people of prayer. After all, Jesus himself tells us, "When you have done all that you were ordered to do, say, 'We are worthless slaves'" (cf. Luke 17:10). Indeed, the true preacher feels unworthy because he feels it is the strength of God's word which brings forth God's kingdom.

A CALL TO LOVE (10:1–16)[2]

The World Day of Prayer for Vocations reminds us of our need to pray, as Jesus himself told his disciples, so that "the Lord of the harvest may send out laborers into his harvest" (v. 2). Jesus's command came in the context of his sending out missionaries. He called not only the twelve apostles, but another seventy-two disciples whom he then sent out, two by two, for the mission. Since the Church "is by her very nature missionary,"[3] the Christian vocation is necessarily born of the experience of mission. Hearing and following the voice of Christ the Good Shepherd means letting ourselves be attracted and guided by him, in consecration to him. It means allowing the Holy Spirit to draw us into this missionary dynamism, awakening within us the desire, the joy, and the courage to offer our own lives in the service of the kingdom of God.

To offer one's life in mission is possible only if we are able to leave ourselves behind. I would like to reflect on that particular "exodus" which is the heart of vocation, or better yet, of our response to the vocation God gives us. When we hear the word "exodus," we immediately think of the origins of the amazing love story between God and his people, a history which passes through the dramatic period of slavery in Egypt, the calling of

Moses, the experience of liberation, and the journey toward the promised land. The Book of Exodus, the second book of the Bible, which recounts these events, is a parable of the entire history of salvation, but also of the inner workings of Christian faith. Passing from the slavery of the old Adam to new life in Christ is an event of redemption that takes place through faith (cf. Eph 4:22–24). This Passover is a genuine "exodus"; it is the journey of each Christian soul and the entire Church, the decisive turning of our lives toward the Father.

At the root of every Christian vocation we find this basic movement, which is part of the experience of faith. Belief means transcending ourselves, leaving behind our comfort and the inflexibility of our ego so that we can center our life in Jesus Christ. It means leaving, like Abraham, our native place and going forward with trust, knowing that God will show us the way to a new land. This "going forward" is not to be viewed as a sign of contempt for one's life, one's feelings, or one's own humanity. On the contrary, those who set out to follow Christ find life in abundance by putting themselves completely at the service of God and his kingdom. Jesus says: "Everyone who has left home or brothers or sisters or father or mother or children or lands, for my name's sake, will receive a hundredfold, and inherit eternal life" (Matt 19:29).

All of this is profoundly rooted in love. The Christian vocation is first and foremost a call to love, a love which attracts us and draws us out of ourselves, "decentering" us and triggering "an ongoing exodus out of the closed inward-looking self toward its liberation through self-giving, and thus toward authentic self-discovery and indeed the discovery of God."[4]

The exodus experience is a paradigm of the Christian life, particularly in the case of those who have embraced a vocation of special dedication to the gospel. This calls for a constantly renewed attitude of conversion and transformation, an incessant moving forward, a passage from death to life like that celebrated in every liturgy, an experience of Passover. From the call of Abraham to that of Moses, from Israel's pilgrim journey through the desert to the conversion preached by the prophets, up to the missionary journey of Jesus, which culminates in his death and resurrection, vocation is always the work of God. He leads us beyond our initial situation, frees us from every enslavement, breaks down our habits and our indifference, and brings us to the joy of communion with him and with our brothers and sisters. Responding to God's call, then, means allowing him to help us leave ourselves and our false security behind and striking out on the path which leads to Jesus Christ, the origin and destiny of our life and our happiness.

This exodus process does not regard individuals alone, but the missionary and evangelizing activity of the whole Church. The Church is faithful to her Master to the extent that she is a Church that "goes forth," a Church that is less concerned about herself, her structures and successes, and more about her ability to go out and meet God's children wherever they are. God goes forth from himself in a Trinitarian dynamic of love: he hears the cry of his people and he intervenes to set them free (cf. Exod 3:7). The Church is called to follow this way of being and acting. She is meant to be a Church that evangelizes, goes out to encounter humanity, proclaims the liberating word of the gospel, heals people's spiritual and physical wounds with the grace of God, and offers relief to the poor and the suffering.

This liberating exodus toward Christ and our brothers and sisters also represents the way for us to understand our common humanity fully and to foster the historical development of individuals and societies. To hear and answer the Lord's call is not a private and completely personal matter fraught with momentary emotion. Rather, it is a specific, real, and total commitment which embraces the whole of our existence and sets it at the service of the growth of God's kingdom on earth. The Christian vocation, rooted in the contemplation of the Father's heart, thus inspires us to solidarity in bringing liberation to our brothers and sisters, especially the poorest. A disciple of Jesus has a heart open to his unlimited horizons, and friendship with the Lord never means flight from this life or from the world. On the contrary, it involves a profound interplay between communion and mission (cf. *Evangelii Gaudium*, 23).

This exodus toward God and others fills our lives with joy and meaning. I wish to state this clearly to the young, whose youth and openness to the future make them open-hearted and generous. At times uncertainty, worries about the future, and the daily problems they encounter can risk paralyzing their youthful enthusiasm and shattering their dreams to the point where they can think that it is not worth the effort to get involved, that the God of the Christian faith is somehow a limit on their freedom. Dear young friends, never be afraid to go out from yourselves and begin the journey! The gospel is the message that brings freedom to our lives; it transforms them and makes them all the more beautiful. How wonderful it is to be surprised by God's call, to embrace his word, and to walk in the footsteps of Jesus, in adoration of the divine mystery and in generous service to our neighbors! Your life will become richer and more joyful each day!

The Virgin Mary, model of every vocation, did not fear to utter her *"fiat"* in response to the Lord's call. She is at our side and she guides us. With the generous courage born of faith, Mary sang of the joy of leaving herself behind and entrusting to God the plans she had for her life. Let us turn to her, so that we may be completely open to what God has planned for each one of us, so that we can grow in the desire to go out with tender concern towards others (cf. Luke 1:39).

THE MISSIONARY JOY (10:17, 21)[5]

The gospel joy that enlivens the community of disciples is a missionary joy. The seventy-two disciples felt it as they returned from their mission (cf. Luke 10:17). Jesus felt it when he rejoiced in the Holy Spirit and praised the Father for revealing himself to the poor and the little ones (cf. Luke 10:21). It was felt by the first converts who marveled to hear the apostles preaching "in the native language of each" (Acts 2:6) on the day of Pentecost. This joy is a sign that the gospel has been proclaimed and is bearing fruit. Yet the drive to go forth and give, to go out from ourselves, to keep pressing forward in our sowing of the good seed, remains ever present. The Lord says: "Let us go on to the neighboring towns, so that I may proclaim the message there also; for that is what I came out to do" (Mark 1:38). Once the seed has been sown in one place, Jesus does not stay behind to explain things or to perform more signs; the Spirit moves him to go forth to other towns.

THE STRENGTH OF THE LITTLE ONES (10:21–24)[6]

Jesus "rejoiced in praise of the Father." What is the reason for Jesus's joy? Because the Lord revealed to the little ones the mysteries of salvation, the mystery of himself—to the little ones, not to the wise and the learned: to little children. For the Lord cherishes children to sow in the hearts of children the mystery of salvation because the little ones are able to understand this mystery.

This is confirmed in the day's first reading, from the Book of Isaiah (11:1–10), which contains many little things, many small details that make us see God's promise of peace to his people, the promise of redemption, the promise to always save them. The text points out that "on that day, a shoot will spring from the stump of Jesse": the prophet does not say: "an army will come to liberate you," but it refers to a small bud, a little thing. And at Christmas we see this smallness, this little thing: a baby, a stable, a mother, a father . . . and thus the importance of having big hearts but the attitude of a child.

Upon this bud will rest the Spirit of the Lord, the Holy Spirit. And this bud will have that *virtue* which is typical of little ones: fear of the Lord. He will walk in fear of the Lord. But fear of the Lord does not mean "dread." It means testifying in our own lives to the commandment that God gave to our father Abraham: "Live in my presence and be blameless." And all this means humility. The fear of the Lord is humility. That's why only the little ones are able to understand fully the meaning of humility, a sense of fear of the Lord, because they walk in the presence of the Lord forever: they, in fact, feel watched by the Lord, guarded by the Lord; they feel that the Lord is with them.

The little ones understand they are a little sprout of a very large trunk, a shoot upon which the Holy Spirit alights. They thus embody Christian humility, which leads them to recognize: "You are God; I am a person. I journey forward in this way with the little things of life, but walking in your presence and trying to be above reproach."

This is true humility, certainly not "theatrical" humility as ostentatious as he who said: "I am humble, but proud of it." The humility of the childlike is that of someone who "walks in the presence of the Lord, does not speak ill of others, seeks only to serve, and feels that he or she is the smallest.... That's where true strength lies. A clear example can be seen in Nazareth. God, in sending his Son, casts his eye upon a humble maiden—very humble—who immediately afterwards hastens to help a cousin in need, and she tells her nothing of what had happened. This is humility: to walk in the presence of the Lord, happily, joyfully, because this is the joy of the humble: to be seen by the Lord.

Therefore, with the humility of which the gospel reading speaks, we must always remember that humility is a gift, a gift of the Holy Spirit. It is what we call the gift of the fear of God—gift, which we must seek from the Lord. By looking at Jesus, who rejoiced because God reveals his mystery to the humble, we can ask for the grace of humility for all of us, the grace of the fear of God, of walking in his presence, of trying to be beyond reproach. Such grace is a gift that will help us to be vigilant in prayer, carrying out works of fraternal charity and rejoicing and giving praise.

THE GOOD SAMARITAN (10:25–37)[7]

This parable has to do with an age-old problem. Shortly after its account of the creation of the world and of man, the Bible takes up the issue of human relationships. Cain kills his brother Abel and then hears God ask: "Where is your brother Abel?" His answer is one that we ourselves all too often give: "Am I my brother's keeper?" (Gen 4:9). By the very question he asks, God leaves no room for an appeal to determinism or fatalism as a justification for our own indifference. Instead, he encourages us to create a different culture, one in which we resolve our conflicts and care for one another.

In earlier Jewish traditions, the imperative to love and care for others appears to have been limited to relationships between members of the same nation. The ancient commandment to "love your neighbor as yourself" (Lev 19:18) was usually understood as referring to one's fellow citizens, yet the boundaries gradually expanded, especially in the Judaism that developed outside of the land of Israel. We encounter the command not to do to others what we would not want them to do to us (cf. Tob 4:15). In the first century before Christ, Rabbi Hillel stated: "This is the entire Torah. Everything else is commentary."[8] The desire to imitate God's own way of acting gradually replaced the tendency to think only of those nearest us: "The compassion of man is for his neighbor, but the compassion of the Lord is for all living beings" (Sir 18:13).

In the New Testament, Hillel's precept was expressed in positive terms: "In everything, do to others as you would have them do to you; for this is the law and the prophets" (Matt 7:12). This command is universal in scope, embracing everyone on the basis of our shared humanity, since the heavenly Father "makes his sun rise on the evil and on the good" (Matt 5:45). Hence the summons to "be merciful, just as your Father is merciful" (Luke 6:36).

TO BE LIKE THE GOOD SAMARITAN (10:25–37)[9]

Jesus's entire person and his life are nothing other than the concrete revelation of the Father's love, reaching its highest expression on the cross: "God proves his love for us in that while we still were sinners Christ died for us" (Rom 5:8). This is love! These are not just words; this is love. From Calvary, where the suffering of God's Son reaches its culmination, the source of love flows, a love that wipes away all sin and transforms everything into new life. We always have within us this indelible certainty of faith: Christ "loved me and gave himself for me" (Gal 2:20). Of this we are very certain: Christ loved me and gave himself for me, for you, for all, for every one of us! Nothing and no one can ever separate us from the love of God (cf. Rom 8:35–39). Love, therefore, is the highest expression of life; it allows us to exist!

Before this essential truth of our faith, the Church can never allow herself to act as that priest or Levite who ignored the man half dead at the side of the road (cf. Luke 10:25–36). She cannot look away and turn her back on the many forms of poverty that cry out for mercy. Turning one's back to avoid seeing hunger, sickness, exploited persons…is a grave sin! It is also a modern sin, a sin of our times! As Christians, we cannot allow ourselves to do this. It is not worthy of the Church or of any Christian to "pass by on the other side" and to pretend to have a clean conscience simply because we have said our prayers or because we have been to Mass on Sunday. No. Calvary is always real; it has not disappeared at all, nor does it remain with us merely as a nice painting in our churches. That culmination of compassion, from which the love of God flows to our human misery, still speaks to us today and spurs us on to offer ever-new signs of mercy. I will never tire of saying that the mercy of God is not some beautiful idea, but rather a concrete action. There is no mercy without being concrete. Mercy is not doing good "in passing," but getting involved where there is something wrong, where there is illness, where there is hunger, wherever there is exploitation. And even human mercy is not authentic—that is, human and merciful— until it has attained tangible expression in the actions of our daily life. The warning of the apostle John has perennial value: "Little children, let us love, not in word or speech, but in truth and action" (1 John 3:18). The truth of mercy is expressed in our daily gestures that make God's action visible in our midst.

Brothers and sisters, you represent the large and varied world of voluntary workers. You are among the most precious things the Church has, you who every day, often silently and unassumingly, give shape and visibility to mercy. You are crafters of mercy: with your hands, with your eyes, with your hearing, with your closeness, with your touch... craftsmen! You express one of the noblest desires of the human heart, making a suffering person feel loved. In the different contexts of need of so many people, your presence is the hand of Christ held out to all, and reaching all. You are the hand of Christ held out: Have you thought about this? The credibility of the Church is also conveyed in a convincing way through your service to abandoned children, to the sick, to the poor who lack food or work, to the elderly, the homeless, prisoners, refugees and immigrants, to all struck by natural disasters.... Indeed, wherever there is a cry for help, there your active and selfless witness is found. In bearing one another's burdens, you make Christ's law visible (cf. Gal 6:2; John 13:34).

You touch the flesh of Christ with your hands: do not forget this. You touch the flesh of Christ with your hands. Be always ready to offer solidarity, to be steadfast in your closeness to others, determined in awakening joy and genuine in giving comfort. The world stands in need of concrete signs of solidarity, especially as it is faced with the temptation to indifference. It requires persons who, by their lives, defy such individualism, which is the tendency to think only of oneself and to ignore the brother or sister in need. Be always happy and full of joy in the service you give, but never presume to think that you are superior to others. Instead, let your work of mercy be a humble and eloquent continuation of the presence of Jesus who continues to bend down to our level to take care of the ones who suffer. For love "builds up" (1 Cor 8:1), day after day helping our communities to be signs of fraternal communion.

OUR CENTER OF GRAVITY (10:25–37)[10]

The parable of the Good Samaritan is a simple and inspiring story that indicates a way of life. Its main focus is not ourselves, but others whom we encounter with their difficulties on our journey and who challenge us. Others challenge us. And when others do not challenge us, something is not right; something in the heart is not Christian. Jesus uses this parable in his dialogue with a lawyer when asked about the twofold commandment that allows us to enter into eternal life: to love God with your whole heart and your neighbor as yourself (cf. vv. 25–28). The lawyer replies, "And who is my neighbor?" (v. 29). We too can ask ourselves this question: Who is my neighbor? Who must I love as myself? My parents? My friends? My fellow countrymen? Those who belong to my religion? Who is my neighbor?

Jesus responds with this parable. A man, along the road from Jerusalem to Jericho, was attacked, beaten, and abandoned by robbers. Along that road a priest passed by, then a Levite, and upon seeing this wounded man, they did not stop, but walked straight past him (vv. 31–32). Then a Samaritan came by, that is, a resident of Samaria, a man who was therefore despised by the Jews because he did not practice the true religion; and yet he, upon seeing that poor wretched man, "was moved with pity. He went to him and bandaged his wounds . . . brought him to an inn and took care of him" (vv. 33–34); and the next day he entrusted him to the care of the innkeeper, paid for him, and said that on his return he would pay for any further costs (cf. v. 35).

At this point, Jesus turns to the lawyer and asks him: "Which of these three—the priest, the Levite, or the Samaritan—do you think was a neighbor to the man who fell victim to the robbers?" And the lawyer, of course—because he was intelligent—said in reply: "The one who had compassion on him" (cf. vv. 36–37).

In this way, Jesus completely overturned the lawyer's initial perspective—as well as our own! I must not categorize others in order to decide who is my neighbor and who is not. *It is up to me whether to be a neighbor or not*—the decision is mine—it is up to me whether or not to be a neighbor to those whom I encounter who need help, even if they are strangers or perhaps hostile. And Jesus concludes by saying: "Go and do likewise" (v. 37).

What a great lesson! And he repeats it to each of us: "Go and do likewise." Be a neighbor to the brother or sister whom you see in trouble. "Go and do likewise." Do good works. Don't just say words that are gone with the wind. A song comes to mind: "Words, words, words." No. Works, works. And through the good works that we carry out with love and joy toward others, our faith emerges and bears fruit. Let us ask ourselves—each of us responding in our own heart—let us ask ourselves: Is our faith fruitful? Does our faith produce good works? Or is it sterile instead, and therefore more dead than alive? Do I act as a neighbor, or do I simply pass by? Am I one of those who selects people according to my own liking? It is good to ask ourselves these questions, and to ask them often, because in the end we will be judged on the works of mercy. The Lord will say to us: "Do you remember that time on the road from Jerusalem to Jericho? That man who was half dead was me. Do you remember? That hungry child was me. Do you remember? That immigrant, who many wanted to drive away, that was me. That grandparent, who was alone, abandoned in a nursing home, that was me. That sick man, alone in the hospital, whom no one visited, that was me."

THE RELEVANCE OF THE PARABLE (10:25–37)[11]

We should be neither paralyzed by fear nor shackled within our conflict. We have to acknowledge the danger but also the opportunity that every crisis brings in order to advance to a successful synthesis. In the Chinese language, which expresses the ancestral wisdom of that great people, the word "crisis" is comprised of two ideograms: *Wēi*, which represents "danger," and *Jī*, which represents "opportunity."

The grave danger is to disown our neighbors. When we do so, we deny their humanity and, without realizing it, our own humanity; we deny ourselves, and we deny the most important

commandments of Jesus. Herein lies the danger: dehumanization. But here we also find an opportunity, that the light of the
love of neighbor may illuminate the Earth with its stunning
brightness like a lightning bolt in the dark; that it may wake us
up and let true humanity burst through with authentic resistance,
resilience, and persistence.

The question that the lawyer asked Jesus in this parable
echoes in our ears today: "Who is my neighbor?" Who is that
other whom we are to love as we love ourselves? Maybe the ques-
tioner expects a comfortable response in order to carry on with
his life: "My relatives? My compatriots? Those who belong to my
religion?" Maybe he wants Jesus to excuse us from the obligation
of loving pagans or foreigners, who during his time were considered unclean. This man wants a clear rule that allows him to classify others as "neighbor" or "non-neighbor," as those who can
become neighbors and those who cannot become neighbors.

Jesus responds with a parable that features two figures belonging to the elite of the day and a third figure, considered a foreigner, a pagan and unclean: the Samaritan. On the road from
Jerusalem to Jericho, the priest and the Levite come upon a dying
man, whom robbers have attacked, stripped, and abandoned. In
such situations, the law of the Lord imposes the duty to offer assistance, but both pass by without stopping. They are in a hurry.
However, unlike these elite figures, the Samaritan stops. Why
him? As a Samaritan, he was looked down upon, no one would
have counted on him, and in any case he would have had his own
commitments and things to do—yet, when he saw the injured
man, he did not pass by like the other two who were linked to
the temple, but "when he saw him, he was moved with pity" (v.
33). The Samaritan acts with true mercy: he bandages the man's
wounds, transports him to an inn, personally takes care of him,
and provides for his upkeep.

All this teaches us that compassion, love, is not a vague sen-
timent, but means, rather, taking care of the other to the point of
personally paying for him. It means committing oneself to take
all the necessary steps so as to "draw near to" the other to the

point of identifying with him: "You shall love your neighbor as yourself." This is the Lord's commandment.

The economic system that has the god of money at its center, and that sometimes acts with the brutality of the robbers in the parable, inflicts injuries that to a criminal degree have remained neglected. Globalized society frequently looks the other way with the pretense of innocence. Under the guise of what is politically correct or ideologically fashionable, one looks at those who suffer without touching them. But they are televised live; they are talked about in euphemisms and with apparent tolerance, but nothing is done systematically to heal the social wounds or to confront the structures that leave so many brothers and sisters by the wayside. This hypocritical attitude, so different from that of the Samaritan, manifests an absence of true commitment to humanity.

Sooner or later, the moral blindness of this indifference comes to light, like when a mirage dissipates. The wounds are there; they are a reality. The unemployment is real, the violence is real, the corruption is real, the identity crisis is real, and the gutting of democracies is real. The system's gangrene cannot be whitewashed forever, because sooner or later the stench becomes too strong. And when it can no longer be denied, the same power that spawned this state of affairs sets about manipulating fear, insecurity, quarrels, and even people's justified indignation in order to shift the responsibility for all these ills onto a "non-neighbor." I am not speaking of anyone in particular; I am speaking of a social and political process that flourishes in many parts of the world and poses a grave danger to humanity.

Jesus teaches us a different path. Do not classify others in order to see who is a neighbor and who is not. You can become neighbor to whomever you meet in need, and you will do so if you have compassion in your heart, that is to say, if you have that capacity to suffer with someone else. You must become a Samaritan. And then also become like the innkeeper at the end of the parable to whom the Samaritan entrusts the person who is suffering. Who is this innkeeper? It is the Church, the Christian community, people of compassion and solidarity, social organizations. It is us, it is you, to whom the Lord Jesus daily entrusts those who are afflicted in body and spirit, so that we can continue pouring out all of his immeasurable mercy and salvation upon them. Here are the roots of the authentic humanity that resists the dehumanization that wears the livery of indifference, hypocrisy, or intolerance. I know that you have committed yourselves to fight for social justice, to defend Mother Earth, and to stand alongside migrants.

Overcoming Indifference (10:25–37)[12]

Jesus taught us to be merciful like our heavenly Father (cf. Luke 6:36). In the parable of the Good Samaritan (cf. Luke 10:29–37), he condemned those who fail to help others in need, those who "pass by on the other side" (cf. Luke 10:31–32). By this example, he taught his listeners, and his disciples in particular, to stop and to help alleviate the sufferings of this world and the pain of our brothers and sisters using whatever means are at hand, beginning with our own time, however busy we may be.

Indifference often seeks excuses: observing ritual prescriptions, looking to all the things needing to be done, hiding behind hostilities and prejudices that keep us apart.

Mercy is the heart of God. It must also be the heart of the members of the one great family of his children: a heart that beats all the more strongly wherever human dignity—as a reflection of the face of God in his creatures—is in play. Jesus tells us that love for others—foreigners, the sick, prisoners, the homeless, even our enemies—is the yardstick by which God will judge our actions. Our eternal destiny depends on this. It is not surprising that the apostle Paul tells the Christians of Rome to rejoice with those who rejoice and to weep with those who weep (cf. Rom 12:15), or that he encourages the Corinthians to take up collections as a sign of solidarity with the suffering members of the Church (cf. 1 Cor 16:2–3). And Saint John writes: "How does

God's love abide in anyone who has the world's goods and sees a brother or sister in need and yet refuses help? (1 John 3:17; cf. Jas 2:15–16).

NEIGHBORS WITHOUT BORDERS (10:37)[13]

Jesus told the parable of the Good Samaritan in answer to the question: Who is my neighbor? The word "neighbor," in the world of Jesus's time, usually meant those nearest us. It was felt that help should be given primarily to those of one's own group and race. For some Jews of that time, Samaritans were looked down upon, considered impure. They were not among those to be helped. Jesus, himself a Jew, completely transforms this approach. He asks us not to decide who is close enough to be our neighbor, but rather that we ourselves become neighbors to all.

Jesus asks us to be present to those in need of help, regardless of whether or not they belong to our social group. In this case, the Samaritan became a neighbor to the wounded Judean. By approaching and making himself present, he crossed all cultural and historical barriers. Jesus concludes the parable by saying: "Go and do likewise" (Luke 10:37). In other words, he challenges us to put aside all differences and, in the face of suffering, to draw near to others with no questions asked. I should no longer say that I have neighbors to help, but that I must myself be a neighbor to others.

The parable, though, is troubling, for Jesus says that the wounded man was a Judean, while the one who stopped and helped him was a Samaritan. This detail is quite significant for our reflection on a love that includes everyone. The Samaritans lived in a region where pagan rites were practiced. For the Jews, this made them impure, detestable, dangerous. In fact, one ancient Jewish text referring to nations that were hated speaks of Samaria as "not even a people" (Sir 50:25); it also refers to "the foolish people that live in Shechem" (50:26).

THE CREATIVE POWER OF LOVE (10:33)[14]

Each one of us is called to change our heart by turning a merciful gaze upon the other, by becoming an artisan of peace and a prophet of mercy. The Samaritan in the parable took care of the dying man on the road because he "saw and had compassion" (cf. v. 33). The Samaritan had no specific responsibility toward the wounded man, and he was a foreigner. Instead, he behaved like a brother, because he had a merciful gaze. A Christian, by vocation, is the brother and sister of every person, especially if he or she is poor, and even an enemy. Never say, "What do I have to do with him or her?" This is just a nice way of washing one's hands! "What do I have in common with him?" A merciful gaze commits us to the creative boldness of love; there is so much need of it! We are everyone's brothers and sisters and, for this reason, prophets of a new world; and the Church is a sign of unity of the human race, among people, families, and cultures.

THE CAPACITY TO LISTEN (10:38–42)[15]

While on his way to Jerusalem, Jesus enters a village and is welcomed into the home of two sisters: Martha and Mary (cf. Luke 10:38–42). Both welcome the Lord, but they do so in different ways. Mary sits at Jesus's feet and listens to his words (cf. v. 39), whereas Martha is completely caught up in preparing things. At a certain point she says to Jesus: "Lord, do you not care that my sister has left me to serve alone? Tell her then to help me" (v. 40). Jesus responds be saying: "Martha, Martha, you are anxious and troubled about many things; one thing is needed. Mary has chosen the good portion, which shall not be taken away from her" (vv. 41–42).

In bustling about and busying herself, Martha risks forgetting —and this is the problem—the most important thing, which is the presence of the guest, in this case Jesus. She forgets about the presence of the guest. A guest is not merely to be served, fed, and looked after in every way. Most importantly, he ought to be listened to. Remember this word: Listen! A guest should be welcomed as a person, with a story, his heart rich with feelings and thoughts, so that he may truly feel like he is among family. If you welcome a guest into your home but continue doing other things, letting him just sit there, both of you in silence, it is as if he were of stone: a guest of stone. No. A guest is to be listened to. Of course, Jesus's response to Martha—when he tells her that there is only one thing that needs to be done—finds its full significance in reference to listening to the very word of Jesus, that word which illuminates and supports all that we are and all that we do. If we go to pray, for example, before the crucifix, and we talk, talk, talk, and then we leave, we do not listen to Jesus. We do not allow him to speak to our heart. Listen: this is the key word. Do not forget! And we must not forget that in the house of Martha and Mary, Jesus, before being Lord and Master, is a pilgrim and guest. Thus, his response has this significance first and foremost: "Martha, Martha why do you busy yourself doing so much for this guest even to the point of forgetting about his presence?—A guest of stone!—Not much is necessary to welcome him; indeed, only one thing is needed: listen to him—this is the word: listen to him—be brotherly to him, let him realize he is among family and not in a temporary shelter."

Understood in this light, hospitality, which is one of the works of mercy, is revealed as a truly human and Christian virtue, a virtue which in today's world is at risk of being overlooked. In fact, nursing homes and hospices are multiplying, but true hospitality is not always practiced in these environments. Various institutions care for many types of disease, of loneliness, of marginalization, but opportunities are decreasing for those who are foreign, marginalized, excluded from finding someone ready to listen to them because they are foreigners, refugees, migrants. Listen to that painful story. Even in one's own home, among one's own family members, it might be easier to find services and care of various kinds rather than listening and providing welcome. Today, we are so taken by excitement, by countless problems—some of which are not important—that we lack the capacity to listen. We are constantly busy and thus we have no time to listen. I would like to pose a question to you, and each one answer in your own heart: Do you, husband, take time to listen to your wife? And do you, wife, take time to listen to your husband? Do you, parents, take time, time to "waste," to listen to your children or your grandparents, the elderly?—"But grandparents always say the same things, they are boring..."—But they need to be listened to! Listen. I ask that you learn to listen and to devote more of your time. The root of peace lies in the capacity to listen.

11

Prayer

What truly is prayer? First, it is a dialogue, a personal relationship with God. As humans, we were created to be in a personal relationship with God and to find our complete fulfillment only in the encounter with the Creator. The path of life leads toward the definitive encounter with the Lord.

The Book of Genesis states that man was created in the image and likeness of God, who is the Father and Son and Holy Spirit, a perfect relationship of love which is unity. From this we can understand that we were all created in order to enter a perfect relationship of love, in the continuous giving and receiving of ourselves so as to be able to find the fulfillment of our being.

When Moses receives God's call before the burning bush, he asks God for a name. And how does God respond? "I am who I am" (Exod 3:14). This expression, in its original sense, signifies presence and favor, and indeed, immediately afterwards God adds: "the Lord, the God of your fathers, the God of Abraham, of Isaac, and of Jacob" (cf. v. 15). Thus, when Christ calls his disciples, he, too, calls them so that they may be with him. This indeed is the greatest grace: being able to feel that the Mass, the

Eucharist, is the privileged moment to be with Jesus and, through him, with God and with our brothers and sisters.

Praying, like every true dialogue, is also knowing how to be in silence—in dialogues there are moments of silence—in silence together with Jesus. When we go to Mass, perhaps we arrive five minutes early and begin to chat with the person next to us. But this is not the moment for small talk; it is the moment of silence to prepare ourselves for the dialogue. It is the moment for recollection within the heart, to prepare ourselves for the encounter with Jesus. Silence is so important! Remember, we are not going to a spectacle. We are going to the encounter with the Lord, and silence prepares us and accompanies us. Pause in silence with Jesus. From this mysterious silence of God springs his word which resonates in our heart. Jesus himself teaches us how it is truly possible to "be" with the Father, and he shows us this with his prayer. The gospels show us Jesus who withdraws to secluded places to pray. Seeing his intimate relationship with God, the disciples feel the desire to be able to take part in it, and they ask him: "Lord, teach us to pray" (Luke 11:1).

As we heard in the first reading, Jesus replies by stating that the first thing necessary for prayer is being able to say "Father." Let us take heed: if I am not able to say "Father" to God, I am not capable of prayer. We must learn to say "Father," that is, to place ourselves in his presence with filial trust. But to be able to learn, we must humbly recognize that we need to be taught; we need to be able to say with simplicity: "Lord, teach me to pray."

This is the first point, to be humble, to recognize ourselves as children, to rest in the Father, to trust in him. To enter the kingdom of heaven, it is necessary to become little, like children, in the sense that children know how to trust, they know that someone will take care of them, of what they will eat, of what they will wear and so on (cf. Matt 6:25–32). This is the first perspective: trust and confidence, as a child toward his parents; to know that God remembers you, takes care of you, of you, of me, of everyone.

The second condition, too, is being precisely like children; it is letting ourselves be surprised. A child always asks thousands of questions because he or she wants to discover the world and even marvels at little things because everything is new. To enter the kingdom of heaven we must let ourselves be astonished. In our relationship with the Lord, in prayer—I ask—do we let ourselves be astonished, or do we think that prayer is speaking with God like parrots do? No, it is trusting and opening the heart so as to let ourselves be astonished. Do we allow ourselves to be surprised by God who is always the God of surprises? The encounter with the Lord is always a living encounter; it is not an artifact. It is a living encounter, and we go to Mass, not to a museum. We go to a living encounter with the Lord.

JESUS ON PRAYER (11:1–13)[2]

The gospel passage opens with the scene of Jesus who is praying alone, apart from the others; when he finishes, the disciples ask him: "Lord, teach us to pray" (v. 1), and he says in reply, "When you pray, say: 'Father...'"(v. 2). This word is the "secret" of Jesus's prayer. It is the key that he himself gives to us so that we too might enter into that relationship of confidential dialogue with the Father who accompanied and sustained his whole life.

With the name "Father" Jesus combines two requests: "hallowed be Thy name, Thy kingdom come" (v. 2). Jesus's prayer, and therefore the Christian prayer, first and foremost, makes room for God, allowing him to show his holiness in us and to advance his kingdom, beginning with the possibility of exercising his Lordship of love in our lives.

Three other supplications complete this prayer that Jesus taught, the "Our Father." They relate to our basic needs: bread, forgiveness, and help in temptation (cf. vv. 3–4). One cannot live without bread, one cannot live without forgiveness, and one cannot live without God's help in times of temptation. The bread that Jesus teaches us to ask for is what is necessary, not superfluous. It is the bread of pilgrims, the righteous; a bread that is neither accumulated nor wasted, and that does not weigh us down as we walk. Forgiveness is, above all, what we ourselves receive from God. Only the awareness that we are sinners forgiven by God's infinite mercy can enable us to carry out concrete gestures of fraternal reconciliation. If a person does not feel that he or she is a sinner who has been forgiven, that person will never be able to make a gesture of forgiveness or reconciliation. It begins in the heart where you feel that you are a forgiven sinner. The last supplication, "lead us not into temptation," expresses awareness of our condition, which is always exposed to the snares of evil and corruption. We all know what temptation is!

Jesus's teaching on prayer continues with two parables, which he modeled on the behavior of a friend toward another friend and that of a father toward his son (cf. vv. 5–12). Both parables are intended to teach us to have full confidence in God, who is Father. He knows our needs better than we do ourselves, but he wants us to present them to him boldly and persistently, because this is our way of participating in his work of salvation. Prayer is the first and principal "working instrument" we have in our hands! In being persistent with God, we don't need to convince him but to strengthen our faith and our patience, meaning our ability to strive together with God for the things that are truly important and necessary. In prayer, there are two of us—God and me—striving together for the important things.

Among these, there is one, the great important thing that Jesus speaks of in today's gospel, which is something we almost never ask for, and that is the Holy Spirit. "Give me the Holy Spirit!" And Jesus says, "If you then, who are evil, know how to give good gifts to your children, how much more will the heavenly Father give the Holy Spirit to those who ask him for it!" (v. 13). The Holy Spirit! We must ask that the Holy Spirit come within us. But what is the use of the Holy Spirit? We need him to live well, to live with wisdom and love, doing God's will. What a beautiful prayer it would be if, this week, each of us were to ask the Father: "Father, give me the Holy Spirit!" Our Lady demonstrates this with her life, which was entirely enlivened by the Spirit of God. May Mary, united to Jesus, help us to pray to the Father so that we might not live in a worldly manner, but according to the gospel, guided by the Holy Spirit.

THE RIGHT SPACE (11:11–12)[3]

There are many problems that you encounter every day. These problems compel you to immerse yourselves with fervor and generosity in apostolic work. And yet, we know that by ourselves we can do nothing: "Unless the Lord build the house, those who build it labor in vain" (Ps 127:1). This awareness calls us to give due space to the Lord every day, to dedicate our time to him, open our hearts to him, so that he may work in our lives and in our mission. That which the Lord promises for the prayer made with trust and perseverance goes beyond what we can imagine (cf. Luke 11:11–12). Beyond that which we ask for, God sends us also the Holy Spirit. The contemplative dimension of our lives becomes indispensable, even in the midst of the most urgent and difficult tasks we encounter. The more our mission calls us to go out into the peripheries of life, the more our hearts feel the intimate need to be united to the heart of Christ, which is full of mercy and love.

HEARTS OF STONE (11:14–23)[4]

The evil heart—of which we all have a little—doesn't allow us to understand God's love. We want to be free, but with a freedom that enslaves us in the end, rather than that freedom of love that the Lord offers us.

This also happens in institutions. For example, Jesus heals a person, but the hearts of the doctors of the law, of the priests, of the legal system are so hard, they are always looking for excuses. And therefore they say to him: "You drive out demons in the name of the demon. You are a demonic sorcerer." The legalists believed that the life of faith is regulated only by the laws that they make. Jesus called them hypocrites, whitewashed tombs, outwardly beautiful but inside filled with iniquity and hypocrisy.

Unfortunately, the same thing happened in the history of the Church. Consider poor Joan of Arc. Today she's a saint! These "experts" burned her alive because, they said, she was a heretic. Or let's think, more recently, of Blessed Rosmini: all of his books were on the Index. You couldn't read them; it was a sin to read them. Today he is a blessed. In this regard, as in the history of God with his people, the Lord sent his prophets to tell them that he loved his people; likewise, in the Church, the Lord sends saints. It is they who lead forth the life of the Church. It is the saints. It isn't the powerful, it isn't the hypocrites. It is the holy man, the holy woman, the child, the holy youth, the holy priest, the holy sister, the holy bishop.... In other words, it is they whose hearts are not hard but instead are always open to the Lord's word of love. It is they who aren't afraid to let themselves be caressed by the mercy of God. This is why saints are men and women who understand misery, human misery, and accompany people closely. They do not scorn people.

With those people who have lost their faithfulness, the Lord is clear: "Those who aren't with me are against me." One could ask: "Isn't there a way to compromise, a little here and a little there?" No! Either you are on the path of love, or you're on the path of hypocrisy. Either you let yourself be loved by the mercy of God, or you do what you want, according to your heart, which grows harder with each step on this path. There is no third path of compromise. Either you're holy or you take the other path. Whoever doesn't gather with the Lord, not only abandons things but worse, scatters and destroys. He or she is a corruptor, one who corrupts.

Because of this unfaithfulness, Jesus weeps over Jerusalem and weeps over each one of us. In Matthew 23, there is a terrible curse against the leaders who have hardened hearts and want to harden the hearts of the people. Jesus says: "Upon you will come all the righteous blood shed on earth, from the blood of righteous

Abel" (Matt 23:35). They will be held accountable for all the innocent blood shed by their wickedness, by their hypocrisy, by their corrupt, hardened, hearts.

STAYING VIGILANT (11:15–26)[5]

Many times the Lord asks us to be vigilant because a Christian is always holding vigil, is always on watch, attentive. He is somewhat of a sentry; he must keep attentive. Yet, today, in the Gospel of Luke (11:15–26), the Lord surprises us with another kind of vigilance that is not easy to understand but is very common.

In this passage, Jesus casts out a demon and then this discussion arises. Some say that "he casts out demons by Beelzebul," and so on. Jesus defends himself and, in the diatribe, ridicules them. Finally, Jesus tells us not a parable but a truth. "When the unclean spirit has gone out of a person, it wanders through waterless regions looking for a resting place, but not finding any, it says, 'I will return to my house from which I came'" (v. 24). And when he comes, he finds it swept and put in order. The man who lives there is free. "Then it goes and brings seven other spirits more evil than itself, and they enter and live there; and the last state of that person is worse than the first (v. 26). In other words, the condition of that man before the demon was driven out of his life was better than this one.

The significance of Jesus's words and of this event is symbolic. The Lord takes the figure of those demons in the desert, wandering, suffering. Let us consider that when Jesus casts out these demons—which are called "legions" because there are so many—they ask to be sent among the swine, because they do not want to roam in the desert. Here it says that the demon passes through waterless places seeking rest," and after a while he returns. But he is surprised to come home and find it swept and put in order: that man's soul is at peace with God and the demon does not enter. And so the demon goes to find seven others, more evil than himself.

The term "more evil" has great force in this passage. How exactly does the demon re-enter that man's "home"? He enters gently. He knocks on the door, rings the bell, asks permission to enter, and returns politely.

This second time, the demons are courteous, and so the man is unaware that they are demons. They enter stealthily. They begin to be a part of the man's life. With their ideas and inspirations they even help the man to live better, and they enter the man's heart and begin to change him from within, but quietly, without making a racket.

This way is different from forceful demonic possession. This is more of a "parlor" demonic possession, and it comes from what the devil does slowly in our lives in order to change the criteria, to lead us to worldliness. He camouflages himself in a manner that is difficult for us to recognize. Thus, that man, liberated from a demon, becomes a wicked man, a man oppressed by worldliness—and that worldliness is precisely what the devil wants.

In fact, worldliness is a step forward for the demon in the course of possession. The adjective that Paul used for the Galatians when they set foot on this road is "foolish": "You foolish Galatians! Who has bewitched you? It was before your eyes that Jesus Christ was publicly exhibited as crucified!'" (Gal 3:1).

It is bewitchment; it is a seduction, because the devil is the father of seduction. Let us consider what he did with Eve: he began with sweet-talking and ended up with "whoever has beguiled you?" However, when the demon enters so gently, politely, and takes possession of our attitudes, our values shift from service to God toward worldliness. In such cases, we become "worldly" and "lukewarm Christians" who make this mishmash, this hodgepodge between the spirit of the world and the spirit of God. However, we cannot live this way. It distances us from the Lord, and it happens very subtly.

We must ask ourselves: How do we avoid falling into this? And how do we find our way out? The answer is, first and foremost, rediscovered in the word "vigilance." "Take heed, be quiet, do not fear," as Isaiah said to Ahaz (Isa 3:4). In other words, employ vigilance and calm. To hold vigil is to understand what enters my heart; it means to stop and examine my life; a personal examination of conscience: "Am I a Christian? Am I raising my children well? Is my life Christian or is it worldly? How might I understand this?"

To respond to such questions we should refer to Paul's recipe: look to the crucified Christ. Indeed, it is only before the Lord's cross that worldliness can be found and destroyed. This is precisely the aim of the crucifix before us: it is not an ornament but precisely what saves us from these bewitchments, from these seductions that lead to worldliness.

Thus, these are the fundamental questions: "Do I look to the crucified Christ? Do I, at times, walk the *Via Crucis* in order to see the price of salvation, the price that has saved us not only from sin but also from worldliness?" We need an *examination of conscience* in order to see what is happening, but always before the crucified Christ in prayer. Furthermore, it would do us well to fracture, not our bones but our convenient attitudes, and this is achieved through acts of charity. Essentially, this means admitting to myself that I am comfortable, but I will do that which costs me. For example, visit a sick person, give help to someone in need—acts of charity—in order to down the spiritual worldliness in the person that the demons seek to create.

In conclusion, let us reflect on these three things: *that the crucified Christ will save us from these courteous demons*, from this gradual slide toward worldliness, from this foolishness, from seduction; that an *examination of conscience* will help us to perceive whether we are falling into any of these transgressions; and that *acts of charity*, those that are costly, will lead us to be more attentive and more vigilant, such that these sly characters cannot enter. We pray that the Lord give us this grace and help us remember the adjective Paul used: "foolish."

THE GOD OF SURPRISES (11:29–32)[6]

In this passage, Jesus addresses the crowds that thronged to listen to him as "an evil generation" because "it seeks a sign." It is evident that Jesus is speaking to the doctors of the law who ask him for "a sign" many times in the gospel. Indeed, they do not see many of Jesus's signs. But this is precisely why Jesus scolds them on various occasions: "You are incapable of seeing the signs of the times," he tells them in the Gospel of Matthew, drawing upon the image of the fig tree. "As soon as its branch becomes tender and puts forth its leaves, you know that summer is near" (Matt 24:32); and you do not understand the signs of the times.

We ask ourselves why the doctors of the law did not understand the signs of the times and asked for an extraordinary sign. The first reason was that they were closed. They were closed within their system. They had organized the law very well. It was a masterpiece. All of the Jews knew what one could and could not do, where one could go. It was all organized. But Jesus caught them unprepared by doing "strange things," such as associating with the sinners and eating with the publicans. And the doctors of the law did not like this, they found it "dangerous," putting at risk the doctrine which they, the theologians, had been creating for centuries.

Certainly, it was a law made out of love, in order to be faithful to God, but it had become a closed regulatory system. They had simply forgotten history. They had forgotten that God is the God of the law, and further, he is also the *God of surprises*. God, many times, had surprises in store for his people: we only need to think of the Red Sea and of how he saved them from slavery in Egypt.

Despite that, however, they did not understand that God is always new. He never denies himself; he never says that something he said was a mistake, never. But he always surprises. They did not understand, and they closed themselves within a system created with much good will. And so they asked that

Jesus give them "a sign," because by maintaining a completely "closed" attitude" they did not recognize the many signs that Jesus had provided.

The second response to his initial question is attributable to the fact that they had forgotten that they were a people on a journey. And when one is on a journey one always finds new things, things one did not know. And they had to accept these things with hearts faithful to the Lord. But a journey is not absolute in itself. It is a journey toward an end point, in this case toward the definitive manifestation of the Lord. In the end, all of life is a journey toward the fullness of Jesus Christ, when the second coming occurs. It is a journey toward Jesus, who will come again in glory, as the angels said to the apostles on the day of the Ascension.

In other words, "this generation seeks a sign, but no sign shall be given to it except the sign of Jonah": that is to say, the sign of the Resurrection, of glory, of that eschatology we are journeying toward. However, many of Jesus's contemporaries were closed within themselves—not open to the God of surprises. They were men and women who did not know the path or even this eschatology, to the point that when, in the Sanhedrin, the priest asks Jesus: "Are you the Messiah, the Son of the Blessed One?" Jesus replies, "I am, and 'you will see the Son of Man seated at the right hand of the Power,' and 'coming with the clouds of heaven.' Then the high priest tore his clothes and said, 'Why do we still need witnesses? You have heard his blasphemy!'" (Mark 14:61–64). For them, the sign that Jesus gave was blasphemy.

This is why Jesus defined them as an "evil generation," for they did not understand that the law they protected and loved was directed toward Jesus Christ. Indeed, if the law does not lead to Jesus Christ, if it does not bring us close to Jesus Christ, it is dead. And this is why Jesus scolds the members of that generation for being closed, for being incapable of recognizing the signs of the times, for not being open to the God of surprises, for not being on a journey toward the Lord's triumphant finale, to the point that, when he explains it, they think it is blasphemy.

We must ask oneself these questions: Am I attached to my things, to my ideas? Am I closed, or am I open to the God of surprises? Also: Am I a stationary person or a person on a journey? And finally: Do I believe in Jesus Christ and in what he has done—that he died and rose again? Do I believe that the journey goes forth toward maturity, toward the manifestation of the glory of the Lord? Am I capable of understanding the signs of the times and of being faithful to the voice of the Lord that is manifested in them?

The Model of a Fool (11:37–41)[7]

The word "fool" is mentioned twice. Jesus says it to the doctors of the law, to some of the Pharisees (cf. Luke 11:37–41); and Paul says it to the pagans: "Claiming to be wise, they became fools" (Rom 1:22). This word said to the doctors of the law, to the pagans, and to Christians who let themselves be bewitched by ideologies is a condemnation. Moreover, it reveals the way of folly, which in turn leads to corruption.

The Three Types of Fool

There are three kinds of fool subject to corruption. First, *the doctors of the law and the Pharisees*, to whom Jesus said: "You are like graves which are not seen"; on the outside they appear beautiful but on the inside they are full of bone and rot. Corrupt. Thus, the Pharisees became corrupt, for they emphasized only appearances, and not what was inside; they were corrupted by vanity, appearances, outward beauty, and external justice. They became corrupt because they were concerned only with polishing, with making beautiful the external aspect of things; they did not delve within. Corruption is buried within, as in a grave.

The second kind of fool refers to *the pagans* who, in the day's reading, Paul accused of having exchanged the glory of the immortal God for images resembling mortal man or birds or animals or reptiles. "Therefore God gave them up in the lusts of their hearts to impurity" (Rom 1:24). In this case too, the pagans exchanged the glory of God—which they could have known through reason—for idols. Such corruption is one of idolatry, of many idolatries, and the corruption of idolatry applies not only to ancient times, but has relevance in the present day, for example, in consumerism and the idolatry of seeking a convenient god.

The third kind of fool refers to *the Galatians*. In allowing themselves to be corrupted by ideologies, they renounce being Christian in order to become ideologues of Christianity. Ultimately, however, all three of these categories, in their own manner, end in corruption by way of this folly.

The Foolishness

What is this foolishness? It is a failure to listen. It is literally a *"nescio,"* an "I don't know how," an incapacity to listen. The word does not enter, because I am not listening to it; I am not allowing it to enter. The fool does not listen. He believes he is listening, but he does not listen. He does his own thing, always, and for this reason, the word of God cannot enter his heart and there is no room for love. Or, and this is often the case, if the word does enter, it does so in a distilled fashion, transformed by one's concept of reality.

Therefore, fools do not know how to listen, and this deafness leads them to corruption. The word of God does not enter; there is no room for love and finally there is no room for freedom. In this respect, Paul was clear: they became slaves. "God gave them up in the lusts of their hearts to impurity, to the degrading of their bodies among themselves" (Rom 1:24). They became slaves because they exchanged the truth of God for falsehood, adoring and serving creatures rather than the Creator. Indeed, they are not free; and this failure to listen, this deafness leaves no room for love or freedom; it always leads to slavery.

Thus, it is appropriate to ask ourselves: "Do I listen to the word of God? Do I let it enter?" The word of God is alive. It is efficacious; it discerns the sentiments and thoughts of the heart; it cuts; it goes inside. We need to question whether we let the word enter our hearts, or if we remain deaf to it. Moreover, do we transform it in appearance? Do we transform it into idolatry, into idolatrous habits? Do we transform it into ideology, and thus it does not enter? This is the folly of Christians.

Finally, just as the icons of the saints do us so much good, we should look at the icon of the fools of today—and there are many of these. There are foolish Christians and also foolish pastors, those whom Saint Augustine "lambasted" vehemently—for the folly of the shepherd harms the flock: the folly of the corrupt shepherd, as well as the folly of the self-satisfied pastor, the pagan, and the folly of the pastor ideologue.

Let us look at the icon of the foolish Christian and compare this folly with the Lord who is always at the door. He knocks at the door and waits. It is a matter of contemplating the Lord's nostalgia, when he remembers the times that were good: "I remember the devotion of your youth, your love as a bride, how you followed me in the wilderness, in a land not sown." God's nostalgia for the love we had for him at first. In fact, if we fall prey to this folly and we distance ourselves, he feels this nostalgia; nostalgia for us, just as Jesus wept with this nostalgia as he wept over Jerusalem. It was the nostalgia for a people whom he had chosen, whom he had loved, but who had distanced themselves through folly; they had preferred appearances, idols, or ideologies.

OPENING THE DOOR TO OTHERS (11:46–54)[8]

This passage from the gospel indicates trouble: "Woe to you, doctors of the law: woe to you, Pharisees." Indeed the Lord, here, is very strong, and strikes a blow. In particular, the passage offers an expression that makes one think: "Woe to you lawyers! For you have taken away the key of knowledge; you did not enter yourselves, and you hindered those who were entering."

People forget that everything is gratuitous, that God took the initiative to save us, and they take the side of the law and try to cling to it—and the more detailed it is, the better. Thus, they cling so tightly to the law that they do not receive the strength of God's justice.

Consequently, they offer a heap of prescriptions and call this salvation. Whereas, instead, the law is a response to God's gratuitous love: it is God who took the initiative to save us. And in response, because God loves me so much, I seek to go on the path that he has shown me. In other words, I fulfill the law.

However, those people lost the key of knowledge because they lost the sense of God's closeness. In truth, the God of revelation is the God who began to journey with us from Abraham up to Jesus: God who journeys with his people. When this close relationship with the Lord is lost, one falls into an obtuse mentality that believes in the self-sufficiency of salvation through fulfillment of the law.

Those people lost the memory of God's mercy. It is mercy that helps us understand what it means to touch Christ's flesh, touch the suffering Christ in a person, both physically and spiritually.

Many times, in my country, I heard of parish priests who did not baptize the children of unwed mothers because they had not been born within a canonical marriage: they closed the door, they scandalized the people of God, because the hearts of these parish priests had lost the key to knowledge. Three months ago, in a country, in a city, a mother wanted to baptize her newly born son, but she had been married civilly with a divorced man. The pastor said, "Yes, yes, I will baptize the baby, but your husband is divorced and must stay out; he cannot be present at the ceremony." This is happening today, because the Pharisees, the doctors of the law, are not just people of days gone by: even today there are many of them.

It is necessary to pray for us pastors, so that we do not lose the key to knowledge and we do not close the door on ourselves and on the people who want to enter.

The gospel says, "When he went outside, the scribes and the Pharisees began to be very hostile toward him and to cross-examine him about many things, lying in wait for him, to catch him in something he might say" (v. 53). This is a corrupt attitude and a second consequence of what happens when one loses the key to knowledge, both in our awareness of the gratuity of salvation and in the closeness of God and in works of mercy; corruption comes to pass.

What did the pastors of those times do? They set traps for the Lord to snare him and then to accuse and condemn him. In conclusion, we ask the Lord for the grace of remembering our salvation, the gratuity of salvation, of God's closeness, and for the concreteness of the works of mercy that the Lord wants from us, whether material or spiritual, but concrete. We close with the hope that the Lord may give us this grace so that we can become people who help open the door to ourselves and others.

12

The Challenges

LIKE GRANDMA'S COOKIES (12:1–7)[1]

In the gospel passage, Saint Luke cites the teaching of Jesus: "Beware of the leaven of the Pharisees." Jesus also spoke of leaven on other occasions, when he explained, for instance, that the kingdom of heaven was like the leaven which the woman kneaded with the flour: it made the dough expand. So it is with the kingdom of heaven. Likewise, the apostle Paul said to the Corinthians: "Clean out the old yeast so that you may be a new batch, as you really are unleavened" (1 Cor 5:7).

In the passage from Luke, Jesus speaks about a leaven that does not make the kingdom of heaven as an evil leaven. There are, therefore, two leavens: one good, one evil—the leaven that makes the kingdom of God grow, and the leaven that only makes what appears to be the kingdom of God. Indeed, the leaven always makes it grow, always; and, when it is good, it makes it grow in a way that is consistent, substantial so that it becomes good bread, a good meal: it grows well. But the leaven of evil does not make it grow well.

I remember that for Carnival, when we were children, grandma made cookies, and it was a very, very thin batter that she made. Then she dropped it into the oil and that batter swelled,

153

and swelled and, when we began to eat it, it was empty. Those cookies were called "liar's cookies," Grandma explained that these cookies are like lies: they seem big, but they have nothing inside, there is nothing true there; there is nothing of substance.

And so Jesus warns us: "Beware of the leaven of the Pharisees." That leaven is hypocrisy. This is why the Lord advises us to be wary of the leaven of the Pharisees, which is hypocrisy.

On many occasions Jesus said "Hypocrites, hypocrites" to the Pharisees, to the doctors of the law. For example, we only have to read Matthew 23.

But in reality, what is this leaven of evil, what is hypocrisy? In several passages of the Bible the Lord laments with the prophet: "This people invoke me with their lips, while their hearts are far from me." This is because hypocrisy is an internal division. You say one thing and do another: it is a sort of spiritual schizophrenia. Furthermore, a hypocrite is a phony; he seems good, courteous, but he has a dagger behind him. Just like Herod, who with fear received the Magi with courtesy and then, as they were leaving, said: "Go and then return and tell me where this child is so that I too can go to adore him." Instead, he wanted to kill him.

A hypocrite is two-faced. He is a phony. Jesus, speaking of these doctors of the law, affirms that they say but do not do. This is another form of hypocrisy. It is existential nominalism: those who believe that, by saying things, everything is in order. No, things must be done, not just said. A hypocrite is a nominalist. He believes that everything is done with words. Moreover, a hypocrite is incapable of blaming himself. He never finds a smudge on himself; instead, he blames others. Just think of the speck and the log. This is precisely how we can describe this leaven which is hypocrisy.

To understand what Jesus wants to tell us, we must undergo a real examination of conscience on our way of acting in life, on our leaven, so that we can be freer to follow the Lord and always tell the truth. For this reason, it is important to ask ourselves: "How am I growing? Am I growing with the old leaven that serves for nothing? Am I growing like my grandmother's cookies, empty, without substance, or am I growing with new leaven, the leaven that makes the kingdom of heaven grow? What is my leaven like? With what spirit do I do things? With what spirit do I pray? With what spirit do I address others? With the spirit that builds or with the spirit that turns into air?

We must never mislead ourselves by saying: "I did this, I did that." Instead take the example of the little ones: Children confess with such truth! Children never, never, ever tell a lie in confession, they never say abstract things: "I did this, I did that." Thus, children are concrete when they are before God and before others. They say concrete things because they have good leaven, the leaven that makes them grow like the kingdom of Heaven.

May the Lord give to us, to all of us, the Holy Spirit and the grace of the clarity to recognize the leaven with which we act in order to always be ready to respond sincerely to the question: Am I a just and transparent person or am I a hypocrite?

THE FATHER CARES FOR ALL (12:6)[2]

Jesus took up the biblical faith in God the Creator, emphasizing a fundamental truth: God is Father (cf. Matt 11:25). In talking with his disciples, Jesus would invite them to recognize the paternal relationship God has with all his creatures. With moving tenderness, he would remind them that each one of them is important in God's eyes: "Are not five sparrows sold for two pennies? Yet not one of them is forgotten in God's sight" (Luke 12:6). "Look at the birds of the air; they neither sow nor reap nor gather into barns, and yet your heavenly Father feeds them" (Matt 6:26).

GOD'S RADIANT PRESENCE (12:6)[3]

Jesus said: "Are not five sparrows sold for two pennies? Yet not one of them is forgotten in God's sight" (Luke 12:6). God our

Father, who created each being in the universe with infinite love, calls us to be his means for hearing the cry of the Amazon region. If we respond to this heartrending plea, it will become clear that the creatures of the Amazon region are not forgotten by our heavenly Father. For Christians, Jesus himself cries out to us from their midst, "because the risen One is mysteriously holding them to himself and directing them toward fullness as their end. The very flowers of the field and the birds which his human eyes contemplated and admired are now imbued with his radiant presence."[4] For all these reasons, we believers encounter in the Amazon region a theological locus, a space where God himself reveals himself and summons his sons and daughters.

PARABLE OF THE RICH FOOL (12:13–21)[5]

This passage from the Gospel of Luke speaks of the rich man concerned with storing the crops from his harvest. Jesus stood firmly against attachment to riches, but not about wealth in and of itself. God, in fact, is rich—he presents himself as rich in mercy, rich in so many gifts—but what Jesus condemns is really the attachment to possessions. Indeed, he clearly states how very difficult it would be for a rich man, in other words, a man attached to possessions, to enter the kingdom of heaven.

The concept is repeated in an even stronger way: "You cannot serve two masters" (cf. Matt 6:24). In this case, Jesus does not place God in opposition to the devil, but God against attachment to wealth, because the opposite of serving God is serving wealth, working for wealth, to have more of it, to be secure. What happens in this case? The riches become security and religion a kind of insurance agency: "I'm insured with God here and I'm insured with riches there." But Jesus is clear: "This is impossible."

The gospel tells us of the young man who was so good that Jesus was moved by him, the wealthy young man who went away "saddened" because he did not want to leave everything in order to give it to the poor. Attachment to possessions is a form of idolatry. Indeed, we are faced with two gods: God, the living One, and the god of gold, in whom I place my security. And this is impossible.

The gospel also presents us with two brothers who argue over their inheritance. This is a circumstance that we experience even today. Consider how many families we know who have argued, who argue, who do not greet each other, who hate each other over an inheritance. What's most important is not love of family, love of children, of brothers and sisters, of parents. No, it's money, which destroys. Everyone knows at least one family torn apart like this.

Covetousness, however, is also at the root of wars. Sure, there is an ideal goal, but behind it is money—the money of arms dealers, the money of those who profit from war. Again, Jesus is clear: "Take care! Be on your guard against all kinds of greed." Covetousness, in fact, gives us a security that is false, and it leads, yes, to prayer—you can pray, go to Church—but also to having an attached heart, and in the end it winds up damaged.

The man spoken of in this gospel was good; he was a successful entrepreneur. His company had produced a plentiful harvest, and he always had many possessions. But rather than thinking of sharing with his workers and their families, he contemplated how to store those possessions. He always sought more. Thus, the thirst of attachment to possessions never ends. If your heart is attached to possessions, then when you have many, you want more. And this is the god of a person attached to possessions. For this reason, Jesus says to take heed and beware of all greed. And, by no coincidence, when he explains the way to salvation, the Beatitudes, the first is poverty of spirit, that is, not to be attached to possessions: "Blessed are the poor in spirit," those who are not attached to riches. Perhaps they have riches but so as to serve others, to share, and to enable many people to move forward.

Someone might ask: "Father, what can I do? What is the sign that I am not engaged in this sin of idolatry, of being attached to possessions?" The answer is simple, and it too is found in the gospel. From the earliest days of the Church, there has been a way: give alms. However, that is not enough. Indeed, if I give to those who are in need, it is a good way, but I must also ask myself: "How much do I give? My leftovers?" If this is the case, it is not a good way. I have to recognize whether in giving I deprive myself of something that might be necessary for me. In that case, my gesture signifies that love for God is greater than my attachment to wealth.

Therefore, the three questions: The first: Do I give? The second: How much do I give? And the third: How do I give? In other words, do I give like Jesus, generously, lovingly, or do I give like one who is paying a tax? When you help people, do you look them in the eye? Do you touch their hand? We must not forget that before us is the flesh of Christ, your brother, your sister. And in that moment you are like the Father who never leaves the birds of the sky without food.

Therefore, let us ask the Lord for the grace to be free of this idolatry, the attachment to possessions. Let us ask him for the grace to look to him, so rich in his love and so rich in his generosity, his mercy, and also for the grace to help others by giving alms, but as he does. Someone might say: "But Father, he isn't depriving himself of anything." In fact, Jesus Christ, being equal to God, deprived himself. He lowered himself, he emptied himself.

THE LITTLE FLOCK (12:32)[6]

One cannot but admire the resources that the Lord used to dialogue with his people, to reveal his mystery to all and to attract ordinary people by his lofty teachings and demands. I believe that the secret lies in the way Jesus looked at people, seeing beyond their weaknesses and failings: "Do not be afraid, little flock, for it is your Father's good pleasure to give you the kingdom" (Luke 12:32); Jesus preaches with that spirit. Full of joy in the Spirit, he blesses the Father who draws the little ones to him: "I thank you, Father, Lord of heaven and earth, because you have hidden these things from the wise and the intelligent and have revealed them to infants" (Luke 10:21). The Lord truly enjoys talking with his people; the preacher should strive to communicate that same enjoyment to his listeners.

ATTENTION TO OTHERS (12:32–48)[7]

In the text of today's gospel, Jesus speaks to his disciples about the attitude to assume regarding the final encounter with him, and he explains that the expectation of this encounter should impel us to live a life full of good works. Among other things he says: "Sell your possessions and give alms. Make purses for yourselves that do not wear out, an unfailing treasure in heaven, where no thief comes near and no moth destroys" (v. 33). It is a call to give importance to almsgiving as a work of mercy, not to place our trust in ephemeral goods, to use things without attachment and selfishness, but according to God's logic, the logic of attention to others, the logic of love. We can be very attached to money and have many things, but in the end we cannot take them with us. Remember that "the shroud has no pockets."

Jesus's lesson continues with three short parables on the theme of vigilance. This is important: vigilance, being alert, being vigilant in life. The first is the parable of the servants waiting for their master to return at night. "Blessed are those slaves whom the master finds alert when he comes" (v. 37): it is the beatitude of faithfully awaiting the Lord, of being ready, with an attitude of service. He presents himself each day, knocks at the door of our heart. Those who open it will be blessed, because they will have a great reward. Indeed, the Lord will make himself a servant to his servants—it is a beautiful reward—in the great banquet of his kingdom. He himself will serve them. With this parable, set at night, Jesus proposes life as a vigil of diligent expectation that heralds the bright day of eternity. To be able to enter one must be ready, awake, and committed to serving others, from the comforting perspective that, "beyond," it will no longer be we who serve God, but he himself who will welcome us to his table. If you think about it, this already happens today each time we meet the Lord in prayer, or in serving the poor, and above all in the Eucharist, where he prepares a banquet to nourish us with his word and his body.

The second parable describes the unexpected arrival of the thief. This situation also requires vigilance. Indeed, Jesus exhorts: "You also must be ready, for the Son of Man is coming at an unexpected hour" (v. 40). The disciple is one who awaits the Lord and his kingdom.

The gospel clarifies this with the third parable: the steward of a house after the master's departure. In the first scene, the steward faithfully carries out his tasks and receives compensation. In the second scene, the steward abuses his authority and beats the servants, and for this, upon the master's unexpected return, he will be punished. This scene describes a situation that is also frequent in our time: so much daily injustice, violence, and cruelty are born from the idea of behaving as masters of the lives of others. We have only one master who likes to be called not "master" but "Father." We are all servants, sinners, and children: He is the one Father.

Jesus reminds us today that the expectation of eternal beatitude does not relieve us of the duty to render the world more just and more livable. On the contrary, this very hope of ours of possessing the eternal kingdom impels us to work to improve the conditions of earthly life, especially for our weakest brothers and sisters. We ask the Virgin Mary to help us not be people and communities dulled by the present, or worse, nostalgic for the past, but to strive toward the future of God, toward the encounter with him, our life and our hope.

WAITING ATTENTIVELY (12:35–36)[8]

Today, I would like to pause on that dimension of hope which is *waiting attentively*. The theme of vigilance is one of the guiding threads of the New Testament. Jesus preaches to his disciples: "Be dressed for action and have your lamps lit; be like those who are waiting for their master to return from the wedding banquet, so that they may open the door for him as soon as he comes and knocks" (Luke 12:35–36). In the time that follows the Resurrection of Jesus, in which peaceful moments continually alternate with painful moments, a Christian never rests. The gospel recommends that we be like servants who never go to sleep until their master has returned. This world requires our responsibility, and we accept all of it with love. Jesus wants our existence to be laborious, that we never lower our guard, so as to welcome with gratitude and wonder each new day given to us by God. Every morning is a blank page on which a Christian begins to write with good works. We have already been saved by Jesus's redemption. However, now we await the full manifestation of his power, when at last God will be everything to every one (cf. 1 Cor 15:28). Nothing is more certain in the faith of Christians than this "appointment," this appointment with the Lord, when he shall come. And when this day arrives, we, as Christians, want to be like those servants who spent the night with their loins girded and their lamps burning: we must be ready for the salvation that comes, ready for the encounter. Have you thought about what that encounter will be like with Jesus, when he comes? It will be an embrace, an enormous joy, a great joy! We must live in anticipation of this encounter!

Christians are not made for boredom; if anything, we are made for patience. We know that hidden in the monotony of certain identical days is a mystery of grace. There are people who with the perseverance of their love become like wells that irrigate the desert. Nothing happens in vain; and no situation in which a Christian finds himself or herself is completely resistant to love. No night is so long as to make us forget the joy of the sunrise. And the darker the night, the closer the dawn. If we remain united with Jesus, the cold of difficult moments does not paralyze us; and if even the whole world preaches against hope, saying that the future will bring only dark clouds, a Christian knows that in that same future there will be Christ's return. No one knows when this will take place, but the thought that at the end of our history there will be the merciful Jesus suffices in order to have faith and to not curse life. Everything will be saved. Everything. We will suffer; there will be moments that give rise to anger and indignation, but the sweet and powerful memory of Christ will drive away the temptation to think that this life is a mistake.

After we have met Jesus, we cannot but look at history with faith and hope. Jesus is as a house, and we are inside, and from the windows of this house we look at the world. For this reason we do not close ourselves in, we do not long with melancholy for a supposedly golden past, but we look ever forward to a future that is not only our handiwork, but that is above all a constant concern of the providence of God. All that is lackluster will one day become light.

Let us consider that God never contradicts himself. Never. God never disappoints. His will in our regard is not nebulous but is a well-defined salvific plan: God "desires everyone to be saved and to come to the knowledge of the truth" (1 Tim 2:4). Therefore, let us not abandon ourselves to the flow of events with pessimism, as if history were a runaway train. Resignation is not a Christian virtue, just as it is not Christian to shrug one's shoulders or give in to a seemingly inescapable destiny.

One who brings hope to the world is never a submissive person. Jesus recommends that we not await him with idle hands: "Blessed are those slaves whom the master finds alert when he comes" (Luke 12:37). There is no peacemaker who at the end of the day has not compromised his personal peace, taking on the problems of others. A submissive person is not a peace-builder but an idler, one who wants to be comfortable. Meanwhile, a Christian is a peacemaker when he takes risks, when he has the courage to take risks in order to bring good, the good which Jesus has given us, as a treasure.

In each day of our life, we repeat that invocation that the first disciples, in their Aramaic language, expressed with the words *Marana tha*, and which we find in the last verse of the Bible,

"Come, Lord Jesus! (Rev 22:20). It is the refrain of every Christian life: in our world we need nothing other than Christ's gentle touch. What a grace if, in prayer, in the difficult days of this life, we hear his voice, which responds and assures us: "Behold, I am coming soon!" (Rev 22:7).

THE CALL TO CONVERSION (12:49–53)[9]

In this passage, Jesus tells us that he came to set fire to the earth. But this fire—the one he set with his word, with his death and resurrection, with the Holy Spirit that he sent us—causes not the wars that we see in the fields of struggle, but the cultural wars, family wars, social wars, even the war in the heart, the inner struggle. Indeed, Jesus calls us to change our lives, to change our path. He calls us to conversion. This is the fire he speaks of: a fire that doesn't leave you alone. It can't, it pushes you to change....

There are no menus for peace. Only the Holy Spirit can give it. This is the fire that causes struggle and brings inner peace, that peace of soul which gives strength to Christians.

Many martyrs in the history of the Church, many men and women have given witness to this interior struggle though giving their lives. Witness is also given by many silent Christians, many men, fathers of families, many women, mothers of families, who carry on their life with silence, educating their children, and go on with work, and try to do God's will.

In the opening prayer today, we asked for the grace of a generous and faithful heart. Conversion requires both things: generosity, which always comes from love, and fidelity, fidelity to the word of God. The prayer then continues by saying: "so we can serve you with loyalty." In other words, we must be loyal to God, transparent, and truthful. And the heart of the Lord is so great that a faithful person is "softened," that is, the Lord is able to get closer and perform the miracle of conversion.

THE CAUSE OF DIVISION (12:51)[10]

The word of God also contains a word of Jesus which alarms us and must be explained, for otherwise it could give rise to misunderstanding. Jesus says to his disciples: "Do you think that I have come to bring peace to the earth? No, I tell you, but rather division!" (v. 51). What does this mean? It means that faith is not a decoration or an ornament; living faith does not mean decorating life with a little religion, as if we were decorating a cake with cream. No, this is not faith. Faith means choosing God as the criterion and basis of life. And God is not empty, God is not neutral, God is always positive, God is love, and love is positive! After Jesus has come into the world it is impossible to act as if we do not know God, or as if he were something that is abstract, empty, a purely nominal reference. No, God has a real face. He has a name. God is mercy; God is faithfulness. He is life which is given to us all.

For this reason, Jesus says, "I came to bring division." It is not that Jesus wishes to divide people. On the contrary, Jesus is our peace, he is our reconciliation! But this peace is not the peace of the tomb. It is not neutrality; Jesus does not bring neutrality. This peace is not a compromise at all costs. Following Jesus entails giving up evil and selfishness and choosing good—truth and justice—even when this demands sacrifice and the renunciation of our own interests. And this indeed divides; as we know, it even cuts the closest ties. However, be careful! It is not Jesus who creates division! He establishes the criterion: whether to live for ourselves or to live for God and for others; to be served or to serve; to obey our own ego or to obey God. It is in this sense that Jesus is "a sign that will be opposed" (Luke 2:34).

Therefore, this word of the gospel does not authorize the use of force to spread the faith. It is exactly the opposite. The Christian's real force is the force of truth and of love, which involves renouncing all forms of violence. Faith and violence are incompatible! Instead, faith and strength go together. Christians are not violent; they are strong. And with what kind of strength? That of meekness, the strength of meekness, the strength of love.

Dear friends, even among Jesus's relatives there were some who at a certain point did not share his way of life and preaching, as the gospel tells us (cf. Mark 3:20–21). His mother, however, always followed him faithfully, keeping the eyes of her heart fixed on Jesus, the Son of the Most High, and on his mystery. And in the end, thanks to Mary's faith, Jesus's relatives became part of the first Christian community (cf. Acts 1:14). Let us ask Mary to help us too to keep our gaze firmly fixed on Jesus and to follow him always, cost what it may.

Valuing God's Time (12:54–56)[11]

It is imperative to return continually to Gibeon (cf. 1 Kings 3:5–12), to remind the Lord in prayer that before him we are perennial "children who do not know how to settle," and to implore "not long life or riches or the life of enemies," but only "discernment in judging among his people." Without this grace, we will not become good meteorologists regarding what can be seen "in the appearance of earth and sky" but rather, we will be unable to "interpret the time of God" (cf. Luke 12:54–56).

Discernment, therefore, is born in the heart and mind of the bishop through his prayer, when he puts the people and situations entrusted to him into contact with the Divine Word pronounced by the Spirit. It is in this intimacy that the pastor nurtures the interior freedom that makes him steadfast in his choices and conduct, both personal and ecclesial. Only in the silence of prayer can one hear the voice of God, perceive the traces of his language, and have access to his truth, which is a very different light that is not above one's mind in the same way that oil is above water but is superior, since only "he who knows the Truth knows that light."[12]

13

Conversion

Repent or Perish (13:1–5)[1]

In today's gospel passage, Jesus refers to two tragic events that had caused a stir: a cruel suppression carried out by Roman soldiers in the temple and the collapse of the tower of Siloam in Jerusalem, which resulted in eighteen deaths (cf. Luke 13:1–5).

Jesus is aware of the superstitious mentality of his listeners and knows that they misinterpreted the second event. In fact, they thought that since those people had died in such a cruel way it was a sign that God was punishing them for some grave sin they had committed, as if to say, "they deserved it." In addition, the fact that they themselves had been saved from such a disgrace made them feel "good about themselves." They "deserved it." "I'm okay."

Jesus clearly rejects this outlook, because God does not allow tragedies in order to punish sins. Jesus affirms that those poor victims were no worse than others. Instead, he invites his listeners to draw a lesson that applies to everyone from such sad events, because we are all sinners; in fact, he said to those who questioned him, "Unless you repent, you will all perish as they did" (v. 3).

Today too, seeing certain misfortunes and sorrowful events, we can be tempted to "unload" the responsibility onto the victims, or even onto God himself. But the gospel invites us to reflect: How do we think of God? Are we truly convinced that God is like that? Couldn't it be just our projection, a god made to "our image and likeness"?

Jesus, on the contrary, invites us to *change our heart*, to make a radical about-face on the path of our lives, to abandon compromises with evil—and this is something we all do, compromise with evil, hypocrisy... many of us have a little hypocrisy—in order to decidedly take up the path of the gospel.

But again, there is the temptation to justify ourselves. What should we convert from? Aren't we basically good people? How many times have we thought this: "But after all I am a good man, I am a good woman"? Isn't that true? "Am I not a believer and a faithful churchgoer?" And we believe that in this way we are justified.

Unfortunately, each of us strongly resembles the tree that, over many years, has repeatedly shown that it's infertile. But, fortunately for us, Jesus is like a farmer who, with limitless patience, still obtains a concession for the fruitless vine. "Leave it alone for one more year," he says to the owner, "we shall see if it bears fruit next year" (cf. v. 9).

A "year" of grace: the period of Christ's ministry; the time of the Church before his glorious return; an interval of our life, marked by a certain number of Lenten seasons, which are offered to us as occasions of repentance and salvation; the duration of a Jubilee Year of Mercy. The invincible patience of Jesus! Have you thought about the patience of God? Have you ever thought as well of his limitless concern for sinners—how it should lead us to impatience with ourselves! It's never too late to convert, never. God's patience awaits us until the last moment.

Remember that little story from St. Thérèse of the Child Jesus, when she prayed for that man who had been condemned to death, a criminal who did not want to receive the comfort of the Church. He rejected the priest; he didn't want forgiveness. He wanted to die like that. And she prayed in the convent, and then, at the moment of being executed, the man turned to the priest, took the crucifix and kissed it. The patience of God! He does the same with us, with all of us. How many times, we don't know—we'll know in heaven—but how many times we are there, about to fall off the edge, and the Lord saves us. He saves us because he has great patience with us. And this is his mercy. It's never too late to convert, but it's urgent. Now is the time! Let us begin today.

THE TWO ROOTS (13:6–9)[2]

Being together in this place makes us realize that we are in one of those "cradles" that have produced countless missionaries. Let's not forget that Saint Turibius of Mogrovejo, the patron of the Latin American bishops, died in this land, during his missionary activity and not while sitting behind a desk. All this invites us to look to our roots, to what enables us through time and the unfolding of history to grow and to bear fruit.... Without roots there are no flowers, no fruits. A poet once said: "Every fruit that a tree has comes from what is beneath the soil"—roots. Our vocations will always have that double dimension: roots in the earth and hearts in heaven. Never forget this. When one of these two is missing, something begins to go wrong and our life gradually withers (cf. Luke 13:6–9), like the tree that has no roots withers.

It is sad to see a bishop, priest, or nun, wither. I am even more saddened when I see seminarians wither. This is very serious. The Church is good, the Church is mother, and if you see that you cannot go further, please speak up before it's too late, before you realize that you no longer have roots and that you are withering away; there is still time to be saved, because Jesus came for this, to save, and he called us to save.

WITNESS OF MERCY (13:7–9)[3]

In many places, evangelization begins with education, to which missionary work dedicates much time and effort, like the merciful vinedresser of the gospel (cf. Luke 13:7–9; John 15:1), patiently waiting for fruit after years of slow cultivation; in this way is brought forth a new people able to evangelize, who will take the gospel to those places where it otherwise would not have been known. The Church can also be defined as "mother" for those who will one day have faith in Christ.

NEVER SLAVES TO THE LAW (13:10–17)[4]

Today's gospel teaches us this difficulty of walking in the law of the Lord and tells us that it is a grace that we must ask for: to walk in law of the Lord.

There are two strong words to describe the woman in this gospel passage: "free" and "prisoner." Luke writes that the devil had imprisoned her with a disease for eighteen years and that Jesus frees her. But he does so on a Saturday, and the law clearly says no work is to be done on Saturdays. That was the old law, while the new law tells us not to work on Sundays.

The healing that Jesus carried out provoked the indignation of the leader of the synagogue, who felt the duty to reprimand the woman by saying: "Come to be healed on other days but not on Saturday, the day on which you cannot work!" To these words, however, Jesus responds forcefully: "You are a hypocrite! For example, what do you do with your ox, with your donkey? Do you not untie him in order to give him a drink and food? But for her you would not?"

The word "hypocrite" is often repeated by Jesus in referring to rigid people, those who have a rigid attitude in carrying out the law and do not have the freedom of children. They feel that the law must be carried out in a particular way and they are slaves to the law. However, the law was not established in order to make us slaves, but to make us free, to make us children. Saint Paul preached a great deal on this; and Jesus, with a few sermons but a great deal of action, made us understand this truth.

"Hypocrite" is a word that Jesus repeats often of the people who are rigid, because there is *always* something else behind the rigidity. In fact, rigidity is not a gift from God; meekness, goodness, benevolence, forgiveness, yes; but rigidity, no!

Therefore, behind the rigidity there is always something hidden, in many cases a double life. Rigidity can also be something like a disease. Those who are rigid suffer greatly when they are sincere, and they realize this, they suffer because they cannot have the freedom of the children of God; they do not know how to walk in the law of the Lord and are not blessed. And they suffer a great deal. Therefore, even if they look good because they follow the law, there is something within that does not make them good: they are either bad, hypocritical, or ill. In any case, they suffer.

We think of the two sons in the parable of the prodigal son in the Gospel of Luke (15:11–32). The eldest son was good, so much so that all of the neighbors, all of his father's friends, said: "This son is so good, he always does what his father says!" But then in their comments they added: "Poor father, with that second child who was a disaster, he left with the money and lived a filthy life, the life of a sinner!"

In the end, however, the story collapses and that sinner, who is gone, realizes he has done wrong and comes back, asks for forgiveness, and his father celebrates. The "good" son, however, is there and shows that what is behind his kindness is the arrogance of believing that he is right: "For that son of yours you throw a celebration, while I have been so good and have always served you, and you don't throw a celebration for me?" (cf. Luke 15:29–30).

This is the hypocritical attitude: behind the good that is done, there is pride. The prodigal son, for his part, knew that he had a father, and in the darkest moment of his life he went to his father. The eldest son, however, only knew his father as a boss, and never saw him as a father. He was rigid; he walked in the law with rigidity. Again: the prodigal son left the law aside, he left without the law, against the law, but at a certain point he thought of his father, he came back, and received forgiveness.

It is not easy to walk in the law of the Lord without falling into rigidity, but those who are rigid suffer a great deal. To the extent that even the leader of the synagogue, whom Luke mentions in the gospel, was ashamed in the end because Jesus talked sense into him, saying: "But don't you do this with your donkey?" Instead, we read in the gospel passage that the entire crowd rejoiced at all the wonders that Jesus carried out.

Let us pray for our brothers and sisters who believe that walking in the law of the Lord is to become rigid. Let us pray that the Lord may make them feel that he is their Father and realize that he delights in mercy, tenderness, goodness, meekness and humility—and that he may teach all of us to walk in the law of the Lord with these attitudes.

ON THE PATH OF THE GOOD SHEPHERD (13:10–17)[5]

In this gospel passage, we do not find Jesus on the road as was his habit, but rather in the synagogue, where there was a woman completely bent over from an illness of the spinal column.

What does Jesus do? I am moved by the verbs used by the evangelist here: "He saw" —he sees her; "he called" —he calls her; "he said to her"; "he laid his hands upon her and he healed her." These are the *verbs of closeness* depicting the attitude of the good shepherd.

Because a good shepherd is always near, we think of the parable of the good shepherd who, as Jesus preached, was so close to the lost sheep he leaves the others and goes to look for her.

After all, the good shepherd cannot be far from his people, and this is the sign of a good shepherd: *closeness*. Instead the others, in this case the head of the synagogue, that small group of clerics, doctors of the law, some Pharisees, Sadducees, the illustrious lived apart from the people, constantly scolding him. But these were not good shepherds. They were closed in their own group and they didn't care about the people: maybe when the religious service had finished they cared about going to see how much money had been collected; this mattered to them, but they weren't close to the people.

Jesus, however, always presents himself as close, and often in the gospel such nearness comes from what he felt in his heart. For this reason, was always with the rejected people: the poor, the sick, sinners, and lepers. He walked among those in need because Jesus had such a capacity to be moved when confronted by sickness. He was a good shepherd. And a good shepherd approaches and has the ability to be moved.

A good shepherd is not ashamed of the flesh, of touching wounded flesh, like Jesus did with this woman; "he touched," "he laid his hands." He touched the lepers; he touched the sinners. A good pastor does not say: "But, yes, I am near to you in spirit."

Instead, the good shepherd does what God the Father did, he approaches, out of compassion, out of mercy, in the flesh of his Son; this is a good shepherd. And the great shepherd, the Father, taught us how to be a good shepherd: he lowered himself, emptied himself, and became a servant.

But those others, who follow the path of clericalism, to whom do they draw near? Such "hypocrites" always draw nearer to the powers that be or to money and are wicked shepherds who do not care about the people and are offended when they are called "hypocrites" by Jesus.

Thus, let us ponder the Good Shepherd, Jesus, who sees, calls, talks, touches, and heals, and the Father, who through his Son became flesh, through compassion. Meditating on the Father and the Son in such a way helps us to comprehend the path of the good shepherd. It is a grace for the people of God to have good shepherds—shepherds like Jesus, who are not ashamed to touch wounded flesh, who know that not only they themselves, but all of us, will be judged by this: I was hungry, I was in jail, I was sick. . . .

THE MYSTERY OF THE KINGDOM (13:18–21)[6]

In today's gospel reading, Jesus uses two simple examples from daily life to explain the kingdom of God: the mustard seed and yeast. Though they both appear insignificant and innocuous, when they begin to germinate, they have a strength that grows within them and that exceeds what we can imagine. This is the mystery of the kingdom.

The fulfillment of the kingdom of God is the horizon of hope for all humanity and for the Church as a community, with its two pillars: the explosive power of the Holy Spirit and the courage to allow this power to be unleashed. Both the seed and the yeast have power within them, just as the power of the kingdom of God comes from within.

This, then, is the reality suggested by the parable. Within us and in all creation, there is a strength which unleashes: there is the Holy Spirit who gives us hope, and living in hope means allowing the Holy Spirit's power to go forth and help us to grow toward this fullness.

In the parable, the mustard seed is taken and sown and the yeast is taken and mixed with flour. Now, if the seed is not taken and sown, if the yeast is not taken by the woman and mixed, they will remain there and their inner will also remain there. In the same way, if we want to store the seed for ourselves, it will only be a seed. If we do not mix the yeast with life, with the flour of life, it will just remain yeast. It is therefore necessary to sow, mix, that courage of hope. Hope grows because the kingdom of God grows from within, not from proselytism but rather with the strength of the Holy Spirit.

The Church has always had the courage to take and sow, to take and mix. So often, we see a preference in our pastoral work to preserve the status quo, rather than one which allows the kingdom to flourish. "If I toss a seed, I lose it," but there is always some loss in sowing the kingdom of God. If I mix the yeast, I will dirty my hands! Woe to those who preach the kingdom with the illusion of not soiling their hands. They are custodians of museums: they prefer beautiful things to the gesture of "tossing" so that the strength may be unleashed, of "mixing" so that the strength may grow.

THE PATH OF SALVATION (13:22–23)[7]

Using the image of a door, Jesus wants his listeners to understand that it is not a question of numbers—how many will be saved—for how many is not relevant, but rather, it is important for everyone to know the way that leads to salvation.

This way means entering through a door. But where is the door? Who is the door? Jesus himself is that door. He says so in the Gospel of John: "I am the door" (10:9). He leads us to communion with the Father, where we find love, understanding, and protection. But why is this door narrow, one might ask? Why does he say it is narrow? It is a narrow door not because it is oppressive but because it demands that we restrain and limit our pride and our fear, in order to open ourselves to him with humble and trusting hearts, acknowledging that we are sinners and in need of his forgiveness. This is why it is narrow, to limit our pride, which inflates us. The door of God's mercy is narrow but is always open to everyone! God does not have preferences, but always welcomes everyone, without distinction. It is a narrow door to restrain our pride and our fear, a door open wide because God welcomes us without distinction. And the salvation that he gives us is an unending flow of mercy that overcomes every barrier and opens surprising perspectives of light and peace. The door is narrow but always open wide: do not forget this.

Again, today, Jesus extends a pressing invitation to us to go to him, to pass through the door of a full, reconciled, and happy life. He awaits each one of us, no matter what sins we have committed, to embrace us, to offer us his forgiveness. He alone can transform our hearts; he alone can bring full meaning to our existence, giving us true joy. By entering Jesus's door, the door of faith and of the gospel, we can leave behind worldly attitudes, bad habits, selfishness, and narrow-mindedness. When we encounter the love and mercy of God, there is authentic change. Our lives are enlightened by the light of the Holy Spirit: an inextinguishable light!

I would like to propose something now. Let us think for a moment, in silence, of the things that we have inside us that prevent us from entering the door: our pride; our arrogance; our sins. Then, let us think of the other door, the one opened wide by the mercy of God who awaits us on the other side to grant us forgiveness.

The Lord offers us many opportunities to be saved and to enter through the door of salvation. This entrance is an occasion that can never be wasted: we don't have to give long, erudite speeches about salvation, like the man who approached Jesus in the gospel. Rather, we have to accept the opportunity for salvation. Because at a certain moment, the master of the house will rise and shut the door (cf. v. 25), as the gospel reminds us. But if God is good and loves us, why would he close the door at a certain point? Because our life is not a video game or a television soap opera. Our life is serious, and our goal of eternal salvation is important.

Let us ask the Virgin Mary, the Gate of Heaven, to help us seize the opportunities the Lord gives us to cross the threshold of faith and thus to enter a broad path: it is the path of salvation that can embrace all those who allow themselves to be enraptured by love. It is love that saves, the love that already on this earth is a source of happiness for all those who, in meekness, patience, and justice, forget about themselves and give themselves to others, especially to those who are most weak.

THE NARROW DOOR (13:22–30)[8]

Today's gospel invites us to reflect on the theme of salvation. Jesus was journeying from Galilee toward Jerusalem—the evangelist Luke recounts—when someone asked him: "Lord, will only a few be saved?" (v. 23). Jesus replied by saying: "Strive to enter through the narrow door; for many, I tell you, will seek to enter and will not be able" (v. 24).

The image of the door recurs in the gospel on various occasions and calls to mind the door of the house, of the home, where we find safety, love, and warmth. Jesus tells us that there is a door which gives us access to God's family, to the warmth of God's house, of communion with him. This door is Jesus himself (cf. John 10:9). He is the door. He is the entrance to salvation. He leads us to the Father and the door that is Jesus is never closed. . . . Because, you know, Jesus does not exclude anyone. Some of you, perhaps, might say to me: "But, Father, I am certainly excluded because I am a great sinner: I have done terrible things, I have done lots of them in my life." No, you are not excluded! Precisely for this reason you are the favorite, because Jesus prefers sinners, always, in order to forgive them, to love them. Jesus is waiting for you to embrace you, to pardon you. Do not be afraid: he is waiting for you. Take heart, have the courage to enter through his door. Everyone is invited to cross the threshold of this door, to cross the threshold of faith, to enter into his life and to have him enter our life, so that he may transform it, renew it, and give it full and enduring joy.

In our day we pass in front of so many doors that invite us to come in, promising a happiness which later we realize lasts only an instant, exhausts itself with no future. But I ask you: Which door do we want to enter? And whom do we want to let in through the door of our life? I would like to say forcefully: let's not be afraid to cross the threshold of faith in Jesus, to let him enter our life more and more, to step out of our selfishness, our closedness, our indifference to others so that Jesus may illuminate our life with a light that never goes out. It is not a firework, not a flash of light! No, it is a peaceful light that lasts forever and gives us peace. Consequently, it is the light we encounter if we enter through Jesus's door.

Of course, Jesus's door is a narrow one, but not because it is a torture chamber. Rather, it is because he asks us to open our hearts to him, to recognize that we are sinners in need of his salvation, his forgiveness, and his love in order to have the humility to accept his mercy and to let ourselves be renewed by him. Jesus tells us in the gospel that being Christian does not mean having a "label"! I ask you: Are you Christians in name only or in the truth? And let each one answer within himself or herself! Not

Christians, never Christians by label! Christians in truth, Christians in the heart. Being Christian is living and witnessing to faith in prayer, in works of charity, in promoting justice, in doing good. The whole of our life must pass through the narrow door which is Christ.

Let us ask the Virgin Mary, Door of Heaven, to help us cross the threshold of faith and to let her Son transform our life as he transformed hers to bring everyone the joy of the gospel.

THE LAMENT OVER JERUSALEM (13:31–35)[9]

In today's gospel, it appears that Jesus has lost his patience, and he uses forceful words: it is not an insult, but neither is it a compliment to call a person a "fox." He uses this term when speaking to the Pharisees about Herod: "Go and tell that fox..." (v. 32). However, there are other occasions when Jesus spoke severely. For instance, he spoke of the evil and adulterous generation. He even referred to the disciples as "hard of heart" and "foolish." In Luke's account, Jesus summarizes what will happen: "Yet today, tomorrow, and the next day I must be on my way, because it is impossible for a prophet to be killed outside of Jerusalem" (v. 33). Essentially, the Lord says what will happen; he prepares for his death.

However, after this very strong outburst, Jesus quickly changes his tone and looks to the people, and upon the city of Jerusalem: "Jerusalem... how often have I desired to gather your children together as a hen gathers her brood under her wings" (v. 34). This is the tenderness of God, the tenderness of Jesus. That day, he wept over Jerusalem. Those tears of Jesus, however, were not the tears of a friend before the tomb of Lazarus, the tears of a friend before the death of another. Instead, those were the tears of a father who weeps; it was God the Father who wept here in the person of Jesus.

Someone once said that God was made man in order to be able to mourn for what had been done to his children. Thus, the tears before the tomb of Lazarus are the tears of a friend. However, the tears recounted in the passage from Luke's Gospel are the tears of the Father.

Consider the father of the prodigal son, when the younger son asked for his inheritance, and then left. This father certainly did not go to his neighbors and say: "Look at what happened to me, what this poor wretch did to me, I condemn this son!" No, he did not do this. Instead, I am certain that the father went away to weep alone.

Admittedly, while the gospel does not give an account of this detail, it nonetheless shows that when the son returns, he sees the father from afar. This indicates that the father would continually go up to the terrace to watch out for his son's return. And a father who does this is a father who lives in tears, waiting for the return of his son. These are the tears of God the Father; and with these tears, the Father recreates, in his Son, all of creation.

When Jesus went with the cross to Calvary, the pious women wept, and he said to them: "Do not weep for me, but weep for yourselves and for your children" (Luke 23:28). These are the tears of a father and mother, which God also continues to shed: even today, faced with disastrous wars that are conducted out of the worship of the god of money, with many innocent people murdered by bombs that are launched by worshipers of the idol of money. Thus, even today the Father weeps, and even today says: "Jerusalem, Jerusalem, my children, what are you doing?" And he says this to the poor victims, as well as to arms traffickers and all those who sell the lives of people.

Consider how God was made man in order to be able to weep. And we would do well to think that God our Father today weeps. He weeps for humanity to understand the peace which he offers us, the peace of love.

LIKE A HEN (13:34–35)[10]

In the Gospel of Luke, we read of Jesus's lament over the city: "Jerusalem, Jerusalem, the city that kills the prophets and stones those who are sent to it" (v. 34). It is a lament which the Lord addresses not only to the city but to everyone, using an image of tenderness: "How often have I desired to gather your children together as a hen gathers her brood under her wings, and you were not willing!" (v. 34). As if to say: "How often I wanted to express this tenderness, this love, as a hen with her brood, and you refused."

This is why Paul, having understood this, can say: "For I am convinced that neither death, nor life, nor angels, nor rulers, nor things present, nor things to come, nor powers, nor height, nor depth, nor anything else in all creation, will be able to separate us from the love of God in Christ Jesus our Lord" (Rom 8:38–39). In fact, God cannot help but love. This is our security.

It is a security that affects everyone, with no exceptions whatsoever. I can reject this love, but that would mean choosing to be like the good thief who rejected love until the end of his life, and there at the end love was waiting for him. Even the most wicked man, the worst blasphemer, is loved by God with the tenderness of a father and, to use Jesus's words, like a hen with her brood.

The mighty God, the Creator, can do all things, yet God weeps, and in those tears is all of his love. God weeps over me, when I am separated from him. God weeps over each of us. God weeps for those wicked ones, who do so many bad things, so much harm to humanity. Indeed, he waits, he does not condemn, and he cries. Why? Because he loves!

14

THE KINGDOM OF GOD

THE COMPASSION OF GOD (14:1–6)[1]

Compassion is one of the virtues, so to speak, one of the attributes of God. Luke speaks about this in today's gospel passage. God has compassion for all of us; he has compassion for humanity and sent his Son to heal, to regenerate, to re-create, and to renew it. This is why it is interesting that the parable of the prodigal son, which we are all familiar with, says that when the father—the image of God who forgives—sees his son arriving, he shows compassion.

God's compassion is not pity: the two things have nothing to do with each other. In fact, I can feel sorry for a little dog who is dying, or about a situation, and I can feel sorry for a person: I feel sorry, I'm sorry that this is happening. Instead, God's compassion is to place himself in the difficulty, to put himself in the situation of the other, with his fatherly heart, and this is why he sent his Son.

Jesus's compassion appears in the gospel. Jesus healed people, but he was not a medicine man. Rather, Jesus, in addition to truly healing them, healed people as a sign. He healed as a sign of God's compassion to save, to bring the lost sheep back to its fold, and to return the woman's lost coins to her purse.

God feels compassion. *He presents his fatherly heart to us.* He presents his heart to each of us. Indeed, when God forgives, he forgives as a father, not as a judicial officer who might read a file and say: "Yes, this person can be released for lack of evidence." God forgives us from within; he forgives because he has placed himself in that person's heart.

When Jesus has to present himself at the synagogue in Nazareth for the first time, and they give him the book to read, the words of the prophet Isaiah come to him: "I was sent to bring the good news, to those who are oppressed." It is significant that Jesus was sent by the Father to be placed within each of us, freeing us from our sins, from our wickedness, and bringing "the good news." God's message is, in fact, a "happy" one.

This too is the mission of every priest: to be moved, to be engaged in people's lives, because a priest is a minister, like Jesus is a minister. However, how often—and we must go to confession for this—have we criticized those priests who are not interested in what happens to their parishioners, and who do not concern themselves with them? "No, he is not a good priest," we have said, because a good priest is one who is involved.

HUMILITY AND HOSPITALITY (14:7–11)[2]

In the scene from today's gospel passage, Jesus, who is in the home of one of the chief Pharisees, observes that the guests at lunch rush to choose the first place. It is a scene that we have seen so often: seeking the best place even with our elbows. Observing this scene, Jesus shares two short parables, and with them two instructions: one concerning the place, the other concerning the reward.

The first parable is set in a wedding banquet. Jesus says: "When you are invited by someone to a wedding banquet, do not sit down in the place of honor, in case someone more distinguished than you has been invited by your host; and the host who invited both of you may come and say to you, 'Give this person your place,' and then in disgrace you would start to take the lowest place" (Luke 14:8–9). With this recommendation, Jesus does not intend to give rules of social behavior, but rather a lesson on the value of humility.

History teaches that pride, careerism, vanity, and ostentation are the causes of many evils. And Jesus helps us to understand the necessity of choosing the last place, that is, of seeking to be small and the hidden: *humility*. When we place ourselves before God in humility, God exalts us; he stoops down to us so as to lift us up to himself; "For all who exalt themselves will be humbled, and those who humble themselves will be exalted" (v. 11).

Jesus's words emphasize completely different and opposing attitudes: the attitude of those who choose their own place and the attitude of those who allow God to assign their place and await a reward from him. Let us not forget this: God pays much more than people do! He gives us a much greater place than that which people give us! The place that God gives us is close to his heart and his reward is eternal life.

This is what is described in the second parable, in which Jesus points out the attitude of selflessness that ought to characterize *hospitality*. He says: "But when you give a banquet, invite the poor, the crippled, the lame, and the blind. And you will be blessed, because they cannot repay you" (vv. 13–14). This means choosing gratuitousness rather than self-seeking and calculating to obtain a reward, seeking interest and trying to increase your wealth. Indeed, the poor, the simple, those who "don't count," can never reciprocate an invitation to a meal.

In this way, Jesus shows his preference for the poor and the excluded, who are the privileged in the kingdom of God, and he launches the fundamental message of the gospel which is to serve others out of love for God. Today, Jesus gives voice to those who are voiceless, and to each one of us he addresses an urgent appeal to open our hearts and to make our own the sufferings and anxieties of the poor, the hungry, the marginalized, the refugees, those who are defeated by life, those who are rejected by society and by the arrogance of the strong. And those who are discarded make up the vast majority of the population.

THE SECRET OF A HAPPY FAMILY (14:12–14)[3]

Open and caring families find a place for the poor and build friendships with those less fortunate than themselves. In their efforts to live according to the gospel, they are mindful of Jesus's words: "As you did it to one of the least of these ... you did it to me" (Matt 25:40). In a very real way, their lives express what is asked of us all: "When you give a luncheon or a dinner, do not invite your friends or your brothers or your relatives or rich neighbors, in case they may invite you in return, and you would be repaid. But when you give a banquet, invite the poor, the crippled, the lame, and the blind. And you will be blessed" (Luke 14:12–14). You will be blessed! Here is the secret to a happy family.

A SIGN OF THE KINGDOM (14:13–14)[4]

Who are the first to whom the gospel message must be proclaimed? The answer, found so often throughout the gospel, is clear: it is the poor, the little ones, and the sick, those who are often looked down upon or forgotten, those who cannot repay us (cf. Luke 14:13–14). Evangelization directed preferentially to the least among us is a sign of the kingdom that Jesus came to bring: "There is an inseparable bond between our faith and the poor. May we never abandon them."[5] This must be clear above all to those who embrace the consecrated missionary life: by the vow of poverty, they choose to follow Christ in his preference for the poor, not ideologically, but in the same way that he identified himself with the poor: by living like them amid the uncertainties of everyday life and renouncing all claims to power, and in this way to become brothers and sisters of the poor, bringing them the witness of the joy of the gospel and a sign of God's love.

OUR FAITH AND THE POOR (14:14)[6]

If the whole Church takes up this missionary impulse, she has to go forth to everyone without exception. But to whom should she go first? When we read the gospel, we find a clear indication: not so much our friends and wealthy neighbors, but above all the poor and the sick, those who are usually despised and overlooked, "those who cannot repay you" (cf. Luke 14:14). There can be no room for doubt or for explanations that weaken so clear a message. Today and always, "the poor are the privileged recipients of the gospel,"[7] and the fact that it is freely preached to them is a sign of the kingdom that Jesus came to establish. We have to state, without mincing words, that there is an inseparable bond between our faith and the poor. May we never abandon them.

GOD'S GRATUITOUSNESS (14:15–24)[8]

When one of those who sat at the table with Jesus exclaimed: "Blessed is he who shall eat bread in the kingdom of God!" In other words, "This would be wonderful!" Jesus replied with the parable of the man who gave a great banquet and whose invitation was rejected. Everyone likes to go to a party, to be invited. The problem was: Invited to what?

The first man, in fact, boasting of having recently bought a field, sets his priority of "vanity," of "pride," of "power," preferring to go and check on his field in order to feel a little powerful, rather than sitting as one of many at that Lord's table. Another speaks about business—"I have bought five yoke of oxen and I need to go to examine them"—and thinks more about his earnings than of going to waste time with those people, thinking: "They will discuss many things, but I won't be at the center. I'll be one of many." Last is the man who offers the excuse of having just gotten married. He could also bring his wife to the banquet, but he wants the attention for himself. In this case, selfishness prevails. In the end, all three have a preference for themselves and don't want to share a party. Because, in reality, they don't know what a party is.

The men in the parable, who exemplify so many, always show an "interest," they seek an "exchange," a "quid pro quo." If the invitation had been, for example, "Come, I have two or three business friends coming from another country, we could do something together," without a doubt, no one would have excused himself. Indeed, what frightens them is the gratuitousness, being one like the others. It is selfishness, the desire to be at the center of everything. When one lives in this dimension, when one revolves around oneself, he ends up without horizons because he himself is the horizon. And so, it is difficult to hear the voice of Jesus, the voice of God. Behind this attitude, there is another thing, even more profound. There is the fear of gratuitousness. God's gratuitousness, in fact, compared with so many life experiences that have caused us to suffer, is so great that it frightens us.

Man is disoriented. This attitude is similar to that of the disciples on the road from Jerusalem to Emmaus. They said to each other: "We had hoped that he was the one to redeem Israel." And also: "The gift was so great that we were disappointed. And we are afraid." The same thing happened with the very practical Thomas, who said to those who spoke of the Risen Jesus: "Don't come with any stories," because "if I don't see, don't touch.... I once believed, and everything collapsed! No. Never again!"

Even Thomas was afraid of God's gratuitousness. In this regard, there is a popular saying: "When the offer is so great, even the holy are suspicious." In other words, when a gift is too large, it puts us on guard, because gratuitousness is too much for us. So, if God offers us such a banquet, we think: "Better not to get involved; it is better to be by ourselves." We are indeed more certain in our sins, within our limits, because there, at least, we are at home.

Nevertheless, to go out from our home at God's invitation, to God's house, with the others, frightens us. And all of us Christians have this fear hidden inside, to a certain extent. Too often, in fact, we are Catholics but not too Catholic, confident in the

Lord, but not too much. And this "not too much," in the end, diminishes us.

After the servant tells the master of the guests' rejection, he is angry, because he has been scorned. So he sends the servant to bring all those who are outcast, the needy, the sick, through the streets and the lanes of the city—the poor, the maimed, the blind, the lame. And when the servant tells him there is still room in the hall, he tells him: "Go out to the highways and hedges, and compel people to come in, so that my house may be filled." One verb, "compel" them, which makes us think: "So many times, the Lord has to do the same with us: with proof, so much proof, he compels the heart, the spirit, to believe that there is gratuitousness in him, that his gift is free, that salvation isn't bought: it is a great gift. God's love is, indeed, the greatest gift.

When we look at the crucifix, we say: "This is the entrance to the celebration. Yes, Lord, I'm a sinner, but I look at you and I go to the Father's feast. I trust. I won't be disappointed, because you have paid for everything." Thus, the Church asks us to trust the gratuitousness of God, even though it can seem foolish. But Paul says: "For the message about the cross is foolishness to those who are perishing, but to us who are being saved it is the power of God" (1 Cor 1:18). We have only to open our heart, do our part, all that we can, but he will provide the grand feast.

THE MEANING OF LOVE (14:15–24)[9]

One of the fellow diners said to Jesus: "Blessed is he who shall eat bread in the kingdom of God!" The Lord, without explanation, responded to him with a parable of this man who held a great banquet and invited many. However, the first ones to be invited did not want to go to the dinner; they did not care about the meal or the people who would be there, or of the Lord who had invited them; they were interested in other things.

In fact, one after the other they began to make excuses. Thus, the first said to him, "I have bought a field"; another, "I have bought five yoke of oxen"; still another, "I have married." They each had their own interests which were more important to them than the invitation. In fact, they clung to their own interests, asking themselves, "What could I gain?" For this reason, their response to the freely given invitation was "I do not care; perhaps another day, I am so busy, I cannot go." They were busy like the man who, after the harvest, after the gathering of the grain, made storehouses in order to further amass goods. Poor man; he died that night.

These people are so attached to their own interests that they fall into slavery of the spirit, and they are incapable of understanding the gratuity of the invitation. Indeed, if one does not understand the gratuity of God's invitation, then one understands nothing.

God's invitation is always free. What should one pay to attend this banquet? The entrance ticket is to be sick, to be poor, to be a sinner. In other words, we must be in need, both in body and in soul, and "neediness" here means being in need of care, healing, and love.

Here one sees two attitudes. The first—that of God—is always free: in order to save, God does not charge anything. God's freely given love is universal, for the gratuity of God has no limits; he receives everyone. Indeed, in the scripture passage, the master gets "angry," saying to his servant, "Go out at once into the streets and lanes of the town and bring in the poor, the crippled, the blind, and the lame" (v. 21), and in Matthew's version of the parable, the master even says to bring the "good and bad" (Matt 22:10).

However, those who mind their own interests do not understand this gratuity. They are like the son who remained by the father's side when the younger son left. When, after much time the younger son returned, poor, the father held a feast, and the older son did not want to attend that banquet. He did not want to enter into that feast because he did not understand. His attitude was: "He has spent all the money; he has spent the inheritance on vice and sin, and you hold him a feast? And I, who am a practicing Catholic, I go to Mass every Sunday, I carry out my duties, and to me, nothing?"

The fact is that he does not understand the gratuity of salvation; he thinks that salvation is the fruit of "I pay, and you save me." Rather, salvation is free, and if we do not enter into such a dynamic of gratuity we will not understand anything.

Salvation is a gift from God to which I respond with another gift—the gift of my heart. There are those, however, who have other interests when they hear talk of gifts. They say to themselves: "I will give this gift and then tomorrow and the next day, or on another occasion, he will give me another." As such, there is always an exchange.

Rather, the Lord does not ask for anything in exchange. He asks only for love and faithfulness, for he is love and he is faithful. Indeed, salvation is not bought. One simply enters the banquet: "Blessed is he who shall eat bread in the kingdom of God!" This is salvation.

I ask myself: "What do they feel, the ones who are indisposed to come to this banquet?" They feel safe, they feel secure, they feel saved in their own way, outside of the banquet, for they have lost the meaning of gratuity. They have lost the meaning of love, and they have lost a greater and more beautiful thing, namely, the capacity to feel themselves loved, and this leaves no hope. When you no longer feel loved, you have lost everything.

Thus, the faithful turn their gaze toward the master of the house who wants his house filled: "He is so full of love that in his gratuity he wants to fill his home." Let us implore the Lord to save us from losing the capacity to feel loved.

FOLLOWING JESUS (14:25)[10]

We heard in the gospel that "large crowds were traveling with Jesus" (v. 25). Today, this "large crowd" is seen in the great number of volunteers who have come together for the Jubilee of Mercy. You are that crowd who follow the Master and who make visible his concrete love for each person. I repeat to you the words of the apostle Paul: "I have indeed received much joy and comfort from your love, because the hearts of the saints have been refreshed through you" (Philem 1:7). How many hearts have been comforted by volunteers? How many hands they have held; how many tears they have wiped away; how much love has been poured out in hidden, humble, and selfless service! This praiseworthy service gives voice to the faith—it gives voice to the faith!—and expresses the mercy of the Father, who draws near to those in need.

Following Jesus is a serious task, and, at the same time, one filled with joy. It takes a certain daring and courage to recognize the divine Master in the poorest of the poor and those who are cast aside and to give oneself in their service. To do so, volunteers, who out of love of Jesus serve the poor and the needy, do not expect any thanks or recompense; rather, they renounce all this because they have discovered true love. And each one of us can say: "Just as the Lord has come to meet me and has stooped down to my level in my hour of need, so too do I go to meet him, bending low before those who have lost faith or who live as though God did not exist, before young people without values or ideals, before families in crisis, before the ill and the imprisoned, before refugees and immigrants, before the weak and defenseless in body and spirit, before abandoned children, before the elderly who are on their own. Wherever someone is reaching out, asking for a helping hand in order to get up, this is where our presence—and the presence of the Church which sustains and offers hope—must be. And I do this, keeping alive the memory of those times when the Lord's hand reached out to me when I was in need.

THE WAR AGAINST EVIL (14:31–32)[11]

In today's gospel, Jesus lays out the conditions for being his disciples: preferring nothing to the love of Christ, carrying one's cross and following him. Many people, in fact, drew near to Jesus, and wanted to be included among his followers, and this would happen especially after some miraculous sign that they saw as indicating that he was the Messiah, the King of Israel. However, Jesus did not want to disappoint anyone. He knew well what awaited him in Jerusalem and which path the Father was asking him to take: it was the way of the cross, the way of sacrificing himself for the forgiveness of our sins. Following Jesus does not mean taking part in a triumphal procession! It means sharing his merciful love, entering his great work of mercy for each and every person and for all people. The work of Jesus is, precisely, a work of mercy, a work of forgiveness and of love! Jesus is so full of mercy! And this universal pardon, this mercy, passes through the cross.

Jesus, however, does not want to do this work alone: he wants to involve us too in the mission that the Father entrusted to him. After the Resurrection, he was to say to his disciples: "As the Father has sent me, so I send you . . . if you forgive the sins of any, they are forgiven" (John 20:21–23). Jesus's disciple renounces all his possessions because in Jesus he has found the greatest good in which every other good receives its full value and meaning: family ties, other relationships, work, cultural and economic goods, and so forth. . . . The Christian detaches himself or herself from all things and rediscovers all things in the logic of the gospel, the logic of love and of service.

To explain this requirement, Jesus uses two parables: that of the tower to be built and that of the king going to war. The second parable says: "What king, going out to wage war against another king, will not sit down first and consider whether he is able with ten thousand to oppose the one who comes against him with twenty thousand? If he cannot, then, while the other is still far away, he sends a delegation and asks for the terms of peace" (Luke 14:31–32). Jesus does not wish to address the topic of war here; it is only a parable. Yet at this moment in which we are praying intensely for peace, this word of the Lord touches us to the core and essentially tells us: there is a more profound war that we must all fight! It is the firm and courageous decision to renounce evil and its enticements and to choose the good, ready to pay in person: this is following Christ, this is what taking up our cross means! This profound war against evil! What is the use of waging war, so many wars, if you aren't capable of waging this profound war against evil? It is pointless! It doesn't work. ... Among other things, this war against evil entails saying "no" to fratricidal hatred and falsehood; saying "no" to violence in all its forms; saying "no" to the proliferation of weapons and to the illegal arms trade. There is so much of it! So much of it! And the doubt always remains: Is this war or that war—because wars are everywhere—really a war to solve problems, or is it a commercial war for selling weapons in illegal trade? These are the enemies to fight, united and consistently, following no other interests than those of peace and the common good.

15

Parables of Mercy

Three Parables of Mercy (15:1–32)[1]

This chapter of the Gospel of Luke is considered the chapter on mercy. It relates three parables with which Jesus responds to the grumbling of the scribes and the Pharisees who are criticizing his actions, saying, "This fellow welcomes sinners and eats with them" (v. 2).

With these three stories, Jesus wants to make us understand that God the Father is the first one to have a welcoming and merciful attitude toward sinners. This is God's attitude.

In the first parable, God is presented as a shepherd who leaves ninety-nine sheep to go and look for the one that is lost. In the second, he is compared to a woman who has lost a coin and searches until she finds it. In the third parable, God is imagined as a father who welcomes the son who distanced himself; the figure of the father reveals the heart of a merciful God, manifested in Jesus.

A common element in these parables is expressed by the verbs that mean *rejoice together, join in celebrating*. Mourning is not spoken of; there is rejoicing, there is celebrating. The shepherd calls his friends and neighbors and says, "Rejoice with me, for I have found my sheep that was lost" (v. 6). The woman calls her friends and neighbors, saying, "Rejoice with me, for I have found the coin that I had lost" (v. 9). And the father says to his other son: "But we had to celebrate and rejoice, because this brother of yours was dead and has come to life; he was lost and has been found" (v. 32).

In the first two parables, the focus is on the joy that is so un-containable that it must be shared with friends and neighbors. In the third parable, the focus is on the joy that springs from the heart of the merciful father and expands to the whole household. God's rejoicing over those who return to him repentant is cele-brated as never before in this Jubilee Year that we are living, as the term itself expresses: "jubilee," that is, jubilation!

With these three parables, Jesus presents to us the true face of God, a God with open arms, a God who deals with sinners with tenderness and compassion. The parable that is most mov-ing for everyone—because it manifests the infinite love of God— is that of the father who enfolds the son who has been found in a close embrace. What strikes us is not so much the sad story of a youth who falls into dissolute ways, but rather his decisive words, "I will get up and go to my father" (v. 18).

The path to return home is the path of hope and new life. God always expects us to resume our journey, he awaits us with patience, sees us when we are still a long way off, runs to meet us, embraces us, kisses us, and forgives us. That is how God is. That is how our Father is. And his forgiveness cancels the past and regenerates us in love. Forgetting the past—this is God's weakness. When he embraces us, he forgives us, and forgets it. He doesn't remember. He forgets the past. When we sinners con-vert and let ourselves be reencountered by God, reproach and sternness do not await us, because God saves. He welcomes us home again with joy and prepares a feast.

In today's gospel, Jesus himself says, "There will be more joy in heaven over one sinner who repents than over ninety-nine righteous persons who need no repentance" (Luke 15:7).

Let me ask you a question: Have you ever thought about how each time we go to confession there is joy and celebration in heaven? Have you ever thought about this? It's beautiful.

This fills us with a great hope, because there is no sin into which we may have fallen from which, with the grace of God, we cannot rise up again. There is never a person who can't be recovered; no one is irrecoverable, because God never stops wanting our good—even when we sin!

May the Virgin Mary, Refuge of Sinners, kindle in our hearts the confidence that was lit in the heart of the prodigal son: "I will get up and go to my father, and I will say to him, 'Father, I have sinned against heaven and before you'" (v. 18). On this path, we can give glory to God, and his glory can become his celebration, and ours.

The Lost Sheep (15:3–7)[2]

We are all familiar with the image of the good shepherd with the little lost lamb on his shoulders. This icon has always been an expression of Jesus's care for sinners and of the mercy of God who never resigns himself to the loss of anyone. Jesus tells us the parable to help us understand that his closeness to sinners should not scandalize us, but more importantly to call us all to reflect on how we live our faith. On the one hand, we have the sinners who approach Jesus to listen to him and, on the other, the suspicious doctors of the law and scribes who move away from him because of his behavior. They move away because Jesus approaches sinners. These men were proud, arrogant, and believed themselves to be just.

Our parable unfolds around three characters: the shepherd, the lost sheep, and the rest of the flock. The one who acts, however, is only the *shepherd*, not the sheep. The shepherd, then, is the only real protagonist and everything depends on him. The parable opens with a question: "Which one of you, having a hundred sheep and losing one of them, does not leave the ninety-nine in the wilderness and go after the one that is lost until he finds it?" (Luke 15:4). It is a paradox that raises doubt about the action of the shepherd: Is it wise to abandon the ninety-nine for one single sheep? And furthermore, to abandon them not in the safety of a pen but in the desert? According to biblical tradition, the desert is a place of death where it is hard to find food and water, where one is without shelter and at the mercy of wild beasts and thieves. What are the ninety-nine defenseless sheep supposed to do? The paradox continues, saying that the shepherd, having found the sheep, "lays it on his shoulders and rejoices. And when he comes home, he calls together his friends and neighbors, saying to them, 'Rejoice with me'" (15:5–6). It seems then that the shepherd didn't go back to the desert to recover the rest of the flock! Reaching out to that single sheep, he seems to forget the other ninety-nine. But it's not like that really.

The lesson that Jesus wants us to learn is, rather, that not a single one of us can be lost. The Lord cannot accept the fact that a single person can be lost. God's action is that of one who goes out seeking his lost children and then rejoices and celebrates with everyone at their recovery. It is a burning desire: not even ninety-nine sheep could stop the shepherd and keep him enclosed in the fold. He could have reasoned like this: "Let me do the sum: If I have ninety-nine of them, I have lost one, but that's no great loss." But he doesn't. Nevertheless, he goes looking for that one, because each one is very important to him, but that one is in the most need; it is the most abandoned, most discarded; and he goes to look for it. We are all warned: mercy to sinners is the style with which God acts, and to this mercy he is absolutely faithful. Nothing and no one can distract him from his saving will. God does not share our current throw-away culture. God throws no one away. God loves everyone, looks for everyone—one by one! He doesn't know what "throwing people away" means, because he is entirely love, entirely mercy.

The Lord's flock is always on the move. It does not possess the Lord; it cannot hope to imprison him in its structures and strategies. The shepherd will be found wherever the lost sheep is. The Lord, then, should be sought precisely where he wants to find us, not where we presume to find him! There is no other way to reassemble the flock except by following the path outlined by the mercy of the shepherd. While he is looking for the lost sheep, he challenges the ninety-nine to participate in the reunification of the flock. Then, not only will the lamb on his shoulders, but the whole flock will follow the shepherd to his home to celebrate with "friends and neighbors."

We should reflect on this parable often, for in the Christian community there is always someone who is missing, and if that person is gone a place is left empty. Sometimes, this is daunting and leads us to believe that a loss is inevitable, like an incurable disease. That is how we run the risk of shutting ourselves in the pen, where there won't be the smell of the sheep but the stench of enclosure! And Christians? We must not be closed in or we will smell, will become stale. Never! We need to go forth, not close in on ourselves, in our little communities, in the parish, holding ourselves to be "righteous." This happens when there is a lack of missionary zeal that leads us to encounter others. In Jesus's vision, there are no sheep that are definitively lost, but only sheep that must be found again. We need to understand this well: to God no one is definitively lost. Never! To the last moment, God is searching for us. Think of the good thief; in the eyes of Jesus there is no one who is definitively lost. The prospect, therefore, is always dynamic, open, challenging, and creative. It urges us to go forth in search of a path to brotherhood. No distance can keep the shepherd away; and no flock can renounce a brother. To find the one who is lost is the joy of the shepherd and of God, but it is also the joy of the flock as a whole! We are all sheep who have been retrieved and brought back by the mercy of the Lord, and we are called to gather the whole flock to the Lord!

SHEPHERDS OF GOD'S TENDERNESS (15:3–7)[3]

How often do I think that we are afraid of the tenderness of God and, because we are afraid of God's tenderness, we do not allow it to be felt within us? Because of this, we are so often hard, serious, punishing.... We are pastors without compassion. What does

Jesus say to us in Luke about that shepherd who noticed that he had ninety-nine sheep because one was missing? He left them well safeguarded, locked away, and went to search for the other, who was ensnared in thorns. . . . And he didn't beat it, didn't scold it. He took it tightly in his arms and cared for it, for it was injured.

Do you do the same with your faithful, when you realize that one of your flock is missing? Or are we accustomed to being a church that has a single sheep in its flock and we let the other ninety-nine get lost on the hill? Are you moved by all this compassion? Are you a shepherd of sheep or have you become one who is "grooming" the one remaining sheep? Do you seek only yourself, having forgotten the tenderness your Father gave you, as we find in chapter 11 of Hosea? Have you forgotten how to give that compassion? The heart of Christ is the tenderness of God. "How can I give you up?

How can I hand you over? When you are alone, disoriented, lost, come to me, and I will save you, I will comfort you" (cf. Hos 11).

Today, I ask you, in this retreat, to be pastors with the compassion of God. To leave the "whip" hanging in the sacristy and to be pastors with tenderness, even with those who create many problems. It is a grace. It is a divine grace.

We do not believe in an ethereal God. We believe in a God who became flesh, who has a heart and this heart today speaks to us thus: "Come to me. If you are tired and oppressed, I will give you rest. But the smallest, treat them with compassion, with the same tenderness with which I treat you." The heart of Jesus Christ says this to us today, and it is what I ask in this Mass for you, and also for me.

The Heart of the Good Shepherd (15:4)[4]

The prophet Ezekiel reminds us that God himself goes out in search of his sheep (Ezek 34:11, 16). As the gospel says, he goes out in search of the one who is lost (cf. Luke 15:4), without fear of the risks. Without delaying, he leaves the pasture and his regular workday. He doesn't demand overtime. He does not put off the search. He does not think: "I have done enough for today; perhaps I'll worry about it tomorrow." Instead, he immediately sets out, his heart anxious until he finds that one lost sheep. Having found it, he forgets his weariness and puts the sheep on his shoulders, fully content. Sometimes he has to go and seek it out, to speak, to persuade; at other times, he must remain in prayer before the tabernacle, struggling with the Lord for that sheep.

Here is the heart that seeks: it is a heart that does not privatize times and spaces. Woe to the shepherds who privatize their ministry! A shepherd is not jealous of his legitimate peace of mind and never demands that he be left alone. A shepherd after the heart of God does not protect his own comfort zone. He is not worried about protecting his good name, but he will be slandered as Jesus was. Unafraid of criticism, he is disposed to take risks in seeking to imitate his Lord. "Blessed are you when people revile you and persecute you…" (Matt 5:11).

A shepherd after the heart of God has a heart sufficiently free to set aside his own concerns. He does not live by calculating his gains or how long he has worked; he is not an accountant of the Spirit, but a Good Samaritan who seeks out those in need. He is a shepherd to the flock, not an inspector, and he devotes himself to the mission, not 50 or 60 percent, but with everything he has. In seeking, he finds, and he finds because he takes risks. Unless a shepherd risks, he does not find. He does not stop when disappointed, and he does not yield to weariness. Indeed, he is stubborn in doing good, anointed with the divine obstinacy that loses sight of no one. Not only does he keep his doors open, but he also goes to seek out those who no longer wish to enter them. Like every good Christian, and as an example for every Christian, he constantly goes out of himself. The epicenter of his heart is outside of himself. He is centered only in Jesus, not in himself. He is not attracted by his own "I," but by the "Thou" of God, and by the "we" of other men and women.

TURNING OUR BACKS ON GOD (15:4–6)[5]

We cannot be reconciled to God by our efforts alone. Truly, sin is the expression of the rejection of his love, with the consequence of closing in on ourselves, deluding ourselves into thinking that we have found greater freedom and autonomy. Far from God, we no longer have a destination, and we are transformed from pilgrims in this world to "wanderers." To use a common expression, when we sin, we "turn away from God." That's just what we do. The sinner sees only himself and presumes this to be sufficient. Thus, sin continues to expand the distance between us and God, and this can become a chasm. However, Jesus comes to find us like a good shepherd who is not content until he has found the lost sheep, as we read in the gospel (cf. Luke 15:4–6). He rebuilds the bridge that connects us to the Father and allows us to rediscover our dignity as children. By the offering of his life, he has reconciled us to the Father and given us eternal life (cf. John 10:15).

THE JOY OF THE SHEPHERD (15:5)[6]

God is "full of joy" (cf. Luke 15:5). His joy is born of forgiveness, of life risen and renewed, of prodigal children who breathe once more the sweet air of home. The joy of Jesus the Good Shepherd is not a joy for himself alone, but a joy for others, and with others, the true joy of love. This is also the joy of the priest. He is changed by the mercy that he freely gives. In prayer, he discovers God's consolation and realizes that nothing is more powerful than his love. He thus experiences inner peace, and is happy to be a channel of mercy, to bring men and women closer to the heart of God. Sadness for him is not the norm, but only a step along the way. Harshness is foreign to him, because he is a shepherd after the meek heart of God.

THE CHURCH'S MISSION (15:7)[7]

We should realize that missionary outreach is paradigmatic for all the Church's activity. Along these lines the Latin American bishops stated that we "cannot passively and calmly wait in our church buildings";[8] we need to move "from a pastoral ministry of mere conservation to a decidedly missionary pastoral ministry."[9] This task continues to be a source of immense joy for the Church: "Just so, I tell you, there will be more joy in heaven over one sinner who repents than ninety-nine righteous persons who need no repentance" (Luke 15:7).

SALVATION (15:11–24)[10]

In accepting the gift of faith, believers become a new creation; they receive a new being; as God's children, they are now "sons in the Son." The phrase "Abba, Father," so characteristic of Jesus's own experience, now becomes the core of the Christian experience (cf. Rom 8:15). The life of faith, as a filial existence, is the acknowledgment of a primordial and radical gift which upholds our lives. We see this clearly in Saint Paul's question to the Corinthians: "What do you have that you did not receive?" (1 Cor 4:7)....Once I think that by turning away from God I will find myself, my life begins to fall apart (cf. Luke 15:11–24). The beginning of salvation is openness to something prior to ourselves, to a primordial gift that affirms life and sustains it in being. Only by being open to and acknowledging this gift can we be transformed, experience salvation, and bear good fruit. Salvation by faith means recognizing the primacy of God's gift. In the words of Saint Paul: "By grace you have been saved through faith, and this is not your own doing; it is the gift of God" (Eph 2:8).

A Society Grounded in Mercy (15:11–32)[11]

Some feel that a vision of society rooted in mercy is hopelessly idealistic or excessively indulgent. But let us try and recall our first experience of relationships within our families. Our parents loved us and valued us for who we are more than for our abilities and achievements. Parents naturally want the best for their children, but that love is never dependent on their meeting certain conditions. The family home is one place where we are always welcome (cf. Luke 15:11–32). I encourage everyone to see society not as a forum where strangers compete and try to come out on top, but above all, as a home or a family, where the door is always open and where everyone feels welcome.

The Father of Mercy (15:11–32)[12]

We shall begin at the end, that is, the joy in the heart of the father who says: "Let us eat and celebrate; for this son of mine was dead and is alive again; he was lost and is found" (Luke 15:23–24). With these words, the father interrupted the younger son just as he was confessing his guilt: "I am no longer worthy to be called your son…" (v. 19). But this expression is unbearable to the heart of the father, who is quick to restore the signs of dignity to the son: the best robe, the fatted calf, shoes. Jesus does not describe a father who is offended and resentful, a father who would, for example, say to his son: "You will pay for this." On the contrary, the father embraces him, awaits him with love. The only thing that the father has on his mind is that his son stands before him healthy and safe; this makes him happy, and he celebrates. The reception of the prodigal son is described movingly: "While he was still far off, his father saw him and was filled with compassion; he ran and put his arms around him and kissed him" (v. 20).

What tenderness! He sees him at a distance. What does this mean? That the father had constantly gone to the balcony to look down the road to see if his son would return—that son who had misbehaved in many ways found the father there waiting for him. How beautiful is the father's tenderness! The father's mercy is overflowing, unconditional, and shows itself even before the son speaks. Certainly, the son knows he erred and acknowledges it: "I have sinned...treat me like one of your hired hands" (vv. 18–19). These words crumble before the father's forgiveness. The embrace and the kiss of his father make him understand that he was always considered a son, despite everything. This teaching of Jesus is very important: our condition as children of God is the fruit of the love of the Father's heart. It does not depend on our merits or on our actions, and thus, no one can take it away, not even the devil! No one can take this dignity away.

Jesus's words encourage us never to despair. I think of the worried mothers and fathers watching their children move away, taking dangerous paths. I think of the parish priests and catechists who wonder at times if their work is in vain. But I also think of the prisoner who feels his life is over. I think of those who have made mistakes and cannot manage to envision the future, of those who hunger for mercy and forgiveness and believe they don't deserve them....In any situation of life, I must not forget that I will never cease to be a child of God, to be a child of the Father who loves me and awaits my return. Even in the worst situation of life, God waits for me. God wants to embrace me. God expects me.

In the parable there is another son, the older one. He too needs to discover the mercy of the father. He always stayed at home, but he is so different from the father! His words lack tenderness: "Listen! For all these years I have been working like a slave for you, and I have never disobeyed your command....But when this son of yours came back" (vv. 29–30). We see the contempt: he never says "father," never says "brother," and thinks only about himself. He boasts of having always remained at his father's side and of having served him, yet he never lived this closeness with joy. And now he accuses the father of never having given him as much as a young goat to feast on. The poor father! One son went away, and the other was never close to him! The suffering of the father is like the suffering of God, the suffering of Jesus when we distance ourselves from him, either because we go far away, or because we are nearby without being close.

The elder son needs mercy too. The righteous, those who believe they are righteous, are also in need of mercy. This son represents us when we wonder whether it is worth all the trouble if we get nothing in return. Jesus reminds us that we do not stay in the house of the Father for a reward but because we have the dignity of being children who share responsibility. There is no "bargaining" with God, but rather following in the footsteps of Jesus who gave himself on the cross without measure.

"Son, you are always with me, and all that is mine is yours. But we had to celebrate and rejoice" (vv. 31–32). The father speaks like this to the elder son. His logic is that of mercy! The younger son thought he deserved punishment for his sins, the elder son was waiting for a recompense for his service. The two brothers don't speak to one another. They live in different ways, but they both reason according to a logic that is foreign to Jesus: if you do good, you get a prize; if you do evil you are punished. This is not Jesus's logic, it's not! This logic is reversed by the words of the father: "But we had to celebrate and rejoice, because this brother of yours was dead and has come to life; he was lost and has been found" (v. 32). The father recovered a lost son, and now he can also give him back to his brother! Without the younger, the elder son ceases to be a "brother." The greatest joy for the father is to see his children recognize one another as brothers.

The sons can decide whether to join in the joy of the father or to reject it. They must ask themselves what they really want and what their vision for their life is. The parable is left open-ended: we do not know what the elder son decided to do. And this is an incentive for us. This gospel passage teaches us that we all need to enter the house of the Father and to share in his joy, in his feast of mercy and of brotherhood. Brothers and sisters, let us open our hearts, in order to be "merciful like the Father"!

16

Parables of Living

THREE TYPES OF PEOPLE (16:1–8)[1]

The biblical readings this Sunday present us with three types of person: the exploiter, the scammer, and the faithful man.

The *exploiter* is the one the prophet Amos tells us about in the first reading (cf. Amos 8:4–7), which is about a person obsessed with earning money, to the point of being annoyed with and intolerant of liturgical days of rest, because they break the frenetic pace of commerce. His only divinity is money, and his actions are dominated by fraud and exploitation. Those who pay for his actions are especially the poor and the destitute, those who are enslaved and whose income equals the price of a pair of sandals (v. 6). Unfortunately, he is the type of person who is found in every age; even today there are many people like him.

The *scammer* is the man who has no loyalty. His method is scamming. The gospel describes such a person in the parable of the dishonest manager (cf. Luke 16:1–8). How did the manager get to the point of cheating, of stealing from his master? From one day to the next? No. It was very gradual. Maybe one day giving a tip here, the other day a bribe there, and so, little by leading to corruption. In the parable, the master praises the dishonest manager for his cunning. Nevertheless, it is still a worldly and strongly sinful cunning, with a bad effect!

Instead, there is a Christian cunning, which involves doing things with shrewdness, but not with the spirit of the world: doing things honestly. And this is good. This is what Jesus means when he invites us to be as cunning as snakes and simple like doves: putting these two dimensions together is a grace of the Holy Spirit, a grace for which we must ask. Even today there are many corrupt scammers. It strikes me to see how corruption is spread everywhere.

The third type of person is the *faithful man*. The profile of a loyal man is what we can find in the second reading (cf. 1 Tim 2:1–8). In fact, he is the one who follows Jesus who gave himself as a ransom for all, who gave his testimony according to the will of the Father (cf. vv. 5–6). The faithful man is a man of prayer, in the double sense that he prays for others and trusts in the prayers of others for himself to be able to "lead a calm and peaceful life, dignified and dedicated to God" (v. 2). The faithful man can walk with his head held high. The gospel also speaks to us of such a faithful person: one who knows how to be faithful in both small and big things (cf. Luke 16:10).

The Choice

God's word leads us to a final choice: "No slave can serve two masters, for a slave will either hate the one and love the other or be devoted to the one and despise the other. You cannot serve God and wealth" (Luke 16:13). The scammer loves scamming and hates honesty. The scammer loves bribes, dark deals, agreements that are made in the dark. And the worst part is that he thinks he's honest. The scammer loves money, loves riches: riches are his idol. He does not mind, as the prophet says, trampling on the poor. Scammers are the ones who own the great "slave labor industries." And today in today's world, slave labor is a management style.

Two Roads (16:1–13)[2]

Today, Jesus invites us to reflect on two opposing ways of life: the way of the world and that of the gospel—and the worldly spirit is not the spirit of Jesus. He recounts the parable of the unfaithful and corrupt manager who is praised by Jesus despite his dishonesty (cf. Luke 16:1–13). We must point out immediately that this manager is not presented as a model to follow, but as an example of deceitfulness. This man is accused of mismanaging his master's affairs, and before being removed, he tries astutely to ingratiate himself with the debtors, dismissing part of their debt so as to ensure himself a future. Commenting on this behavior, Jesus observes: "For the children of this age are more shrewd in dealing with their own generation than are the children of light" (v. 8).

We are called to respond to such worldly astuteness with Christian astuteness, which is a gift of the Holy Spirit. This is a matter of departing from the worldly spirit and values, which the devil really favors, in order to live according to the gospel. How is worldliness manifested? Worldliness is manifested in attitudes of corruption, deception, and subjugation. It constitutes the most ill-chosen road—the road of sin—because one leads you to the other! It's like a chain, even if it is generally the easiest road to travel. The spirit of the gospel, on the other hand, requires a serious lifestyle—serious but joyful, full of joy!—serious and challenging, marked by honesty, fairness, respect for others and their dignity, and a sense of duty. And this is Christian astuteness!

The journey of life necessarily involves a choice between two roads: between honesty and dishonesty, between fidelity and infidelity, between selfishness and altruism, between good and evil. You cannot waver between one and the other, because they are based on different and conflicting forms of logic. The prophet Elijah asked the people of Israel: "How long will you go limping with two different opinions?" (cf. 1 Kings 18:21). It's a fine image. It is important to decide which direction to take and then, once you have chosen the right one, to walk in it with enthusiasm and determination, trusting in God's grace and the support of his

Spirit. The conclusion of the gospel passage is powerful and insistent: "No slave can serve two masters; for a slave will either hate the one and love the other or be devoted to the one and despise the other" (Luke 16:13).

With this teaching, Jesus today urges us to make a clear choice between him and the worldly spirit—between the logic of corruption, of the abuse of power and greed, and that of righteousness, meekness, and sharing. Some people conduct themselves with corruption as they do with drugs: they think they can use it and stop when they want. It starts out small: a tip here, a bribe there. . . . And between this and that, one's freedom is slowly lost. Corruption is also habit-forming, and it generates poverty, exploitation, and suffering. How many victims there are in the world today! How many victims of widespread corruption? However, when we try to follow the gospel logic of integrity, clarity in intentions and behavior, of fraternity, we become artisans of justice and we open horizons of hope for humanity. In gratuitousness and by giving of ourselves to our brothers and sisters, we serve the right master: God.

AGAINST INJUSTICE (16:1–31)[3]

Nor can we overlook the social degeneration brought about by sin, as, for example, when human beings tyrannize nature, selfishly and even brutally ravaging it. This leads to the desertification of the earth (cf. Gen 3:17–19) and those social and economic imbalances denounced by the prophets, beginning with Elijah (cf. 1 Kings 21) and culminating in Jesus's own words against injustice (cf. Luke 12:13; 16:1–31).

DISHONEST WEALTH (16:9–15)[4]

In the parable of the dishonest manager, Jesus urges us to take responsibility for our friends with dishonest wealth, in order to be welcomed in the eternal habitations (cf. Luke 16:9–15). All of the Fathers of the Church have interpreted these words to mean that wealth is good when it is placed at the service of our neighbors; otherwise, it is unjust.[5] Thus, money must serve, not rule. This is a key principle: money must serve, not rule. Money is only a technical instrument of intermediation, of comparison of values and rights, of the fulfillment of duties and saving. Like any technical instrument, money does not have a neutral value but acquires value based on the aims and circumstances in which it is used. When we claim that money is neutral, we fall under its power. Enterprises must not exist to earn money, even though money serves to measure their functioning. Enterprises exist to serve.

As If They Don't Exist (16:19–31)[6]

In the opening antiphon from Psalm 139[138], we prayed: "Search me, O God, and know my heart!... See if there be any wicked way in me, and lead me in the way everlasting" (cf. vv. 23–24). Since we can live a life of lies, of appearances, we ask the Lord that he search the truth of our life, and if I am leading a life of lies that he guide me to the way of life, of true life.

This was exactly what happened to the rich man of this gospel passage. When a person lives in his closed environment, breathes in that air of his possessions, his satisfaction, his vanity, of feeling safe, trusting only in himself, he loses direction; he loses the compass and does not know where the boundaries are. His problem is that he lives only there; he does not come out of himself.

But the rich man knew who that poor man was—he knew! Because later, when he speaks with father Abraham, he says: "Send me Lazarus." Therefore, he even knew his name, but he did not care. Was he therefore a sinful man? Yes. But one can return from sin; one asks for forgiveness and the Lord forgives.

As for that rich man, however, his heart led him to a path of death, to the point of no return. There is a point, a moment, there is a limit from which it is difficult to turn back. And it is precisely the point at which sin transforms into corruption. Here, we are reminded of the powerful words of Jeremiah: "Cursed are those who trust in mere mortals... the heart is devious above all else" (Jer 17: 5, 9); and when you are on that path of sickness, it will be difficult for you to heal.

Today, I will ask a question of all of us: What do we feel in the heart when we are walking along the street and we see the homeless, we see children on their own, begging? Perhaps we think they are from that ethnic group that steals. What do I feel when I see the homeless, the poor, the abandoned, even the well-dressed homeless, who do not have money to pay rent because they have no work?... What do I feel when, on the television news, in the newspapers, I see that a bomb has fallen on a hospital, on a school, and many children have died, poor people? Perhaps I say a Hail Mary, an Our Father, for them and I continue to live as if nothing has happened. Instead, it is good to ask ourselves if such human drama has entered my heart or if I am like that rich man that the gospel speaks about, whose heart never welcomed Lazarus—Lazarus, for whom the dogs had more pity than the rich man did. And, if I were like that rich man, I would be on the path from sin to corruption.

This is why we ask the Lord: "Search me, O God, and know my heart!... And see if there be any wicked way in me; see if my way is wrong, if I am on the slippery path from sin to corruption from which there is no return."

POVERTY AND MERCY (16:19–31)[7]

I should like to pause with you today to consider the parable of the rich man and the poor Lazarus. The lives of these two people seem to run on parallel tracks: their life status is opposite and not at all connected. The gate of the rich man's house is always closed to the poor man, who lies outside it, seeking to eat the leftovers from the rich man's table. The rich man is dressed in fine clothes, while Lazarus is covered with sores; the rich man feasts sumptuously every day, while Lazarus starves. Only the dogs take care of him, and they come to lick his wounds. This scene recalls the harsh reprimand of the Son of Man at the Last Judgement: "I was hungry and you gave me no food, I was thirsty and you gave me nothing to drink...naked and you did not give me clothing" (Matt 25:42–43). Lazarus is a good example of the silent cry of the poor throughout the ages and the contradictions of a world in which immense wealth and resources are in the hands of the few.

Jesus says that one day that rich man died. The poor and the rich die. They have the same destiny, like all of us—there are no exceptions to this. Thus, that man turned to Abraham, imploring him with the name of "father" (vv. 24, 27), thereby claiming to be his son, belonging to the people of God. Yet in life he showed no consideration toward God. Instead, he made himself the center of all things, closed inside his world of luxury and wastefulness. In excluding Lazarus, he did not take into consideration the Lord or his law. *To ignore a poor man is to scorn God!* We must learn this well: to ignore the poor is to scorn God.

There is a detail in the parable that is worth noting: *the rich man has no name*, but only an adjective: "the rich man," while the name of the poor man is repeated five times, and "Lazarus" means "God helps." Lazarus, who is lying at the gate, is a living reminder to the rich man to remember God, but the rich man does not receive that reminder. Therefore, he will be condemned not because of his wealth but for being incapable of feeling compassion for Lazarus and for not coming to his aid.

The Rich Man and Lazarus after Death

In the second part of the parable, we again meet Lazarus and the rich man after they have died (vv. 22–31). Now, in the hereafter, the situation is reversed: the poor Lazarus is carried by the angels to Abraham's bosom in heaven, while the rich man is thrown into torment. Thus the rich man "lifted up his eyes and saw Abraham far off and Lazarus in his bosom." He seems to see Lazarus for the first time, but his words betray him: "Father Abraham," he calls, "have mercy upon me, and send Lazarus to dip the end of his finger in water and cool my tongue; for I am in anguish in this flame." Now the rich man recognizes Lazarus and asks for his help, while in life he pretended not to see him. How often do many people pretend not to see the poor! To them the poor do not exist. Before he denied him even the leftovers from his table, and now he would like him to bring him a drink! He still believes he can assert rights through his previous social status.

Declaring it impossible to grant his request, Abraham personally offers the key to the whole story. He explains that good things and evil things have been distributed so as to compensate for earthly injustices, and the door that in life separated the rich from the poor is transformed into "a great chasm." As long as Lazarus was outside his house, the rich man had the opportunity for salvation, to thrust open the door, to help Lazarus, but now that they are both dead, the situation has become irreparable. God is never called upon directly, but the parable clearly warns: God's mercy toward us is linked to our mercy toward our neighbor; when this is lacking, there is no room to be found in our closed heart, and he cannot enter. If I do not thrust open the door of my heart to the poor, the door remains closed. Even to God. This is terrible.

At this point, the rich man thinks about his brothers who risk suffering the same fate, and he asks that Lazarus return to the world in order to warn them. But Abraham replies: "They have Moses and the prophets; let them hear them." In order to convert, we must not wait for exceptional events, but open our heart to the word of God, which calls us to love God and neighbor. The word of God may revive a withered heart and cure it of its blindness. The rich man knew the word of God but did not let it enter his heart; he did not listen to it, and thus was incapable of opening his eyes and of having compassion for the poor man. No messenger and no message can take the place of the poor whom we meet on the journey, because in them Jesus himself comes to meet us. Jesus says, "As you did it to one of the least of these who are members of my family, you did it to me" (Matt 25:40). Hidden in the reversal of fate that the parable describes lies the mystery of our salvation in which Christ links poverty with mercy. Dear brothers and sisters, listening to this gospel passage, all of us, together with the poor of the earth, can sing with Mary: "He has brought down the powerful from their thrones, and lifted up the lowly; he has filled the hungry with good things, and sent the rich away empty" (Luke 1:52–53).

THE ONE STANDING AT THE DOOR (16:20)[8]

In the parable, there is a rich man who does not notice Lazarus and a poor man who is "at his gate" (Luke 16:20). This rich man, in fact, does not do evil toward anyone; nothing says that he is a bad man. But he has a sickness much greater than that of Lazarus, who was "full of sores" (v. 20). This rich man suffers from terrible blindness, because he is not able to look beyond his world filled with banquets and fine clothing. He cannot see beyond the door of his house to where Lazarus lies, because what is happening outside does not interest him. He does not see with his eyes, because he cannot feel with his heart. For into it a worldliness has entered which anaesthetizes the soul. This worldliness is like a "black hole" that swallows up what is good and extinguishes love; it consumes everything in its very self. And so, here a person sees only outward appearances, no longer noticing others because one has become indifferent to everyone. The one who suffers from grave blindness often takes on "squinting" behavior: he looks with adulation at famous people, of high rank, admired by the world, yet turns his gaze away from the many Lazaruses of today—from the poor, from the suffering who are the Lord's beloved.

But the Lord looks at those who are neglected and discarded by the world. On the one hand, Lazarus is the only one named in all of Jesus's parables. His name means "God helps." God does not forget him; he will welcome him to the banquet in his kingdom, together with Abraham, in communion with all who suffer. The rich man in the parable, on the other hand, does not even have a name; his life passes by forgotten, because whoever lives for himself does not write history. And a Christian must write history! He and she must go out from themselves to write history! But whoever lives for themselves cannot write history. Today's callousness causes chasms to be dug that can never be crossed. And we have fallen, at this time, into the sickness of indifference, selfishness, and worldliness.

There is another detail in the parable, a contrast. The opulent life of this nameless man is described as being ostentatious; everything about him concerns needs and rights. Even when he is dead, he insists on being helped and demands what is to his benefit. Lazarus's poverty, however, is articulated with great dignity — from his mouth no complaints or protests or scornful words issue. This is a valuable teaching. As servants of the word of Jesus we have been called not to parade our appearances and not to seek for glory; nor can we be sad or full of complaints. We are not prophets of gloom who take delight in unearthing dangers or deviations; we are not people who become ensconced in our own surroundings, handing out bitter judgments on our society, on the Church, on everything and everyone, polluting the world with our negativity. Pitiful skepticism does not belong to whoever is close to the word of God.

Whoever proclaims the hope of Jesus carries joy and sees a great distance; such persons have the horizon open before them. There is no wall closing them in; they can see a great distance because they know how to see beyond evil and beyond their problems. At the same time, they can see clearly from up close, because they are attentive to their neighbor and to their neighbor's needs. The Lord is asking this of us today: before all the Lazaruses whom we see, we are called to be disturbed, to find ways of meeting and helping without always delegating to others or saying: "I will help you tomorrow; I have no time today, I'll help you tomorrow." This is a sin. The time taken to help others is time given to Jesus. It is love that remains: it is our treasure in heaven, which we earn here on earth.

TRUE HAPPINESS AND ETERNAL LIFE (16:19–31)[9]

Let us consider the parable of the rich man and Lazarus (cf. Luke 16:19–31). We can find inspiration in this meaningful story, for it provides a key to understanding what we need to do in order to attain true happiness and eternal life. It exhorts us to sincere conversion.

The Gift of the Other

The parable begins by presenting its two main characters. The poor man is described in greater detail: he is wretched and lacks the strength even to stand. Lying before the door of the rich man, he feeds on the crumbs falling from the rich man's table. His body is full of sores and dogs come to lick his wounds (cf. vv. 20–21). The picture is one of great misery; it portrays a man disgraced and pitiful.

The scene is even more dramatic if we consider that the poor man is called Lazarus: a name full of promise, which literally means "God helps." This character is not anonymous. His features are clearly delineated, and he appears as an individual with his own story. While practically invisible to the rich man, we see and know him as someone familiar. He has a face, and so he is a gift, a priceless treasure, a human being whom God loves and cares for, despite his concrete condition as an outcast.

Lazarus teaches us that every other person is a gift. A right relationship with people consists in gratefully recognizing their value. Even the poor person at the door of the rich is not a nuisance, but a summons to conversion and to change. The parable first invites us to open the doors of our heart to others because each person is a gift, whether it be our neighbor or an anonymous pauper. Lent is an opportune season for opening our doors to all those in need and recognizing in them the face of Christ. Each of us meets people like this every day. Each life that we encounter is a gift deserving acceptance, respect, and love. The word of God helps us to open our eyes to welcome and love life, especially when it is weak and vulnerable. But in order to do this, we have to take seriously what the gospel tells us about the rich man.

Sin Blinds Us

The parable is unsparing in its description of the contradictions associated with the rich man (cf. v. 19). Unlike poor Lazarus, he does not have a name; he is simply called "a rich man." His opulence is evident in his extravagant and expensive robes. In those days purple cloth was even more precious than silver and gold and was thus reserved to divinities (cf. Jer 10:9) and kings (cf. Jdg 8:26), while fine linen gave one an almost sacred character. The man was clearly ostentatious about his wealth and in the habit of displaying it daily: he "feasted sumptuously every day" (v. 19). In him we can catch a dramatic glimpse of the corruption of sin, which progresses in three successive stages: love of money, vanity, and pride.

The apostle Paul tells us that "the love of money is the root of all kinds of evil" (1 Tim 6:10). It is the main cause of corruption and a source of envy, strife, and suspicion. Money can come to dominate us, even to the point of becoming a tyrannical idol.[10] Instead of being an instrument at our service for doing good and showing solidarity toward others, money can chain us and the entire world to a selfish logic that leaves no room for love and hinders peace.

The parable shows that the rich man's greed makes him vain. His personality finds expression in appearances, in showing others what he can do. But his appearance masks an interior emptiness. In his life he is a prisoner to outward appearances, to the most superficial and fleeting aspects of existence.[11]

The lowest rung of this kind of moral degradation is pride. The rich man dresses like a king and acts like a god, forgetting that he is merely mortal. For those corrupted by love of riches, nothing exists beyond their own ego. People around them do not come into their line of sight. The result of attachment to money is a sort of blindness. The rich man does not see the poor man who is starving, hurting, lying at his door.

Looking at this character, we can understand why the gospel so bluntly condemns the love of money: "No one can serve two masters; for a slave will either hate the one and love the other or be devoted to the one and despise the other. You cannot serve God and wealth" (Matt 6:24).

The Gift of the Word

The parable of the rich man and Lazarus helps us to prepare for Easter. The liturgy of Ash Wednesday invites us to an experience quite similar to that of the rich man. When the priest places the ashes on our heads, he repeats the words: "Remember that you are dust, and to dust you shall return." As it turned out, the rich man and the poor man both died, and the greater part of the parable takes place in the afterlife. The two characters suddenly discover that "we brought nothing into the world, and we can take nothing out of it" (1 Tim 6:7).

We too see what happens in the afterlife. There the rich man speaks at length with Abraham, whom he calls "father" (Luke 16:24, 27), as a sign that he belongs to God's people. This detail makes his life appear all the more contradictory, for until this moment, there had been no mention of his relationship with God. In fact, there was no place for God in his life. His only god was himself.

The rich man recognizes Lazarus only amid the torments of the afterlife. He wants the poor man to alleviate his suffering with a drop of water. What he asks of Lazarus is similar to what he could have done but never did. Abraham tells him: "Remember that during your lifetime you received your good things, and Lazarus in like manner evil things; but now he is comforted here, and you are in agony" (v. 25). In the afterlife, a kind of fairness is restored, and life's evils are balanced by good.

The parable goes on to offer a message for all Christians. The rich man asks Abraham to send Lazarus to warn his brothers who are still alive. But Abraham answers: "They have Moses and the prophets; they should listen to them" (v. 29). Countering the rich man's objections, he adds: "If they do not listen to Moses and the prophets, neither will they be convinced even if someone rises from the dead" (v. 31).

The rich man's real problem thus comes to the fore. At the root of all his ills was *the failure to heed God's word*. As a result, he no longer loved God and grew to despise his neighbor. The word of God is alive and powerful, capable of converting hearts and leading them back to God. When we close our heart to the gift of God's word, we end up closing our heart to the gift of our brothers and sisters.

17

Faith

To Welcome and Not Scandalize (17:2)[1]

"Whoever welcomes one such child in my name welcomes me, and whoever welcomes me welcomes not me but the one who sent me" (Mark 9:37; cf. Matt 18:5; Luke 9:48; John 13:20). With these words, the evangelists remind the Christian community of Jesus's teaching, which both inspires and challenges. This phrase traces the sure path that leads to God. It begins with the smallest and, through the grace of our Savior, it grows into the practice of welcoming others. To be welcoming is a necessary condition for making this journey a concrete reality: God made himself one of us. In Jesus, God became a child, and the openness of faith in God, which nourishes hope, is expressed in loving proximity to the smallest and the weakest. Charity, faith, and hope are all actively present in the spiritual and corporal works of mercy, as we have rediscovered during the recent Extraordinary Jubilee.

But the evangelists reflect also on the responsibility of the one who works against mercy: "It would be better for you if a millstone were hung around your neck and you were thrown into the sea than for you to cause one of these little ones to stumble" (Matt 18:6; cf. Mark 9:42; Luke 17:2). How can we ignore this severe warning when we see the exploitation carried out by unscrupulous people? Such exploitation harms young girls and boys who are led into prostitution or into the mire of pornography; who are enslaved as child laborers or soldiers; who are caught up in drug trafficking and other forms of criminality; who are forced to flee from conflict and persecution, risking isolation and abandonment.

For this reason, on the occasion of the annual World Day of Migrants and Refugees, I feel compelled to draw attention to the reality of child migrants, especially the ones who are alone. In doing so, I ask everyone to take care of the young, who in a three-fold way are defenseless. They are children, they are foreigners, and they have no means to protect themselves. I ask everyone to help those who, for various reasons, are forced to live far from their homeland and are separated from their families.

INCREASE OUR FAITH (17:5)[2]

"Lord, 'increase our faith!'" (v. 5). This cry sprang up spontaneously from the disciples as the Lord spoke to them of mercy and told them that they must forgive seventy times seven times. Let us make this cry our own—"increase our faith!"—as we begin this conversation. Let us ask this in the simple words of the *Catechism*, where we read: "To live, grow and persevere in the faith until the end we must nourish it with the word of God; we must beg the Lord to increase our faith; it must be 'working through charity,' abounding in hope, and rooted in the faith of the Church."[3]

I would like to return for a moment to the theme of "growth." If you go back and attentively read *Evangelii Gaudium*—a programmatic document—you will see that it always speaks of "growth" and "maturation" both in faith and love, in solidarity and in the understanding of the word. *Evangelii Gaudium* has a positive dynamic. "The Lord's missionary mandate includes a call to growth in faith: 'Teach them to observe all

219

that I have commanded you' (Matt 28:20). Hence it is clear that that the first proclamation also calls for ongoing formation and maturation."[4]

I emphasize a *journey of formation and maturation in faith*. Taking this seriously means "it would not be right to see this call to growth exclusively or primarily in terms of doctrinal formation."[5] Growth in faith takes place by encountering the Lord over the course of one's life. These encounters are to be kept in memory as a treasure; they constitute a living faith within a personal history of salvation.

Our experience of these encounters is that of incomplete fullness. Incomplete, because we have to keep walking; full, because in all things human and divine, the whole is found in each individual part. This continual maturation pertains as much to the disciple as to the missionary, as much to the seminarian as to the priest or bishop.

INCREASE OUR FAITH (17:5–7)[6]

Today, the gospel passage begins: "The apostles said to the Lord, 'Increase our faith!'" (v. 5). It seems that we can all make this our invocation. Let us , like the apostles, say to the Lord: "Increase our faith!" Yes, Lord, our faith is small, our faith is weak and fragile, but we offer it to you as it is, so that you can make it grow....

And how does the Lord answer us? He responds: "If you had faith the size of a mustard seed, you could say to this mulberry tree, 'Be uprooted and planted in the sea,' and it would obey you" (v. 6). A mustard seed is tiny, yet Jesus says that faith this size, small but true and sincere, suffices to achieve what is humanly impossible, unthinkable. And it is true! We all know people who are simple, humble, but whose faith is so strong it can move mountains! Let us think, for example, of some mothers and fathers who face very difficult situations; or of some sick and even gravely ill people who transmit serenity to those who come to visit them. These people, because of their faith, do not boast about what they do, but rather, as Jesus asks in the gospel, they say: "We are worthless slaves; we have done only what we ought to have done!" (Luke 17:10). How many people among us have such strong, humble faith, and what good they do!

FAITH GROWS (17:5–10)[7]

The word of God presents us today with two essential aspects of the Christian life: faith and service. With regard to faith, two specific requests are made of the Lord.

The first is made by the prophet Habakkuk, who implores God to intervene in order to re-establish the justice and peace which men have shattered by violence, quarrels, and disputes: "O Lord, how long shall I cry for help, and you will not listen?" (Hab 1:2). God, in response, does not intervene directly, does not resolve the situation in an abrupt way, and he does not make himself present by a show of force. Rather, he invites patient waiting, without ever losing hope; above all, he emphasizes the importance of faith, since it is by faith that man will live (cf. Hab 2:4). God treats us in the same way. He does not indulge our desire to change the world and other people immediately and repeatedly. Instead, he intends primarily to heal the heart—my heart, your heart, and the heart of each person. God changes the world by transforming our hearts, and this he cannot do without us. The Lord wants us to open the door of our hearts so that he can enter into our lives. And this act of opening to him, this trust in him, is precisely "the victory that conquers the world, our faith" (1 John 5:4), for when God finds an open and trusting heart, then he can work wonders there.

But to have faith, a lively faith, is not easy, and so we pass to the second request, which the apostles bring to the Lord in the gospel: "Increase our faith!" (Luke 17:6). It is a good prayer, one that we also can direct to the Lord each day. But the divine response is surprising, and here too he turns the request around: "If you had faith. . . ." It is the Lord who asks us to have faith.

Because faith, which is always God's gift and always to be asked for, must be nurtured by us. It is no magic power that comes down from heaven; it is not a "talent" that is given once and for all, not a special force for solving life's problems. A faith useful for satisfying our needs would be a selfish one, centered entirely on ourselves. Faith must not be confused with well-being or feeling well, with having consolation in our heart that gives us inner peace. Faith is the golden thread that binds us to the Lord, the pure joy of being with him, united to him; it is a gift that lasts our whole life but bears fruit only if we do our part.

LIBERATED SERVANTS (17:7–10)[8]

In this gospel passage, Jesus states, "We are unworthy servants" (cf. v. 7). But what does this expression mean?

In the opening prayer for the day, we prayed, *asking for three graces*, namely: "Lord, graciously keep from us every obstacle, so that, in serenity of body and spirit alike, we may pursue in freedom of heart the things that are yours." This prayer summarizes the steps necessary to enter into a true dimension of service: that is, of being "unworthy servants."

The Obstacles
The first thing that we asked is that the Lord keep obstacles from us so that we can serve him well, serve him freely, like sons and daughters. Among the obstacles that the Christian faces on his journey, and that prevent him or her from becoming servants, we should remember at least two. One, of course, is *the desire for power*. It is a common difficulty that is frequently encountered in daily life. For instance, how often—perhaps in our home—is it said: "Here I am in charge"? Or how often, without saying it, have we ensured that others were aware of our desire for power? In contrast, Jesus taught us that the leader becomes as one who serves, and that if anyone would be first, he must be servant of all. Thus, Jesus overturns the values of worldliness, of the world.

This is because the desire for power is not the way of becoming a servant of the Lord. On the contrary, it is an obstacle, one of those obstacles that we prayed that the Lord might keep us from.

There is, moreover, another obstacle—one that can be observed even in the life of the Church—which is *disloyalty*. We encounter it when someone wishes to serve the Lord but also serves things that are not of the Lord. Jesus told us that no one can have two masters; we serve God or we serve money. And disloyalty, he stressed, is not the same as being a sinner. Indeed, we are all sinners, and we feel sorry because of this. However, being disloyal is like double-crossing. And this is an obstacle. Therefore, those who want power and those who are disloyal can hardly serve, can hardly become free servants of the Lord.

After having asked the Lord to keep away obstacles, the prayer continues: in order that—the second request—in serenity of body and spirit, we might dedicate ourselves to service. The second key word, therefore, is *serenity*—serving the Lord in peace. Obstacles—either the desire for power, or disloyalty—take away peace, and cause a yearning of the heart that cannot be in peace, which is always anxious... without peace.

This causes a dissatisfaction that leads us to live in the tension of worldly vanity, to live for appearances. One sees many people who live only to be in a shop window, for appearances, in order to say: "Ah, what a good thing it is!"... for fame, worldly fame. In doing this, however, we cannot serve the Lord. That is why we ask the Lord to remove obstacles, because it is in serenity—of body or spirit—we can dedicate ourselves freely to his service.

The third key word is *freedom*. Serving God is free. We are sons and daughters, not slaves. To serve God in peace—with serenity, when he has removed from us the obstacles that rid us of peace and serenity—is serving him with freedom. It is no coincidence that, when we serve the Lord freely, we feel an ever more profound peace. It is like hearing once again the Lord say: "Come, come, come, good and faithful servant!"

To do this, however, we need his grace, for we are unable to do it by ourselves. However, this does not mean that, when we arrive at the state of free service of sons and daughters with the Father, we can say: "We are good servants of the Lord." Above all, we are "unworthy servants." This expression demonstrates the unworthiness of our work: by ourselves, we are unable to accomplish it. We must simply ask and make space in order that God may transform us into liberated servants, into sons and daughters who are not slaves.

Recognizing God's Gifts (17:11–19)[9]

This gospel passage invites us to acknowledge God's gifts with wonder and gratitude. On the way to his death and resurrection, Jesus meets ten lepers who approach him, keep their distance, and tell their troubles to the one whom their faith has perceived as a possible savior: "Jesus, Master, have mercy on us!" (v. 13). They are sick and they are looking for someone to heal them. Jesus responds by telling them to go and present themselves to the priests, who according to the law were charged with certifying presumed healings. In this way, Jesus does not simply make them a promise; he tests their faith. At that moment, in fact, the ten had not yet been healed. They were restored to health after they set out in obedience to Jesus's command. Then, rejoicing, they showed themselves to the priests and continued on their way. They forgot the Giver, the Father, who cured them through Jesus, his Son made man.

All but one—a Samaritan, a foreigner living on the fringes of the chosen people, practically a pagan! This man was not content with being healed by his faith but brought that healing to completion by returning to express his gratitude for the gift received. He recognized in Jesus the true Priest, the one who raised him up and saved him, who can now set him on his way and accept him as one of his disciples.

To be able to offer thanks, to be able to praise the Lord for what he has done for us: this is important! So we can ask ourselves: Are we capable of saying "thank you"? How many times do we say "thank you" in our family, our community, in our church? How many times do we say "thank you" to those who help us, to those close to us, to those who accompany us through life? Often, we take everything for granted! This also happens with God. It is easy to approach the Lord to ask for something, but to return and give thanks. . . . That is why Jesus emphasizes the failure of the nine ungrateful lepers: "Were not ten made clean? But the other nine, where are they? Was none of them found to return and give praise to God except this foreigner?" (Luke 17:17–18).

It also takes humility to be able to give thanks. In the first reading, we heard the singular story of Naaman, the commander of the army of the king of Aram (cf. 2 Kgs 5:14–17). In order to be cured of his leprosy, he accepts the suggestion of a poor slave and entrusts himself to the prophet Elisha, whom he considers an enemy. Naaman is nonetheless ready to humble himself. Elisha asks nothing of him, but simply orders him to bathe in the waters of the River Jordan. This request leaves Naaman perplexed, even annoyed. Can a God who demands such banal things truly be God? He would like to turn back, but then he agrees to be immersed in the Jordan and immediately he is cured. . . .

Significantly, Naaman and the Samaritans were two foreigners. How many foreigners, including persons of other religions, give us an example of values that we sometimes forget or set aside! Those living beside us, who may be scorned and sidelined because they are foreigners, can teach us how to walk on the path that the Lord wishes. The Mother of God, together with Joseph her spouse, knew what it was to live far from home. She too was long a foreigner in Egypt, far from her relatives and friends. Yet her faith was able to overcome the difficulties. Let us cling to this simple faith of the Holy Mother of God. Let us ask her that we may always come back to Jesus and express our thanks for the many benefits we have received from his mercy.

Gratitude (17:18)[10]

Sometimes we have to wonder if we are turning into a civilization of bad manners and bad words, as if this were a sign of self-liberation. It's not uncommon to hear bad words publicly. Kindness and the ability to say "thank you" are often considered signs of weakness and raise the suspicion of others. This tendency is encountered even within the nucleus of the family. We must become firmly determined to educate others to be grateful and appreciative: both the dignity of the person and social justice must pass through the portal of the family. If family life neglects this style of living, social life will also reject it. Gratitude, moreover, stands at the very core of the faith of the believer. A Christian who does not know how to give thanks has lost the very "language" of God. This is terrible! Let's not forget Jesus's question after he heals the ten lepers and only one of them returns to thank him (cf. Luke 17:18). I remember once listening to a very wise old person, someone who was very simple but had an uncommon wisdom of life and piety: "Gratitude is a plant that grows only in the soil of noble souls." Nobility of soul, that grace of God in the soul, compels us to say "thank you" with gratitude. It is the flower of a noble soul. This really is something beautiful.

God Comes in Humility (17:20)[11]

The apostle Paul tells us of God's great plan: "When the fullness of time had come, God sent his Son, born of a woman" (Gal 4:4). But history tells us that when this "fullness of time" came, when God became man, humanity was not especially well-disposed, nor was there even a period of stability and peace: there was no "Golden Age." The scenario of this world did not merit the coming of God; indeed, "his own people did not accept him" (John 1:11). The fullness of time was thus a gift of grace. God filled our time out of the abundance of his mercy. Out of sheer love, he inaugurated the fullness of time.

It is particularly striking how the coming of God into history came about. He was "born of a woman." There was no triumphal entrance or striking epiphany of the Almighty. He did not reveal himself as a brilliantly rising sun, but entered the world in the simplest of ways, as a child from his mother, with that "style" that scripture tells us is like a rainfall upon the land (cf. Isa 55:10), like the smallest of seeds that sprouts and grows (cf. Mark 4:31–32). Thus, contrary to our expectations and perhaps even our desires, the kingdom of God, now as then, "is not coming with things that can be observed" (Luke 17:20), but rather *in smallness, in humility.*

BEWARE OF FIREWORKS (17:20–25)[12]

At that time, there was curiosity regarding the time of the kingdom of God: when the liberation of the Romans would come or the liberation of the people of God. The people did not have a good understanding of what the kingdom of God was, and so they asked Jesus. And he responded clearly: "It is among you" (cf. v. 21). He explained that the kingdom of God in our midst is like a mustard seed that is small but is planted and grows, grows, grows, and grows, but with time. And it is the same with the seed of wheat.

In the gospel, the image of the seed is precisely suggested in this regard, but also the yeast with the flour that the woman kneads in order to make bread, and that which was small then grows, grows, and grows and we do not know how. Jesus, when he explains this, says that we do not know how the seed grows, how it sprouts; we do not know how the yeast exapands the dough, but the kingdom of God is this way: it is among you, as a seed that grows, as yeast in the dough.

It is up to us to safeguard it and to hope that it will grow, that it will bear fruit. We hope, so that *the kingdom of God becomes strong in hope.* Paul also said, "In hope we were saved" (Rom 8:24). Moreover, our salvation is always the intention of hope; it is not a possession, now, as if to say, "I am saved, I am all right." No, they are intentions of hope, and the kingdom of God grows in this way, with our work. We work to safeguard the grain that grows, that also germinates with our rest. Jesus teaches us that the kingdom of God is like the grain that is planted: man goes through his days and nights and, even when he is asleep, it grows on its own because it is God who ensures its growth. And so, whether during our work or during our rest, the kingdom of God grows. However, it takes hope to see that growth. And this is truly the first thing that Jesus tells us today: the kingdom of God is among us.

Jesus also tells us another thing: how it grows. In fact, the kingdom of God does not come about by attracting attention, and no one will say "here it is" or "there it is." No, the kingdom of God is among you. It is not a religion of entertainment with which we are always searching for new things, revelations, and messages.

God has spoken in Jesus Christ: this is God's final say. The rest is like the fireworks that light up for a moment, and then what remains? Nothing, there is no growth, there is no light, there is nothing: an instant. However, so often we were tempted by this religion of entertainment, searching for strange things rather than revelation and the meekness of the kingdom of God that is among us and grows. And this religion of entertainment is not hope: it is the desire to have something in one's hand. However, our salvation is measured in hope, the hope that belongs to the man who sowed wheat or the woman who prepared the bread, mixing yeast and flour: the hope that it will grow. Artificial light, on the contrary, is all about an instant and then vanishes, as fireworks do. It is not enough to illuminate a house; it is a show.

There is the kingdom of God, but the question remains: When will the Son of Man come? And this is the other question that underlies the first. It is Jesus who gives us an explanation:

"For as the lightning flashes and lights up the sky from one side to the other, so will the Son of Man be in his day" (v. 24). Therefore, this will be the fullness of God's kingdom, when the Lord returns, and he will return in this way. But before this fullness comes, the Lord says, it is necessary that he, the Son of Man, suffer greatly, and that he be rejected by this generation: it is the suffering of the cross, of work, of all of this that we carry forward.

If God's kingdom is already among us, and if we must not let ourselves be lured by the spectacular things, which are fireworks and serve no purpose, what must we do while awaiting the coming of the kingdom of God, the coming of the Lord? The keyword is *"to guard."* Yes, to guard with patience, patience in our work and in our suffering; to guard as the man who planted and guarded the seed, guarding it so that no weeds would grow near it, so that the plant would grow. In practice this means guarding hope.

Let us ask ourselves: How do I guard hope? Do I prefer specific things, fireworks? Do I have the patience, even mortification, willingness to accept the cross, to guard the hope that was sown in our hearts in baptism? It is a hope that does not disappoint, because hope never disappoints!

The truth that the kingdom of God is among us challenges us in how we guard the kingdom of God, this hope. Someone might want to ask, "Do I hope?" That is why it is proper to ask ourselves: Do I hope or move forward as I can, not knowing how to discern the good from the bad, the wheat from the weeds, the light, the gentle light of the Holy Spirit from the brightness of this artificial thing?

It is good to question our own hope in this seed that is growing within us, and how we guard our hope that the kingdom of God is among us, but with rest, with work, with discernment, we must guard the hope of the kingdom of God that grows, to the very moment when the Lord comes and everything is transformed. Yes, in one moment, everything, the world, us; everything! And, as Paul says to the Christians in Thessalonica, in that moment, we will all remain with him.

LISTENING DEEPLY (17:21)[13]

We need, then, to learn how to listen carefully to his word and the story of his life, but also to be attentive to the details of our own daily lives, so as to learn how to view things with the eyes of faith and to keep ourselves open to the surprises of the Spirit.

Yet, as we know, the kingdom of God comes quietly and unobtrusively (cf. v. 21), and we can gather its seeds only when, like the prophet Elijah, we enter into the depths of our soul and are open to the imperceptible whisper of the divine breeze (cf. 1 Kgs 19:11–13).

THINKING ABOUT DEATH (17:26–37)[14]

What Jesus says in this passage attracts my attention, especially his response when he is asked what the end of the world will be like. But in the meantime let's think about what my end will be like. In this passage, Jesus uses the expressions "as it was in the days of Noah" and "just as it was in the days of Lot." It says that "they were eating and drinking, and marrying and being given in marriage, until the day Noah entered the ark," and, likewise with Lot (cf. vv. 27–28).

But here comes "the day that the Lord makes it rain fire and sulfur from heaven." In short, there is normality, life is normal and we are used to this normality: I get up at six, I get up at seven, I do this, I do that work, I'm going to find this tomorrow, Sunday is a holiday, I do this. And so we are used to living the normality of life, and we think this will always be the case. But it will be like the day that Noah went up on the ark, until the day the Lord made fire and brimstone fall from heaven. Because surely there will come a day when the Lord will say to each of us: "Come." And the call for some will be sudden, for others it will be after an illness, in an accident; we do not know. But the call will be there, and it will be a surprise: not God's last surprise, because after this one there will be another—the surprise of eternity—but it will be the surprise of God for each of us. . . .

Thinking about death is not a bad fantasy, it is a reality: whether it is bad or not bad depends on me, and on how I think about it, but there will be the encounter with the Lord. This will be the beauty of death. It will be the meeting with the Lord. It will be him and he will come to meet us and say: "Come, come, blessed by my Father, come with me." It is useless to say: "But, Lord, wait as I have to fix this, or this." Because you will not be able to fix anything; on that day . . . you will leave everything.

But we will have the Lord, this is the beauty of the encounter. The other day I met a priest, who was around sixty-five years old. He was not feeling well. He went to the doctor, who after the visit told him: "Look, you have this serious thing, but maybe we have time to stop it, we will do this; if this doesn't stop it, we will do that, and if that doesn't stop it, we will start walking and I will accompany you to the end." That doctor was so good! How sweetly he told the truth. Let us also accompany each other on this path. Let us go together, as we work and do good, but always looking to that moment.

18

The Treasure

PERSEVERANCE (18:1–8)[1]

In today's gospel, Jesus tells a parable about the need to pray always, never wearying. The main character is a widow whose insistent pleading with a dishonest judge succeeds in obtaining justice from him. Jesus concludes that if the widow succeeded in convincing that judge, do you think that God will not listen to us if we pray to him with insistence? Jesus's words are very strong: "And will not God grant justice to his chosen ones who cry to him day and night?" (v. 7).

"Crying day and night" to God! This image of prayer is striking, but let us ask ourselves: Why does God want this? Doesn't he already know what we need? What does it mean to "persevere" with God?

This is a good question that makes us examine an important aspect of our faith. God invites us to pray insistently not because he is unaware of our needs or because he is not listening to us. On the contrary, he is always listening, and he lovingly knows everything about us. On our daily journey, especially in times of difficulty, in the battle against the evil that is outside and within us, the Lord is not far away, he is by our side. We battle with him beside us, and our weapon is prayer, which makes us feel his presence beside us, his mercy, and also his help. But the battle against evil is a long and hard one; it requires patience and endurance, as it did of Moses who had to keep his arms outstretched for the people to prevail (cf. Exod 17:8–13). This is how it is: there is a battle to be waged each day, but God is our ally, faith in him is our strength, and prayer is the expression of this faith. Jesus assures us of the victory, but at the end he asks: "When the Son of man comes, will he find faith on earth?" (v. 8). If faith is snuffed out, then prayer is snuffed out and we walk in the dark. We become lost on the path of life.

Therefore, let us learn from the widow of the gospel to pray always without growing weary. This widow was very good! She knew how to battle for her children! I think of the many women who fight for their families, who pray and never grow weary. Today let us all remember these women who by their attitude provide us with a true witness of faith and courage and a model of prayer. Our thoughts go out to them!

Pray always, but not in order to convince the Lord by dint of words! He knows our needs better than we do! Indeed, persevering prayer is the expression of faith in a God who calls us to fight with him every day and at every moment in order to conquer evil with good.

Prayer as a Source of Mercy (18:1–8)[2]

This gospel parable contains an important teaching: we "need to pray always and not to lose heart" (v. 1). This means, then, praying constantly, not just when I feel like it. No, Jesus says that we ought "to pray always and not lose heart." And he offers the example of the widow and the judge.

The judge is a powerful person, called to issue judgment on the basis of the law of Moses. That is why the biblical tradition recommended that judges be people who fear God, who are worthy of faith, impartial and incorruptible (cf. Exod 18:21). However, this judge "neither feared God nor had respect for people"

(v. 2). As a judge, he was unfair and unscrupulous; he did not take the law into account but did whatever he wanted, according to his own interests. It was to him that a widow turned for justice. Widows, along with orphans and foreigners, were the most vulnerable groups in society. The rights afforded them by the law could be easily disregarded because, being isolated and defenseless, they could hardly be assertive. A poor widow, alone and with no one to defend her, might be ignored, might even be denied justice, like the orphan, the foreigner, the migrant. In those days, this was a very serious problem. Faced with the judge's indifference, the widow has recourse to her only weapon: to bother him incessantly with her request for justice. And because of her insistence, she achieves her end. At a certain point, the judge grants her request, not because he is moved by mercy or because his conscience has been working on him. He simply admits: "because this widow keeps bothering me, I will grant her justice, so that she may not wear me out by continually coming" (v. 5).

From this parable Jesus draws two conclusions: if the widow could manage to bend the dishonest judge with her incessant requests, how much more will God, who is the good and just Father, "grant justice to his chosen ones who cry to him day and night"; moreover, he will not "delay long in helping them," but will act speedily (vv. 7–8).

That is why Jesus urges us to pray and "not to lose heart." We all go through times of tiredness and discouragement, especially when our prayers seem ineffective. But Jesus assures us that, unlike the dishonest judge, God promptly answers his children, even though this doesn't mean he will necessarily do it when and how we would like.

Prayer does not work like a magic wand! It helps us keep faith in God and to entrust ourselves to him even when we do not understand his will. In this, Jesus himself—who prayed constantly!—is our model. The Letter to the Hebrews reminds us that "In the days of his flesh, Jesus offered up prayers and supplications, with loud cries and tears, to the one who was able to save him from death, and he was heard because of his reverent submission" (Heb 5:7). At first glance, this statement seems far-fetched, because Jesus died on the cross. Yet, the Letter to the Hebrews makes no mistake: God has indeed saved Jesus from death by giving him complete victory over it, but the path to that victory is through death itself! The supplication that God has answered referred to Jesus's prayer in Gethsemane. Assailed by overwhelming anguish, Jesus prays to the Father to deliver him of this bitter cup of the Passion, but his prayer is pervaded by trust in the Father, and he entrusts himself entirely to his will: "not what I want," Jesus says, "but what you want" (Matt 26:39). What he is praying for is of secondary importance; what matters above all is his relationship with the Father. This is what prayer does: it transforms the desire and models it according to the will of God, whatever that may be, because the one who prays aspires first of all to union with God, who is merciful Love.

The parable ends with a question: "When the Son of man comes, will he find faith on earth?" (v. 8). And with this question we are all warned: we must not cease to pray, even if our prayer seems to be left unanswered. It is prayer that conserves the faith; without it, faith falters! Let us ask the Lord for a faith that is incessant in prayer, persevering, like that of the widow in the parable, a faith that nourishes our desire for his coming. And in prayer, let us experience that compassion of God, a Father comes to encounter his children, full of merciful love.

Humble Prayer (18:9–14)[3]

With another parable, Jesus wants to show us the right attitude for prayer and for invoking the mercy of the Father: how one must pray, the right attitude for prayer. It is the parable of the Pharisee and the tax collector (cf. Luke 18:9–14). Both men went up into the temple to pray, but they did so in very different ways, obtaining opposite results.

The Pharisee

The Pharisee stood and prayed using many words. His is, yes, a prayer of thanksgiving to God, but it is really just a display of his own merits, with a sense of superiority over "other people," whom he describes as "thieves, rogues, adulterers, or even," for example, referring to the other person there, "like this tax collector" (v. 11). But this is the real problem: the Pharisee prays to God, but in truth he is just self-laudatory. He is praying to himself! Instead of having the Lord before his eyes, he has a mirror. Although he is standing in the temple, he doesn't feel the need to prostrate himself before the majesty of God; he remains standing. He feels secure, as if he were the master of the temple! He lists all the good works he has done. He is beyond reproach, observing the law beyond measure; he fasts "twice a week" and pays tithes on all he possesses. In short, he is satisfied with his observance of the precepts. Yet, his attitude and his words are far from the way of God's words and actions, the God who loves all people and does not despise sinners. In contrast, this Pharisee despises sinners, even by comparing himself to and judging the other person there. In short, the Pharisee, who holds himself to be just, neglects the most important commandment: love of God and of neighbor.

It is not enough, therefore, to ask ourselves how much we pray. We have to ask ourselves how we pray, or better, about the state of our heart. It is important to examine our prayer so as to evaluate our thoughts and our feelings and root out arrogance and hypocrisy. But can one pray with arrogance? No. Can one pray with hypocrisy? No. We must pray simply by placing ourselves before God just as we are—not like the Pharisee who prays with arrogance and hypocrisy. We are all taken up by the frenetic pace of daily life, often at the mercy of feelings, dazed and confused. It is necessary to learn how to rediscover the path to our heart, to recover the value of intimacy and silence, because the God who encounters us and speaks to us is there. Only by beginning there can we in our turn encounter others and speak with them. The Pharisee walked toward the temple, sure of himself, but he was unaware of the fact that his heart had lost the way.

The Tax Collector

The tax collector—the other man—instead presents himself in the temple with a humble and repentant spirit: "standing far off, he would not even look up to heaven, but was beating his breast" (v. 13). Unlike the Pharisee's long prayer, his prayer was very brief: "God, be merciful to me a sinner." Nothing more. A beautiful prayer!

Indeed, tax collectors—then called "publicans"—were considered impure, subject to foreign rulers. They were disliked by the people and socially associated with "sinners." The parable teaches us that a man is just or sinful not because of his social class but because of his way of relating to God and how he relates to his brothers and sisters. Gestures of repentance and the few and brief words of the tax collector bear witness to his awareness of his own miserable condition. His prayer is essential. He acts out of humility, certain only that he is a sinner in need of mercy. If the Pharisee asked for nothing because he already had everything, the tax collector can only beg for the mercy of God. And this is beautiful: to beg for the mercy of God! Presenting himself with "empty hands," with a bare heart and acknowledging himself to be a sinner, the tax collector shows us all the condition that is necessary to receive the Lord's forgiveness. In the end, he who is so despised is the one who becomes an icon of the true believer.

Jesus concludes the parable with the judgment: "I tell you, this man went down to his home justified rather than the other; for all who exalt themselves will be humbled, but all who humble themselves will be exalted" (v. 14). Of these two, who is the corrupt one? The Pharisee. The Pharisee is the very icon of a corrupt person who pretends to pray, but only manages to strut in front of a mirror. He is corrupt and he is pretending to pray. Thus, in life whoever believes himself to be just, and criticizes and despises others, is corrupt and a hypocrite. Pride compromises every good deed, empties prayer, and creates distance from God and from others.

If God prefers humility, it is not to dishearten us. Rather, humility is the necessary condition for being raised by him, for experiencing the mercy that comes to fill our emptiness. If the prayer of the proud does not reach God's heart, the humility of the poor opens it wide. God has a weakness for the humble ones. Before a humble heart, God opens his heart entirely. It is this humility that the Virgin Mary expresses in the canticle of the *Magnificat*: "for he has looked with favor on the lowliness of his servant.... His mercy is for those who fear him from generation to generation" (Luke 1:48, 50). Let us ask our Mother to help us to pray with a humble heart. And let us repeat that beautiful prayer three times: "Oh God, be merciful to me a sinner."

The Merciful Gaze of God (18:9–14)[4]

What can the Lord give to one whose heart is already filled with one's self-importance, with one's own success? Nothing, because a presumptuous person is incapable of receiving forgiveness, as he is satisfied by his presumed righteousness. Let us consider the parable of the Pharisee and the tax collector, where only the latter—the tax collector—returns home justified, that is, forgiven (cf. vv. 9–14). One who is aware of his own wretchedness and lowers his gaze with humility feels God's merciful gaze upon him. We know through experience that only one who is able to acknowledge his mistakes and apologize receives the understanding and forgiveness of others.

Quietly listening to the voice of our conscience allows us to recognize that our thoughts are far from divine thoughts, and that our words and our actions are often worldly, guided, that is, by choices contradictory to the gospel.

THE SEPARATIST LOGIC (18:11)[5]

Consider the biblical image of the Pharisee. When praying, he said to the Lord: "God, I thank you that I am not like other people: thieves, rogues, adulterers, or even like this tax collector" (v. 11). One of the temptations to which we are continually exposed is that of fostering a separatist logic.[6] It is interesting that, to protect ourselves, we think that we strengthen our identity and security each time that we distinguish or isolate ourselves from others, especially from those who are from a different background. But identity does not depend on separation: identity is strengthened in belonging. My belonging to the Lord: this gives me identity. Not distancing myself from others because I think they do not "count."

We must take an important step: we cannot analyze, reflect on, much less pray about reality as if we were on different shores or paths, as if we were outside of history. We all need to repent; we all need to place ourselves before the Lord and each time renew the covenant with him and together say like the tax collector: "My God, have mercy on me because I am a sinner!" With this attitude, we stay on the same "side"—not separated, but together on the same side—and we place ourselves before the Lord in a contrite attitude of listening.

THE RICH YOUNG MAN (18:18–23)[7]

Once I asked you the question: "Where is your treasure? In what does your heart find its rest?"[8] Our hearts can be attached to true or false treasures. They can find genuine rest or they can simply slumber, becoming lazy and lethargic. The greatest good we can have in life is our relationship with God. Are you convinced of this? Do you realize how much you are worth in the eyes of God? Do you know that you are loved and welcomed by him unconditionally, as indeed you are? Once we lose our sense of this, we human beings become an incomprehensible enigma, for it is the knowledge that we are loved unconditionally by God which gives meaning to our lives. Do you remember the conversation that Jesus had with the rich young man (cf. Mark 10:17–22)? The evangelist Mark observes that the Lord looked upon him and loved him (v. 21) and invited him to follow him and thus to find true riches. I hope, dear young friends, that this loving gaze of Christ will accompany each of you throughout life.

LEAVING EVERYTHING (18:18–30)[9]

Like the rich young man, Jesus challenges us with a question that touches us deeply: Do you want to be perfect? (cf. Matt 19:21, 5:48). It is not about theoretical knowledge, or even sincere adherence to the precepts of the divine law "from youth" (Mark 10:20); but Jesus looks us in the eye and loves us, asking us to leave everything to follow him. Love is appraised in the fire of risk, in the ability to put all the cards on the table and to stake everything for that hope that does not disappoint. However, very often, the personal and community decisions that cost us the most are those that affect our small and, sometimes, worldly securities. We are all called to live the joy that springs from the encounter with Jesus, to overcome our selfishness, to leave behind our own comfort, and to dare to reach out to all the peripheries in need of the light of the gospel.[10] We can respond to the Lord with generosity when we experience that we are loved by God despite our sin and our inconsistency.

THREE CLASSES OF PEOPLE (18:35–43)[11]

This gospel passage begins with an unseeing man, a blind man, and ends with him receiving his sight, "and all the people, when they saw it, praised God" (v. 43). There are three categories of people in this passage: the blind man, those who were with Jesus, and the people.

The Outcast

The blind man, because of the illness that had taken his sight, couldn't see; he was begging. And perhaps he was often saddened and wondered: "Why did this happen to me?" In other words, he was a man who couldn't find a way out—he was an outcast. And thus, the blind man was sitting by the roadside like so many outcasts here in the various streets and public squares of Rome. Today, there are so many, so many, sitting by the roadside.

That man couldn't see, but he wasn't foolish. He knew all that went on in the city. After all, he was right at the entrance to the city of Jericho, and thus he knew everything, and he wanted to know everything. And so, when he heard all the noise he inquired: What's happening? He was a man who had found a way of life along this road, a beggar, an outcast, a blind man. However, when he heard Jesus was coming, he cried out. And when they told him to be silent, he cried out even louder. What was the reason for his behavior? This man wanted salvation, he wanted to be healed. And thus, the gospel tells us that Jesus saw his faith. Indeed, the blind man gambled and won, even though it's difficult to gamble when a person is so "debased"—so marginalized. However, he gambled and knocked at the door of Jesus's heart.

The Disciples

The second category of people that we meet in this passage is comprised of those who walked with the Lord: they were walking ahead, leading the way. These were the disciples, and the apostles too, those who followed the Lord and went with him. They were also the converts, those who had accepted the kingdom of God and who were happy about this salvation.

This is exactly why they rebuked the blind man, trying to silence him by telling him: "Calm down, be polite! It's the Lord. Please, don't make a scene!" In this way, they distanced the Lord

THE GOSPEL OF LUKE

from the periphery. In fact, this peripheral man was unable to reach the Lord, because this band—albeit with much good will—closed the door.

Unfortunately, this happens frequently among us believers: when we've found the Lord, without realizing it we create this ecclesiastical microclimate. And this is an attitude not only of priests and bishops, but also the faithful. It's a manner of conduct that leads us to say: "We are the ones who are with the Lord." However, it often happens that in looking at the Lord, we end up not seeing the Lord's needs—we don't see the Lord who is hungry, who is thirsty, who is in prison, who is in the hospital. Indeed, we fail to see the Lord in the outcast, and this is a very harmful condition.

The problem is that these people who were with Jesus had forgotten the harshness of their own marginalization; they had forgotten the moment and the place where Jesus had called them. Therefore they said: "Now we are chosen, we're with the Lord." They were happy with this "little world," but they wouldn't allow people to disturb the Lord, to the point that they didn't even allow children to approach, to draw near. They had forgotten the journey that the Lord had made with them, the journey of conversion, of calling, of healing.

This is a reality that the apostle John describes with a very beautiful phrase that we heard in the first reading, they had forgotten, they had abandoned their first love (cf. Rev 1:1–5; 2:1–5). And this is a sign: in the Church, the faithful, the ministers, become a group like this, not ecclesial but ecclesiastical. When a group is privileged with closeness to the Lord, there is the temptation of forgetting their first love. It is precisely that beautiful love which we all had when the Lord called us, saved us, said to us: "I love you so much." Even the disciples are tempted to forget the first love, that is, to forget the peripheries, where they were before, even should they be ashamed of it. It is an attitude that can be expressed this way: "Lord, this one has an odor. Don't let him come to you." But the Lord's response is clear: "Did you not have an odor when I kissed you?"

In facing the temptation of the groups of the chosen, which are found in every age, the conduct of Jesus in the Church, in the history of the Church, is described in this way by Luke: "Jesus stopped." This is a grace. It is a grace when Jesus stops and says: "Look over there, bring him to me," as he did with the blind man in Jericho. In this way, the Lord makes the disciples turn their heads to the suffering peripheries, as if to say: "Do not look only at me. Yes, you must see me, but not only me! See me in others too, in the needy."

Indeed, when God stops, he always does so with mercy and justice, but also, sometimes, he does so with anger. This happens when the Lord is stopped by the ruling class, which he defines as "the evil and adulterous generation." Certainly, this was no caress. Returning to the gospel and the episode of the blind man in Jericho, Jesus himself wants the man brought near and heals him, recognizing his faith: "Your faith has saved you."

The Faithful

The third group presented by Luke is the simple people who needed signs of salvation. The gospel passage reads: "all the people, when they saw it, praised God" (v. 43). These people were, therefore, capable of celebrating, of praising God, of wasting time with the Lord. So often, we find simple people, so many elderly women who walk and sacrifice so much to go and pray at a shrine of Our Lady. They are people who don't ask for privileges; they ask only for grace. They are the faithful people who know how to follow the Lord without asking for any privileges.

See then, the three categories of people who directly call upon us: "the outcast; the privileged, those who have been chosen and who are now subject to temptation; and the faithful people who follow the Lord to praise him because he is good, and also to ask him for health, to ask him for so much grace.

This reflection should lead us to consider the Church, our Church, which is sitting by this roadside in Jericho. Because, in the Bible, according to the fathers, Jericho is the symbol of sin. So, let us consider the Church watching Jesus pass, this *outcast*

Church. Let us consider these nonbelievers, those who have sinned so much and who don't want to get up, because they don't have the strength to start over. And let us also consider the *church of the Children,* of the sick, of the imprisoned, the Church of the simple people asking the Lord that we may all have the grace of having been called and that we never, never, ever distance ourselves from this Church. Let us never enter into this microclimate of privileged ecclesiastical disciples who distance themselves from the Church of God that is suffering, that is asking for salvation, that is asking for faith, and that is asking for the word of God. Finally, let us ask for the grace to be faithful people of God, without asking the Lord for any privilege that may distance us from the people of God.

19

Jerusalem

ZACCHAEUS (19:1–10)[1]

On his way to Jerusalem, Jesus enters the city of Jericho. This is the final stage of a journey that sums up the meaning of the whole of Jesus's life, which was dedicated to searching for and saving the lost sheep of the house of Israel. But the closer this journey comes to an end, the more hostility envelops Jesus.

Yet the conversion with Zacchaeus, one of the most joyful events recounted by Saint Luke, happens in Jericho. This man is a lost sheep. He is despised and "excommunicated" because he is a tax collector. Indeed, he is the head of the tax collectors of the city, a friend of the hated Roman occupants. He is a thief and an exploiter.

Being short in stature and prevented from approaching Jesus, most likely because of his bad reputation, Zacchaeus climbs a tree to be able to see the Teacher who is passing by. This exterior action, which is a bit ridiculous, expresses the interior act of a man seeking to bring himself above the crowd in order to be near Jesus. Zacchaeus himself does not realize the deep meaning of his action; he doesn't understand why he does it, but he does it anyway. Nor does he dare to hope that the distance which separates him from the Lord may be overcome; he resigns himself to seeing Jesus only as he passes by. But then Jesus comes close to the tree and he calls him by name: "Zacchaeus, hurry and come down; for I must stay at your house today" (Luke 19:5). The man of small stature, rejected by everyone and far from Jesus, is lost in anonymity—but Jesus calls him. And the name "Zacchaeus" in the language of the time has a beautiful meaning, full of allusion. "Zacchaeus" in fact, means "God remembers."

So Jesus goes to Zacchaeus's house, drawing criticism from all the people of Jericho—even in those days there was a lot of gossip!—who said: How can this be? With all the good people in the city, how can he go stay with a tax collector? Because he was lost. Jesus said: "Today salvation has come to this house, because he too is a son of Abraham" (v. 9). From that day forward, joy entered, peace entered, salvation entered, and Jesus entered Zacchaeus's house.

There is no profession or social condition, no sin or crime of any kind that can erase from the memory and the heart of God even one of his children. "God remembers," always. He never forgets those whom he created. He is the Father, who watchfully and lovingly waits to see the desire to return home be reborn in the hearts of his children. And when he sees this desire, even simply hinted at and so often almost unconsciously, he is immediately there, and through his forgiveness, he lightens the path of conversion and return. Let us look at Zacchaeus today in the tree—a ridiculous act, but an act of salvation. And I say to you: if your conscience is weighed down, if you are ashamed of many things that you have done, stop for a moment, do not be afraid. Think about the fact that someone is waiting for you, because he has never ceased to remember you; and this someone is your Father. It is God who is waiting for you! Climb up, as Zacchaeus did, climb the tree of desire for forgiveness. I assure you that you will not be disappointed. Jesus is merciful and never grows tired of forgiving! Remember that this is the way Jesus is.

Brothers and sisters, let Jesus also call us by name! In the depths of our hearts, let us listen to his voice, which says: "Today

I must stop at your house," that is, in your heart, in your life. And let us welcome him with joy. He can change us; he can transform our stony hearts into hearts of flesh; he can free us from selfishness and make our lives a gift of love. Jesus can do this; let Jesus turn his gaze to you!

THE LORD ALLOWS HIMSELF TO BE INVITED (19:1–10)[2]

The Lord also wants to "be invited." As we read in the scene with Zacchaeus from Luke's Gospel, the tax collector from Jericho feels that curiosity, a curiosity that comes from grace, which was sown by the Holy Spirit and brings Zacchaeus to say: "I want to see the Lord." The initiative comes from the Spirit. Hence the Lord looks up and says: "Come down, invite me to your house!"

God, therefore, always acts with love: either to correct us, to invite us to dinner, or to be invited. He is going to tell us: "Wake up." He is going to tell us: "Open." He is going to tell us: "Come down."

MERCY AND CONVERSION (19:1–10)[3]

Jesus makes conversion the first word of his preaching: "Repent, and believe in the good news" (Mark 1:15). With this proclamation he presents himself to the people, asking them to accept his word as God's final and definitive words to humanity (cf. Mark 12:1–11). Speaking of conversion with regard to the preaching of the prophets, Jesus insists even more on the interior dimension. In fact, conversion involves the whole person, heart and mind, in order to become a new creature, a new person. Change your heart and you will be renewed.

When Jesus calls one to conversion, he does not set himself up as judge of persons. He calls from a position of closeness, because he shares in the human condition, and therefore he calls from the street, from the home, from the table.... Mercy toward those who needed to change their lives came about through his loving presence so as to involve each person in his salvation history. Jesus persuaded people with his kindness, with his love. With his way of being he touched the depths of people's hearts and they were attracted by the love of God and urged to change their lifestyle. For example, the conversion of Matthew (cf. Matt 9:9–13) and of Zacchaeus (cf. Luke 19:1–10) happened in exactly this manner, because they felt loved by Jesus and, through him, by the Father. True conversion happens when we accept the gift of grace, and a clear sign of its authenticity is when we become aware of the needs of our brothers and sisters and are ready to draw near to them.

Jesus Enters Jerusalem (19:28–40)[4]

The liturgy invites us to share in the joy and celebration of the people who cry out in praise of their Lord, a joy that will fade and leaves a bitter and sorrowful taste by the end of the account of the Passion. This celebration seems to combine stories of joy and suffering, mistakes and successes that are part of our daily lives as disciples. It somehow expresses the contradictory feelings that we too, the men and women of today, experience: the capacity for great love...but also for great hatred; the capacity for courageous self-sacrifice, but also the ability to "wash our hands" at the right moment; the capacity for loyalty, but also for great abandonment and betrayal.

We also see clearly throughout the gospel account that the joy Jesus awakens is, for some, a source of anger and irritation.

Jesus enters the city surrounded by his people and by a cacophony of singing and shouting. We can imagine that, amid the outcry, we hear at the same time the voice of the forgiven son and the healed leper, or the bleating of the lost sheep. Then too, the song of the publican and the unclean man; the cry of those living on the edges of the city; and the cry of those men and women who had followed Jesus because they felt his compassion for their pain and misery. That outcry is the song and the spontaneous joy of all those left behind and overlooked, who, having been touched by Jesus, can now shout: "Blessed is he who comes in the name of the Lord." How could they not praise the one who had restored their dignity and hope? Theirs is the joy of so many forgiven sinners who are able to trust and hope once again. And they cry out. They rejoice. This is joy.

All this joy and praise is a source of unease, scandal, and upset for those who consider themselves righteous and "faithful" to the law and its ritual precepts.[5] It is a joy that is unbearable for those hardened against pain, suffering, and misery. Many of these think to themselves: "Such ill-mannered people!" It is a joy that is intolerable for those who have forgotten the many chances they themselves have been given. How hard it is for the comfortable and the self-righteous to understand the joy and the celebration of God's mercy! How hard it is for those who trust only in themselves and look down on others, to share in this joy.[6]

And so here is where another kind of shouting comes from, the fierce cry of those who shout out: "Crucify him!" It is not spontaneous but already armed with disparagement, slander, and false witness. It is a cry that emerges in moving from the facts to an account of the facts; it comes from this "story." It is the voice of those who twist reality and invent stories for their own benefit, without concern for the good name of others. This is a false account, the cry of those who have no problem in seeking ways to gain power and to silence dissonant voices. The cry that comes from "spinning" facts and painting them in such a way that they disfigure the face of Jesus and turn him into a "criminal." It is the voice of those who want to defend their own position, especially by discrediting the defenseless. It is the cry born of the show of self-sufficiency, pride, and arrogance, which sees no problem in shouting: "Crucify him, crucify him."

And so the celebration of the people ends up being stifled. Hope is demolished, dreams are killed, joy is suppressed; the heart is shielded, and charity grows cold. It is the cry of "save yourself," which would dull our sense of solidarity, dampen our ideals, and blur our vision...the cry that wants to erase compassion—that "suffering with" that is compassion, which is the weakness of God.

Faced with such people, the best remedy is to look at Christ's cross and let ourselves be challenged by his final cry. He died crying out his love for each of us: young and old, saints and sinners, the people of his times and of our own. We have been saved by his cross, and no one can repress the joy of the gospel; no one, in any situation whatsoever, is far from the Father's merciful gaze. Looking at the cross means allowing our priorities, choices, and actions to be challenged. It means questioning ourselves about our sensitivity to those experiencing difficulty.

Brothers and sisters, where is our heart focused? Does Jesus Christ continue to be a source of joy and praise in our heart, or do our priorities and concerns make us ashamed to look at sinners, the least and the forgotten?

And you, dear young people, the joy that Jesus awakens in you is a source of anger and even irritation to some, since a joyful young person is hard to manipulate. A joyful young person is hard to manipulate!

But today, a third kind of shouting is possible: "Some of the Pharisees in the crowd said to him, 'Teacher, order your disciples to stop.' He answered, 'I tell you, if these were silent, the stones would shout out'" (Luke 19:39–40).

The temptation to silence young people has always existed. The Pharisees themselves rebuke Jesus and ask him to silence them.

There are many ways to silence young people and make them invisible, many ways to anaesthetize them, to make them keep quiet, to ask nothing, and to question nothing. "Keep quiet, you!" There are many ways to sedate them, to keep them from getting involved, to make their dreams flat and dreary, petty and plaintive.

On this Palm Sunday, as we celebrate World Youth Day, we do well to hear Jesus's answer to all those Pharisees past and present, even the ones of today: "If these were silent, the stones would cry out" (v. 40).

Dear young people, you have it in you to shout. It is up to you to opt for Sunday's "Hosanna!" so as not to fall into Friday's "Crucify him!" . . . It is up to you not to keep quiet. Even if others keep quiet, if we older people and leaders—so often corrupt—keep quiet, if the whole world keeps quiet and loses its joy, I ask you: Will you cry out?

Please, make that choice, before the very stones themselves cry out.

A SONG OF PRAISE AND WONDER (19:40)[7]

It is the silent night of the disciples who remained numb, paralyzed, and uncertain of what to do amid so many painful and disheartening situations. It is also that of today's disciples, speechless in the face of situations we cannot control, that make us feel and, even worse, believe that nothing can be done to reverse all the injustices that our brothers and sisters are experiencing in their flesh.

It is the silent night of those disciples who are disoriented because they are plunged into a crushing routine that robs memory, silences hope, and leads one to thinking that "this is the way things have always been done"—those disciples who, overwhelmed, have nothing to say and end up considering the words of Caiaphas as "normal" and unexceptional: "You do not understand that it is better for you to have one man die for the people than to have the whole nation destroyed" (John 11:50).

In the midst of our silence, our overpowering silence, the stones begin to cry out (cf. Luke 19:40) and to clear the way for the greatest message that history has ever heard: "He is not here; for he has been raised" (Matt 28:6). The stone before the tomb cried out and proclaimed the opening of a new way for all. Creation itself was the first to echo the triumph of life over all that had attempted to silence and stifle the joy of the gospel. The stone before the tomb was the first to leap up and in its own way intone a song of praise and wonder, of joy and hope, in which all of us are invited to join.

The Cry of Jesus (19:41)[8]

As true man, Jesus showed his emotions. He was hurt by the rejection of Jerusalem (cf. Matt 23:27) and this moved him to tears (cf. Luke 19:41). He was also profoundly moved by the sufferings of others (cf. Mark 6:34). He felt deeply their grief (cf. John 11:33), and he wept at the death of a friend (cf. John 11:35). These examples of his sensitivity showed how much his human heart was open to others.

The Way of Peace (19:41–44)[9]

Indeed, as he drew near Jerusalem, the Lord wept at the sight of the city. Why? Jesus himself provides the answer to this question: "If you, even you, had only recognized on this day the things that make for peace! But now they are hidden from your eyes" (v. 42). Thus, he wept because Jerusalem did not know the way of peace and chose the way of hostility, of hatred, of war.

Today, Jesus is in heaven, watching us, and he will come to us here, on the altar. But today too, Jesus weeps, because we have chosen the way of war, the way of hatred, the way of hostility. This is even more glaring now that we are approaching Christmas: there will be lights, there will be celebrations, trees lit up, even nativity scenes... all decorated: the world continues to wage war, to wage wars. The world has not comprehended the way of peace.

And yet, last year we commemorated the centenary of the Great War. And this year there will be other commemorations for the anniversary of the bombing of Hiroshima and Nagasaki, to name only two. And everyone laments, saying: "What awful stories!"

What remains of a war, of the one that we are experiencing now? What remain are ruins, thousands of uneducated children, the deaths of so many innocent people: so many! And also so much money in the pockets of arms dealers.

It is a crucial issue. Jesus once said: "No one can serve two masters: either God or wealth." And war is choosing wealth: "Let's make weapons so that the economy will balance out somewhat and we can continue with our interests." In this regard, there is a horrible word of the Lord: "accursed," because he said: "Blessed are the peacemakers!" So those who work for war, who wage wars, are accursed. They are criminals.

But when the whole world, as it is today, is at war—the whole world!—it is a world war being fought piecemeal: here, there, there, everywhere. And there is no justification. God weeps; Jesus weeps.

Thus, we hear again the Lord's words before Jerusalem, expressed in the Gospel according to Luke: "If you, even you, had only recognized on this day the things that make for peace!" Today, this world is not at peace. And while arms dealers do their work, there are poor peacemakers who, simply in order to help one person, and another and another, give their life. And they carry out this mission by taking as their model a symbol, an icon of our times: Teresa of Calcutta. In fact, with the cynicism of the powerful it could be asked: But what did that woman do? She lost her life helping people to die? The issue is that today, the way of peace isn't comprehended. Indeed, Jesus's proposal of peace has not been heard. And this is why he wept looking at Jerusalem, and he weeps now.

OUR DAILY STRUGGLE (19:45–48)[10]

In recent days, the Church has called us to ponder the process of worldliness, of apostasy that ends in persecution. The scripture passage of the day proposes a reflection on that worldliness of the people of God who wanted to replace their covenant with the customs of all the pagan people. And those who did not go along were persecuted; there were many martyrs and much suffering. An example can be found in the readings over the previous few days, in the story of the elderly scribe Eleazar, who was an example of fidelity to the law to the very end.

The same happened to Jesus when he went to the temple and began to drive out those who were selling, chasing them all away, saying to them: "It is written, 'My house shall be a house of prayer; but you, however, have made it a den of robbers'" (v. 46). The leaders of the temple, the chief priests and scribes, had changed things a bit. They had entered into a process of decay and had rendered the temple impure; they had blemished the temple.

This message is also relevant for Christians today, because the temple is a symbol of the Church. And the Church will always —always!—suffer the temptation of worldliness and the temptation of power that is not the power Jesus Christ wills for her. Jesus does not say: "No, do not do this here; do it outside," but instead: "You have made a den of robbers here!" When the Church enters into this process of degradation the end is awful. Very bad!

The chief priests and scribes were angry. Jesus did not chase them from the temple, but those who were doing business, the businessmen of the temple. The chief priests and the scribes, however, were connected to them, because they evidently received money from them. This was the "holy bribe." They were attached to money and worshiped it as "holy."

The words in the gospel passage are very strong. They tell us that the chief priests, the scribes, and the leaders of the people sought to destroy him. The same had happened in the time of

Judah Maccabee. Why? They did not know what to do because all the people hung on his every word, listening. Jesus's strength, therefore, was his word, his testimony, and his love. And where there is Jesus, there is no place for worldliness, no place for corruption.

All this is clear even today. This is the struggle each one of us faces. This is the daily struggle of the Church, which is called to be always with Jesus. And Christians must always hang on his every word, hear his word, and never seek security where there are things of another master. After all, you cannot serve two masters: it is either God or riches; God or power.

That's why it is good for us to pray for the Church, to think of the many martyrs today who suffer and die in order to avoid entering into this spirit of worldliness and apostasy. Today! Today the Church has more martyrs than in the early days. It is good for us to think about them, and also to ask for the grace never to enter into this process of degrading worldliness that leads us to become attached to money and power.

20

The Authority of Jesus

GOD AND CAESAR (20:20–26)[1]

This Sunday's gospel presents us with a new face-to-face encounter between Jesus and his adversaries. The theme addressed is that of the tribute to Caesar, a "thorny" issue about whether or not it was lawful to pay taxes to the Roman emperor, to whom Palestine was subject in Jesus's time. There were various positions. Thus, the question that the Pharisees posed — "Is it lawful for us to pay taxes to the emperor, or not?" (v. 22) — was meant to ensnare the Teacher. In fact, depending on how he responded, he could have been accused of being either for or against Rome.

But in this case too, Jesus responds calmly and takes advantage of the malicious question in order to teach an important lesson, rising above the polemics and the alliance of his adversaries. He tells the Pharisees: "Show me a denarius." They present him with a coin, and, observing the coin, Jesus asks: "Whose head and whose title does it bear?" The Pharisees can only answer: "The emperor's." Jesus concludes: "Then give to the emperor the things that are the emperor's, and to God the things that are

God's" (v. 25). On the one hand, in suggesting they return to the emperor what belongs to him, Jesus declares that paying tax is not an act of idolatry, but a legal obligation to the earthly authority; on the other—and it is here that Jesus presents the "thrust" of his response: recalling the primacy of God, he asks them to render to God that which is his due as the Lord of the life and history of humankind.

The reference to Caesar's image engraved on the coin says that it is right that they feel fully—with rights and duties—citizens of the State; but symbolically, it makes them think about the other image that is imprinted on every man and woman: the image of God. He is the Lord of all, and we, who were created "in his image," belong to him first and foremost. From the question posed to him by the Pharisees, Jesus draws a more radical and vital question for each of us, a question we can ask ourselves: To whom do I belong? To family, to the city, to friends, to work, to politics, to the state? Yes, of course. But first and foremost—Jesus reminds us—you belong to God. This is the fundamental belonging. It is God who has given you all that you are and have. And therefore, day by day, we can and must live our life in recognition of this fundamental belonging and in heartfelt gratitude toward our Father, who creates each one of us individually, unrepeatably, but always in the image of his beloved Son, Jesus. It is a wondrous mystery.

Christians are called to commit themselves concretely in the human and social spheres without comparing "God" and "Caesar"; comparing God and Caesar would be a fundamentalist approach. Christians are called to commit themselves concretely in earthly realities but illuminating them with the light that comes from God. Primary entrustment to God and hope in him do not imply an escape from reality, but rather the diligent rendering to God of that which belongs to him. This is why a believer looks to the future reality, that of God, so as to live earthly life to the fullest and to meet its challenges with courage.

THE RESURRECTION FROM THE DEAD (20:27–38)[2]

The gospel presents Jesus confronted by several Sadducees, who did not believe in the resurrection and considered the relationship with God only in the dimension of earthly life. Therefore, in order to ridicule the concept of resurrection and to create difficulty for Jesus, the Sadducees submit a paradoxical and absurd case: that of a woman who had had seven husbands, all brothers, who died one after the other. Thus came the malicious question posed to Jesus: "In the resurrection, whose wife will the woman be?" (v. 33).

Jesus does not fall into the snare. He emphasizes the truth of the resurrection, explaining that life after death will be different from life on earth. He makes his interlocutors understand that it is not possible to apply the categories of this world to the realities that transcend and surpass what we see in this life. He says, in fact: "Those who belong to this age marry and are given in marriage; but those who are considered worthy of a place in that age and in the resurrection from the dead neither marry nor are given in marriage" (vv. 34–35). With these words, Jesus explains that in this world we live a provisional reality, which ends. Conversely, in the afterlife, after the resurrection, we will no longer have death as the horizon and will experience all things, even human bonds, in the dimension of God, in a transfigured way. Even marriage, a sign and instrument of God in this world, will shine brightly, transformed in the full light of the glorious communion of saints in Paradise.

The "sons of heaven and of the resurrection" are not a few privileged ones, but are all men and all women, because the salvation that Jesus brings is for each one of us. And the life of the risen shall be equal to that of angels (cf. v. 36), meaning wholly immersed in the light of God, completely devoted to his praise, in an eternity filled with joy and peace. But pay heed! Resurrection is not only the fact of rising after death but is a new genre of life which we already experience now....

Resurrection is the foundation of the faith and of Christian hope. Were there no reference to Paradise and to eternal life, Christianity would be reduced to ethics, to a philosophy of life. Instead, the message of Christian faith comes from heaven. It is revealed by God and goes beyond this world. Belief in resurrection is essential in order that our every act of Christian love not be ephemeral and an end in itself but may become a seed destined to blossom in the garden of God and to produce the fruit of eternal life.

THE GOD WHO BEARS MY NAME (20:27–38)[3]

This Sunday's gospel sets before us Jesus grappling with the Sadducees, who deny that there is a resurrection. They pose a question to Jesus on this very matter, in order to trip him up and ridicule faith in the resurrection of the dead. They begin with an imaginary case: "A woman had seven husbands, who died one after the other," and they ask Jesus: "Whose wife will the woman be after her death?" Jesus, ever humble and patient, first replies that life after death does not have the same parameters as earthly life. Eternal life is another life, in another dimension where, among other things, there will be no marriage, which is tied to our existence in this world. Those who rise—Jesus says—will be like the angels, and they will live in a different state, which now we can neither experience nor imagine. This is the way Jesus explains it.

But then Jesus, as it were, moves to the counterattack. And he does so by citing the sacred scripture with a simplicity and originality that leave us full of admiration for our Teacher, the only Teacher! Jesus finds proof for the resurrection in the account of Moses and the burning bush (cf. Exod 3:1–6), where God reveals himself as the God of Abraham, and of Isaac, and of Jacob. The name of God is bound to the names of men and women to whom he binds himself, and this bond is stronger than death. And we can also say this about God's relationship with us—with each one of us: He is our God! He is the God of each one of us! It is as though he bears each of our names. It pleases him to say it, and this is the covenant. This is why Jesus states: "He is God not of the dead, but of the living; for to him all of them are alive" (v. 38). And this is the decisive bond, the fundamental covenant, the covenant with Jesus: he himself is the covenant, he himself is the life and the resurrection, for by his crucified love he has triumphed over death. In Jesus, God gives us eternal life. He gives it to everyone, and thanks to him, everyone has the hope of a life even truer than this one. The life that God prepares for us is not a mere embellishment of the present one. It surpasses our imagination, for God continually amazes us with his love and with his mercy.

Therefore, what will happen is quite the opposite of what the Sadducees expected. It is not this life that will serve as a reference point for eternity, for the other life that awaits us; rather, it is eternity—that life—which illumines and gives hope to the earthly life of each one of us! If we look at things from only a human perspective, we tend to say that the human journey moves from life to death. This is what we see! But this is only the case if we look at things from a human perspective. Jesus turns this perspective upside down and states that our pilgrimage goes from death to life: the fullness of life! We are on a journey, on a pilgrimage toward the fullness of life, and that fullness of life is what illumines our journey!

Therefore, death stands behind us, not before us. Before us is the God of the living, the God of the covenant. The God who bears my name, our names, stands before us. He is the "God of Abraham, the God of Isaac, and the God of Jacob" (v. 37), and also the God with my name, with your name...with our names. The God of the living! Before us stands the final defeat of sin and death, the beginning of a new time of joy and of endless light. But already on this earth, in prayer, in the sacraments, in fraternity, we encounter Jesus and his love, and thus we may already taste something of the risen life. The experience we have of his love and his faithfulness sets our hearts on fire and increases our faith in the resurrection. In fact, if God is faithful love, he cannot be thus for only a limited time. Faithfulness is eternal, it cannot change. God's love is eternal, it cannot change! It is not only for a time: it is forever! It is for going forward! He is faithful forever, and he is waiting for us, each one of us. He accompanies each one of us with his eternal faithfulness.

THE TRUE FACE OF GOD (20:38)[4]

In the gospel, we have heard how Jesus, with a simple yet complete answer, demolishes the banal casuistry that the Sadducees have set before him. His response—"He is God not of the dead, but of the living; for to him all of them are alive" (v. 38)—reveals the true face of God, who desires only life for all his children. The hope of being born to a new life, then, is what we must make our own if we are to be faithful to the teaching of Jesus.

Hope is a gift of God. We must ask for it. It is placed deep within each human heart in order to shed light on this life, so often troubled and clouded by situations that bring sadness and pain. We need to nourish the roots of our hope so that they can bear fruit—especially the certainty of God's closeness and compassion, despite whatever evil we have done. There is no corner of our heart that cannot be touched by God's love. Whenever someone makes a mistake, the Father's mercy is all the more present, awakening repentance, forgiveness, reconciliation, and peace.

21

Signs of the Times

TRUE GREATNESS (21:1–4)[1]

Whoever becomes like a little child, Jesus tells us, is the greatest in the kingdom of heaven (cf. Matt 18:4). The true greatness of a person consists in making oneself small before God. This is because God is not known through grand ideas and extensive study, but rather through the littleness of a humble and trusting heart. To be great before the Most High does not require the accumulation of honor and prestige or earthly goods and success, but rather a complete self-emptying. A child has nothing to give and everything to receive. A child is vulnerable and depends on his or her father and mother. The one who becomes like a little child is poor in self but rich in God.

Children, who have no problem in understanding God, have much to teach us. They teach us that God accomplishes great things in those who put up no resistance to him, who are simple and sincere and open, without duplicity. The gospel shows us how great wonders are accomplished with small things: with a few loaves and two fishes (cf. Matt 14:15–20), with a tiny mustard seed (cf. Mark 4:30–32), with a grain of wheat that dies in the earth (cf. John 12:24), with the gift of just a single glass of water (cf. Matt 10:42), with the two coins of a poor widow (cf. Luke 21:1–4), with the humility of Mary, the servant of the Lord (cf. Luke 1:46–55).

THE ONE TREASURE (21:1–4)[2]

The character that draws the most attention in this gospel is the widow. In the Bible, widows appear many times, so many times, both in the Old and New Testaments. A widow is a woman who is alone. She does not have a husband to protect her. She is a woman who must make do as she can, who lives on public charity.

In particular, the widow of this passage of the gospel, whom Jesus points out to us, was a widow whose only hope was in the Lord. And when Jesus saw those who put in offerings at the temple, he saw this woman who put in only two coins and said: "This poor widow has put in more than all of them, for all of them have contributed out of their abundance, but she out of her poverty has put in all she had to live on" (vv. 3–4).

In the widows of the gospel, I like seeing the image of the "widowhood" of the Church who is awaiting Jesus's return. Indeed, the Church is the bride of Jesus, but her Lord—her one treasure—has left. And the Church, when she is faithful, leaves everything while she waits for her Lord. However, when the Church is not very faithful or does not have much trust in her Lord's love, she too seeks to make do with other things, with other securities, more from the world than from God.

In the widows of the gospel Jesus gives us a beautiful image of the Church. Similarly, there is the woman leaving Nain with her son's casket: crying alone. Yes, very kind people accompanied her, but her heart is alone! It is the widow Church that cries when her children die to the life of Jesus.

There is then the other woman who, in order to protect her children, goes to the evil judge. She makes his life impossible, knocking on his door every day, saying, "Do justice for me!" And, in the end, that judge does justice. And it is the widow Church who prays, who intercedes for her children.

But the heart of the Church is always with her Bridegroom, with Jesus. He is above. Our soul, too, according to the fathers of the desert, is very much like the Church. And when our soul, our life, is closer to Jesus, it is separated from many worldly things, useless things that do not help and that separate us from Jesus. Thus, it is our Church that seeks her Bridegroom, that awaits her Bridegroom, waits for that meeting, cries for her children, fights for her children, and gives all that she has because her interest is her Bridegroom alone.

In these final days of the liturgical year, it will be good for us to ask ourselves whether our soul is like this Church that wants Jesus, whether our soul turns to its Bridegroom and says: "Come Lord Jesus! Come."

The "widowhood" of the Church refers to the fact that the Church is waiting for Jesus. she can be a Church faithfully anticipating, trustfully awaiting her husband's return, or a Church unfaithful to this "widowhood," seeking security anew in other realities—the lukewarm Church, the mediocre Church, the worldly Church. Let us also think about our soul. Does our soul seek security in the Lord alone or does it seek other securities that do not please the Lord? Thus, in these final days, it will be good for us to repeat that last verse of the Bible: "Come, Lord Jesus!"

AN EXAMPLE OF GENEROSITY (21:1–4)[3]

The poor are not just people to whom we can give something. They have much to offer us and to teach us. How much we have to learn from the wisdom of the poor! Think about it. Several hundred years ago, a saint, Benedict Joseph Labré, who lived on the streets of Rome on the alms he received, became a spiritual guide to all sorts of people, including nobles and prelates. In a very real way, the poor are our teachers. They show us that people's value is not measured by their possessions or how much money they have in the bank. A poor person, a person lacking material possessions, always maintains his or her dignity. The poor can teach us much about humility and trust in God. In the parable of the Pharisee and the tax-collector (cf. Luke 18:9–14), Jesus holds the tax-collector up as a model because of his humility and his acknowledgment that he is a sinner. The widow who gave her last two coins to the temple treasury is an example of the generosity of all those who have next to nothing and yet give away everything they have (Luke 21:1–4).

THE MEANING OF EXISTENCE (21:5–11)[4]

Jesus is in Jerusalem for the last and most important stage of his earthly life: his death and resurrection. He is in the precincts of the temple, "adorned with beautiful stones and gifts" (Luke 21:5). People are speaking of the beautiful exterior of the temple when Jesus says: "The days will come when not one stone will be left upon another; all will be thrown down" (v. 6). He adds that there will be no lack of conflicts, famine, convulsions on earth and in the heavens. Jesus does not want to frighten us but to tell us that everything we now see will inevitably pass away. Even the strongest kingdoms, the most sacred buildings, and the surest realities of this world do not last forever; sooner or later they fall.

In response, people immediately put two questions to the Master: "When will this be, and what will be the sign that this is about to take place?" (v. 7). When and what.... We are constantly driven by curiosity. We want to know when and we want to see signs. Yet Jesus does not care for such curiosity. On the contrary, he exhorts us not to be taken in by apocalyptic preachers. Those who follow Jesus pay no heed to prophets of doom, the nonsense of horoscopes, or terrifying sermons and predictions that distract from the truly important things. Amid the din of so many voices, the Lord asks us to distinguish between what is from him and what is from the false spirit. This is important: to distinguish the word of wisdom that God speaks to us each day from the shouting of those who seek in God's name to frighten, to nourish division and fear.

Jesus firmly tells us not to be afraid of the upheavals in every period of history, not even in the face of the most serious trials and injustices that may befall us. He asks us to persevere in the good and to place all our trust in God, who does not disappoint: "Not a hair of your head will perish" (v. 18). God does not forget his faithful ones, his precious possession. He does not forget us.

Today, however, he questions us about the meaning of our lives. Using an image, we could say that these readings serve as a "strainer" through which our life can be poured: they remind us that almost everything in this world is passing away, like running water. But there are treasured realities that remain, like a precious stone in a strainer. What endures? What has value in life? What riches do not disappear? Surely these two: the Lord and our neighbor. These two riches do not disappear! These are the greatest goods; these are to be loved. Everything else—the heavens, the earth, all that is most beautiful, even this basilica— will pass away; but we must never exclude God or others from our lives.

Today, though, when we speak of exclusion, we immediately think of actual people, not useless objects but precious persons. The human person, set by God at the pinnacle of creation, is often discarded, set aside in favor of ephemeral things. This is unacceptable, because in God's eyes humans are the most precious good. It is ominous that we are growing used to this rejection. We should be worried when our consciences are anaesthetized, and we no longer see the brother or sister suffering at our side or notice the grave problems in our world, which become a mere refrain familiar from the headlines on the evening news.

THE DAY OF JUSTICE (21:5–11)[5]

It is good for us to think about this: What will that day be like when I am before Jesus, when the Lord will ask me for an account of talents that he gave me, or how my heart was when the seed fell? How do I receive the word? With an open heart? Do I let it grow for the good of others or keep it hidden? This examination of conscience is good and useful, because we will all be judged and everyone will find oneself in front of Jesus. We do not know the date, but it will happen.

Even in the gospel (Luke 21:5–11), we find advice regarding this from Jesus himself, who exhorts: "Beware that you are not led astray" (v. 8). What deception is he referring to? It is the deception of alienation and that of estrangement: the deception by which I am distracted, I do not think, and I live as if I were never going to die. However, when the Lord comes—and he will come like lightning—how will he find me? Waiting, or in the midst of so many distractions of life, deceived by things that are superficial, that have no transcendence?

We are therefore faced with a real and true call from the Lord to think seriously about the end: about my end, the judgment—about my judgment. This is why when we are children we go to catechism class, and are taught four things: death, judgment, hell, or glory.

Of course, some might say: "Father, this frightens us." However, it is the truth. If you do not take care of your heart, and you always live far away from the Lord, perhaps there is the danger of continuing in this way, far away from the Lord for eternity. This is very bad!

This is why, today, it is good to consider what our end will be like. How will it be when I find myself before the Lord? And for those who may be frightened or saddened by this reflection, we recall the passage in the gospel acclamation taken from the Book of Revelation: "Be faithful until death," says the Lord, "and I will give you the crown of life" (2:10). Here is the solution to our fears: fidelity to the Lord: this does not disappoint. Indeed, if each one of us is faithful to the Lord, when our death comes, we shall say what Saint Francis said: "Sister Death, come." It will not frighten us. And even on the Day of Judgment, we will look to the Lord and say: "Lord I have many sins, but I tried to be faithful." And since the Lord is good, we will not be afraid.

WISDOM (21:15)[6]

The ultimate interpreter of God's mysteries is Jesus. He is the wisdom of God in person (cf. 1 Cor 1:24). Jesus did not teach us his wisdom with long speeches or grand demonstrations of political or earthly power but by giving his life on the cross. Sometimes we can fall into the trap of believing in our own wisdom, but the truth is that we can easily lose our sense of direction. At those times, we need to remember that we have a sure compass before us in the crucified Lord. In the cross, we find the wisdom that can guide our life with the light that comes from God.

From the cross also comes healing. There, Jesus offered his wounds to the Father for us, the wounds by which we are healed (cf. 1 Pet 2:24). May we always have the wisdom to find in the wounds of Christ the source of all healing! I know that many in Myanmar bear the wounds of violence, wounds both visible and invisible. The temptation is to respond to these injuries with a worldly wisdom that, like that of the king in the first reading, is deeply flawed. We think that healing can come from anger and revenge. Yet the way of revenge is not the way of Jesus.

Jesus's way is radically different. When hatred and rejection led him to his passion and death, he responded with forgiveness and compassion. In today's gospel, the Lord tells us that, like him, we too may encounter rejection and obstacles, yet he will give us a wisdom that cannot be resisted (cf. Luke 21:15). He is speaking of the Holy Spirit, through whom the love of God has been poured into our hearts (cf. Rom 5:5). By the gift of his Spirit, Jesus enables us each to be signs of his wisdom, which triumphs over the wisdom of this world, and his mercy, which soothes even the most painful of injuries.

On the eve of his passion, Jesus gave himself to his apostles under the signs of bread and wine. In the Eucharist, we not only recognize, with the eyes of faith, the gift of his body and blood; we also learn how to rest in his wounds, and there be cleansed of all our sins and foolish ways. By taking refuge in Christ's wounds, dear brothers and sisters, may you know the healing balm of the Father's mercy and find the strength to bring it to others, to anoint every hurt and every painful memory. In this way, you will be faithful witnesses of the reconciliation and peace that God wants to reign in every human heart and in every community....

Jesus wants to give this wisdom in abundance. He will surely crown your efforts to sow seeds of healing and reconciliation in your families, in your communities, and in the wider society of this nation. Does he not tell us that his wisdom is irresistible (cf. Luke 21:15)? His message of forgiveness and mercy uses a logic that will encounter obstacles, and that not all will want to understand. Yet his love, revealed on the cross is ultimately unstoppable. It is like a spiritual GPS that unfailingly guides us toward the inner life of God and the heart of our neighbor.

COME TO THE BANQUET (21:20–28)[7]

This passage from the Gospel of Luke concludes with Jesus saying: "When these things begin to take place" —namely the destruction of pride, vanity, all of this—"stand up and raise your heads, because your redemption is drawing near" (v. 28). This means that you are invited to the wedding of the Lamb. Thus, the Lord will give us the grace to wait for that voice, to prepare ourselves to hear this voice: "Come, come, come, faithful servant, a sinner but faithful: come, come to the banquet of your Lord."

ONE WORD IS ENOUGH (21:34–36)[8]

The Lord, in fact, asks only this: that we open our heart. . . . Jesus knows what we have done. For this reason, open your hearts and he will forgive you; but do not go on your own, do not go down your own path. Let Jesus touch you. Let yourself be forgiven. It is enough to say just one word, "Lord"; he will do the rest, he will do everything else.

22

The Passion of Jesus

Memory is a dimension of our faith which we might call "deuteronomic," not unlike the memory of Israel itself. Jesus leaves us the Eucharist as the Church's daily remembrance of, and deeper sharing in, the event of his Passover (cf. Luke 22:19). The joy of evangelizing always arises from grateful remembrance. It is a grace we constantly need to implore. The apostles never forgot the moment when Jesus touched their hearts: "It was about four o'clock in the afternoon" (John 1:39). Together with Jesus, this remembrance makes present to us "a great cloud of witnesses" (Heb 12:1), some of whom, as believers, we recall with great joy: "Remember your leaders, those who spoke to you the word of God" (Heb 13:7). Some of them were ordinary people who were close to us and introduced us to the life of faith: "I am reminded of your sincere faith, a faith that dwelt first in your grandmother Lois and your mother Eunice" (2 Tim 1:5). The believer is essentially "one who remembers."

The Logic of Memory (22:19)[2]

The Church celebrates the Eucharist. She celebrates the memory of the Lord, the sacrifice of the Lord, because the Church is a community of remembrance. Hence, in fidelity to the Lord's command, she never ceases to say: "Do this in remembrance of me" (Luke 22:19). Generation after generation, throughout the world, she celebrates the mystery of the Bread of Life. She makes it present, truly real, and she gives it to us. Jesus asks us to share in his life, and through us he allows this gift to multiply in our world. We are not isolated individuals, separated from one another, but rather a people of remembrance, a remembrance ever renewed and ever shared with others.

A life of remembrance needs others. It demands exchange, encounter, and a genuine solidarity capable of entering into the mindset of taking, blessing and giving. It demands the logic of love.

Equal Worthiness (22:26)[3]

Let us also keep in mind that Jesus had no use for adults who looked down on the young or lorded it over them. On the contrary, he insisted that "the greatest among you must become like the youngest" (v. 26). For him age did not establish privileges and being young did not imply lesser worth or lesser dignity.

Service (22:26–27)[4]

Christ embraces all of humanity and wishes no one to be lost. "For God sent the Son into the world, not to condemn the world, but that the world might be saved through him" (John 3:17). He does it without oppressing or constraining anyone to open to him the doors of heart and mind. "Let the greatest among you become as the youngest, and the leader as one who serves"—Jesus Christ says. "I am among you as one who serves" (Luke 22:26–27). Every activity therefore must be distinguished by an attitude of service to persons, especially those furthest away and least known. Service is the soul of that fraternity that builds up peace.

WISDOM OF THE HEART (22:27)[5]

Wisdom of the heart means serving our brothers and sisters. Job's words: "I was eyes to the blind, and feet to the lame," point to the service which this just man, who enjoyed a certain authority and a position of importance amongst the elders of his city, offered to those in need. His moral grandeur found expression in the help he gave to the poor who sought his help and in his care for orphans and widows (Job 29:12–13).

Today too, how many Christians show, not by their words but by lives rooted in a genuine faith, that they are "eyes to the blind" and "feet to the lame"! They are close to the sick in need of constant care and help in washing, dressing, and eating. This service, especially when it is protracted, can become tiring and burdensome. It is relatively easy to help someone for a few days, but it is difficult to look after a person for months or even years, in some cases when he or she is no longer capable of expressing gratitude. And yet, what a great path of sanctification this is! In those difficult moments we can rely in a special way on the closeness of the Lord, and we become a special means of support for the Church's mission.

Wisdom of the heart means being with our brothers and sisters. Time spent with the sick is holy time. It is a way of praising God who conforms us to the image of his Son, who "came not to be served but to serve, and to give his life as a ransom for many" (Matt 20:28). Jesus himself said: "I am among you as one who serves" (Luke 22:27).

CONFIRMED IN FAITH (22:32)[6]

Christ, on the eve of his passion, assured Peter: "I have prayed for you that your faith may not fail" (Luke 22:32). He then told him to strengthen his brothers and sisters in that same faith. Conscious of the duty entrusted to the successor of Peter, Benedict XVI proclaimed the present Year of Faith, a time of grace that is helping us to sense the great joy of believing and to renew our wonder at the vast horizons that faith opens up, so as then to profess that faith in its unity and integrity, faithful to the memory of the Lord and sustained by his presence and by the working of the Holy Spirit. The conviction born of a faith which brings grandeur and fulfilment to life, a faith centered on Christ and on the power of his grace, inspired the mission of the first Christians. In the acts of the martyrs, we read the following dialogue between the Roman prefect Rusticus and a Christian named Hierax: "'Where are your parents?' the judge asked the martyr. He replied: 'Our true father is Christ, and our mother is faith in him.'"[7] For those early Christians, faith, as an encounter with the living God revealed in Christ, was indeed a "mother," for it had brought them to the light and given birth within them to divine life, a new experience and a luminous vision of existence for which they were prepared to bear public witness to the end.

THE PATH OF CONVERSION (22:33, 49–51)[8]

We may be tempted to think that everything is wrong, and instead of professing "good news," what we profess is only apathy and disillusionment. So we close our eyes to pastoral challenges, believing that the Spirit has nothing to say. We forget that the gospel is a path of conversion, not only "of others," but also ours.

Like it or not, we are invited to face reality as it presents itself to us—personal, community, and social reality. The nets, say the disciples, are empty, and we can understand the feelings this generates. They return home with no great adventures to tell; they return home empty-handed; they return home downcast.

What remained of those strong, courageous, lively disciples, who felt chosen and had left everything to follow Jesus (cf. Mark 1:16–20)? What was left of those self-confident disciples, who were willing go to prison and even give their lives for their Master (cf. Luke 22:33), who wanted to hurl fire on the earth to defend him (cf. Luke 9:54); who would have drawn the sword and gone to battle for him (cf. Luke 22:49–51)? What is left of Peter after scolding his Master about how he would have had to lead his own life (cf. Mark 8:31–33), his program of redemption? Desolation.

It was the hour of truth in the life of the first community. It was the time when Peter was confronted with part of himself — with the part of his truth that many times he didn't want to see. He experienced his limitation, his fragility, his sinfulness. Peter, the instinctive, impulsive leader and savior, with a good dose of self-sufficiency and excess confidence in himself and in his possibilities, had to submit to his own weakness and sin. He was as much a sinner as the others; he was very needy like the others; he was as fragile as the others. Peter disappointed the one to whom he had sworn protection — a crucial hour in Peter's life!

As disciples, as a Church, the same can happen to us: there are moments when we confront ourselves not with our glories, but with our weakness. Crucial hours in the life of the disciples, but also the hour in which the apostle is born.

PRAYER AND VIGILANCE (22:39–46)[9]

At the hour which God had appointed to save humanity from its enslavement to sin, Jesus came here, to Gethsemane, to the foot of the Mount of Olives. We now find ourselves in this holy place, a place sanctified by the prayer of Jesus, by his agony, by his sweating of blood, and above all by his "yes" to the loving will of the Father. In some sense, we dread approaching what Jesus went through at that hour; we tread softly as we enter that inner space where the destiny of the world was decided.

In that hour, Jesus felt the need to pray and to have with him his disciples, his friends, those who had followed him and shared most closely in his mission. But here, at Gethsemane, following him became difficult and uncertain. They were overcome by doubt, weariness and fright. As the events of Jesus's passion rapidly unfolded, the disciples would adopt different attitudes before the Master: attitudes of closeness, distance, hesitation.

Here, in this place, each of us might do well to ask: Who am I, before the sufferings of my Lord?

Am I among those who, when Jesus asked them to keep watch with him, fell asleep instead, and rather than praying, sought to escape, refusing to face reality?

Or do I see myself in those who fled out of fear, who abandoned the Master at the most tragic hour in his earthly life?

Is there perhaps duplicity in me, like that of the one who sold our Lord for thirty pieces of silver, who was once called Jesus's "friend" and yet ended up by betraying him?

Do I see myself in those who drew back and denied him, like Peter? Earlier, he had promised Jesus that he would follow him even unto death (cf. Luke 22:33), but then, put to the test and assailed by fear, he swore he did not know him.

Am I like those who began planning to go about their lives without him, like the two disciples on the road to Emmaus, foolish and slow of heart to believe the words of the prophets (cf. Luke 24:25)?

Or, thanks be to God, do I find myself among those who remained faithful to the end, like the Virgin Mary and the apostle John? On Golgotha, when everything seemed bleak and all hope seemed pointless, only love proved stronger than death—the love of the Mother and the beloved disciple that made them stay at the foot of the cross, sharing in the pain of Jesus, to the very end.

Do I recognize myself in those who imitated their Master to the point of martyrdom, testifying that he was everything to them, the incomparable strength sustaining their mission and the ultimate horizon of their lives?

Jesus's friendship with us, his faithfulness, and his mercy are a priceless gift which encourages us to follow him trustingly, notwithstanding our failures, our mistakes, also our betrayals.

But the Lord's goodness does not dispense us from the need for vigilance before the tempter, before sin, before the evil and the betrayal which can enter even into the religious and priestly life. We are all exposed to sin, to evil, to betrayal. We are fully conscious of the disproportion between the grandeur of God's call and of our own littleness, between the sublimity of the mission and the reality of our human weakness. Yet the Lord in his great goodness and his infinite mercy always takes us by the hand lest we drown in the sea of our fears and anxieties. He is ever at our side; he never abandons us. And so, let us not be overwhelmed by fear or disheartened, but with courage and confidence let us press forward on our journey and our mission.

The Heart of an Apostle (22:61–62)[10]

The first face I ask you to guard in your hearts is that of your priests. Do not leave them exposed to loneliness and abandonment, easy prey to a worldliness that devours the heart. Be attentive and learn how to read their expressions so as to rejoice with them when they feel the joy of recounting all that they have "done and taught" (Mark 6:30). Also, do not step back when they feel humiliated and can only cry because they "have denied the Lord" (cf. Luke 22:61–62), And why not also offer your support, in communion with Christ, when one of them, already disheartened, goes out with Judas into "the night" (cf. John 13:30). As bishops in these situations, your paternal care for your priests must never be found wanting. Encourage communion among them; seek the perfection of their gifts; involve them in great ventures, for the heart of an apostle was not made for small things.

23

The Death of Jesus

We can contemplate even more clearly the great mystery of God's love by directing our gaze to Jesus crucified. As the Innocent One is about to die for us sinners, he pleads the Father: "Father, forgive them; for they do not know what they are doing" (v. 34). It is on the cross that Jesus presents the sin of the world to the mercy of the Father: the sin of all people, my sins, your sins, everyone's sins. There, on the cross, he presents them to the Father. And along with the sin of the world, all our sins are wiped away. Nothing and no one is left out of this sacrificial prayer of Jesus. That means that we must not be afraid of acknowledging and confessing ourselves as sinners.

How many times have we said: "Well, this one is a sinner, he did this and that." We judge others. And you? Every one of us ought to ask ourselves: "Yes, he is a sinner. And me?" We are all sinners, but we are all forgiven. We all have the opportunity to receive this forgiveness which is the mercy of God. Therefore, we mustn't be afraid to acknowledge that we are sinners, to confess that we are sinners, because every sin was borne by the Son on the cross. When we confess our sin, repenting, entrusting ourselves to him, we can be certain of forgiveness. The sacrament of reconciliation makes present to each one of us that power of forgiveness that flows from the cross and renews in our life the grace of mercy that Jesus purchased for us! We must not be afraid of our defects: we each have our own. The power of the love of the Crucified One knows no bounds and never runs dry. This mercy wipes away our defects.

Mary, Mother of Mercy (23:34)[2]

Mary is the Mother of God, the Mother of God who forgives, who bestows forgiveness, and for this reason we can call her Mother of forgiveness. This word "forgiveness"—so misunderstood in today's world—points to the new and original fruit of Christian faith. A person who does not know how to forgive has not yet known the fullness of love. Only those who truly love are able to forgive and forget. At the foot of the cross, Mary sees her Son offering offering himself totally and thus testifying to what it means to love as God loves. At that moment, she hears Jesus utter words that probably reflect what he learned from her as a child: "Father, forgive them because they don't know what they are doing" (Luke 23:34). In that moment, Mary became the Mother of forgiveness for all of us. She herself, following the example of Jesus and by his grace, she was able to forgive those who were killing her innocents.

For us, Mary is an icon of how the Church must offer forgiveness to those who seek it. The Mother of forgiveness teaches the Church that the forgiveness granted on Golgotha knows no limits. Neither the law with its quibbles, nor the wisdom of this world with its distinctions, can hold it back. The Church's forgiveness must be every bit as broad as that offered by Jesus on the cross and by Mary at his feet. There is no other way.

A Paradox (23:35–43)[3]

The solemnity of Our Lord Jesus Christ, King of the Universe, is the crown of the liturgical year and this Holy Year of Mercy. The gospel in fact presents the kingship of Jesus as the culmination of his saving work, and it does so in a surprising way. "The Messiah [Christ] of God, the chosen one, the king" (cf. Luke 23:35, 37) appears without power or glory: he is on the cross, where he seems more to be conquered than conqueror. His kingship is paradoxical: his throne is the cross; his crown is made of thorns; he has no scepter, but a reed is put into his hand; he does not have luxurious clothing but is stripped of his tunic; he wears no shiny rings on his fingers, but his hands are pierced with nails; he has no treasure, but is sold for thirty pieces of silver.

Jesus's reign is truly not of this world (cf. John 18:36), but for this reason, Saint Paul tells us in the second reading, we find redemption and forgiveness (cf. Col 1:13–14). The grandeur of his kingdom is not power as defined by this world, but the love of God, a love capable of encountering and healing all things. Christ lowered himself to us out of this love. He lived our human misery, and he suffered the lowest point of our human condition: injustice, betrayal, abandonment. He experienced death, the tomb, hell. And so our king went to the ends of the universe in order to embrace and save every living being. He did not condemn us, nor did he conquer us, and he never disregarded our freedom, but he paved the way with a humble love that forgives all things, hopes all things, sustains all things (cf. 1 Cor 13:7). This love alone overcame and continues to overcome our worst enemies: sin, death, fear.

Dear brothers and sisters, today we proclaim this singular victory by which Jesus became the king of every age, the Lord of history, with the sole power of love, which is the nature of God, his very life, and which has no end (cf. 1 Cor 13:8). We joyfully share the splendor of having Jesus as our King. His rule of love transforms sin into grace, death into resurrection, and fear into trust.

It would mean very little, however, if we believed Jesus was king of the universe but did not make him Lord of our lives. All this is empty if we do not personally accept Jesus and if we do not also accept his way of being king. The people presented to us in today's gospel, however, help us. In addition to Jesus, three figures appear: the people who are looking on, those near the cross, and the criminal crucified next to Jesus.

First, the people: the gospel says that "the people stood by, watching" (Luke 23:35): no one says a word, no one draws any closer. The people keep their distance, just to see what is happening. They are the same people who were pressing in on Jesus when they needed something, and who now keep their distance. Given the circumstances of our lives and our unfulfilled expectations, we too can be tempted to keep our distance from Jesus's kingship, to refuse to accept completely the scandal of his humble love, which unsettles and disturbs us. We prefer to remain at the window, to stand apart, rather than draw near and be with him. A people who are holy, however, who have Jesus as their king, are called to follow his way of tangible love; they are called to ask themselves, each one each day: "What does love ask of me, where is it urging me to go? What answer am I giving Jesus with my life?"

There is a second group, and it includes various individuals: the leaders of the people, the soldiers, and a criminal. They all mock Jesus. They provoke him in the same way: "Save yourself!" (cf. Luke 23:35, 37, 39).... They tempt Jesus, just as the devil did at the beginning of the gospel (cf. Luke 4:1–13), to give up reigning as God wills, and instead to reign according to the world's ways: to come down from the cross and destroy his enemies! If he is God, let him show his power and superiority! This temptation is a direct attack on love: "Save yourself" (vv. 37, 39)—not others, but yourself. Claim triumph for yourself with your power, with your glory, with your victory. It is the most terrible temptation, the first and the last of the gospel. When confronted with this attack on his very way of being, Jesus does not speak, he does not react. He does not defend himself, he does not try to convince them, and he does not mount a defense of his kingship. He continues, rather, to love; he forgives, he lives this moment of trial according to the Father's will, certain that love will bear fruit.

In order to receive the kingship of Jesus, we are called to struggle against this temptation, called to fix our gaze on the crucified one, to become ever more faithful to him. How many times, even among ourselves, do we seek out the comforts and certainties offered by the world? How many times are we tempted to come down from the cross? The lure of power and success seem an easy, quick way to spread the gospel; we soon forget how the kingdom of God works. This Year of Mercy invites us to rediscover the core, to return to what is essential. This time of mercy calls us to look to the true face of our king, the one that shines out at Easter, and to rediscover the youthful, beautiful face of the Church, the face that is radiant when it is welcoming, free, faithful, poor in means but rich in love, on mission. Mercy, which takes us to the heart of the gospel, urges us to give up habits and practices that may be obstacles to serving the kingdom of God. Mercy urges us to orient ourselves only in the perennial and humble kingship of Jesus, not in submission to the precarious regalities and changing powers of every age.

In the gospel another person appears, closer to Jesus. It is the thief who begs him: "Jesus, remember me when you come into your kingdom" (v. 42). This person, simply looking at Jesus, believed in his kingdom. He was not closed in on himself, but rather—with his errors, his sins and his troubles—he turned to Jesus. He asked to be remembered, and he experienced God's mercy: "Today you will be with me in Paradise" (v. 43). As soon as we give God the chance, he remembers us. He is ready to completely and forever cancel our sin, because his memory—unlike our own—does not record evil that has been done or keep score of injustices experienced. God has no memory of sin, but only of us, of each of us, we who are his beloved children. And he believes that it is always possible to start anew, to raise ourselves up.

Let us also ask for the gift of this open and living memory. Let us ask for the grace of never closing the doors of reconciliation and pardon, but rather of knowing how to go beyond evil and differences, opening every possible pathway of hope. As God believes in us, infinitely beyond any merits we have, so too we are called to instill hope and provide opportunities to others. Because even if the Holy Door closes, the true door of mercy which is the heart of Christ always remains open wide for us. From the lacerated side of the Risen One until the very end of time flow mercy, consolation, and hope.

So many pilgrims have crossed the threshold of the Holy Doors, and far away from the clamor of the daily news they have tasted the great goodness of the Lord. We give thanks for this, as we recall how we have received mercy in order to be merciful, in order that we too may become instruments of mercy. Let us go forward on this road together. May our Blessed Lady accompany us, she who was also close to the cross, she who gave birth to us there as the tender Mother of the Church, who desires to gather all under her mantle. Beneath the cross, she saw the good thief receive pardon, and she took Jesus's disciple as her son. She is the Mother of Mercy, to whom we entrust ourselves

THE EMBRACE OF GOD (23:39–43)[4]

"Paradise" is one of the last words spoken by Jesus on the cross, addressed to the good thief. Let us pause for a moment to consider this scene. On the cross, Jesus is not alone. Beside him, on the right and on the left, there are two criminals. Perhaps, passing before those three crosses raised on Golgotha, someone drew a sigh of relief, thinking that at last justice had been done by putting such people to death.

One of the criminals recognizes that he deserves that dreadful torture. We call him the "good thief," who, as opposed to the other, says: "We are receiving the due reward of our deeds" (Luke 23:41).

On Calvary, on that tragic and holy Friday, Jesus reaches the finality of his Incarnation, of his solidarity with us sinners.

Fulfilled there is what the prophet Isaiah had said of the Suffering Servant: "he was numbered with the transgressors" (cf. 53:12; cf. Luke 22:37).

It is there, on Calvary, that Jesus has his final appointment with a sinner, to throw open the gates of his kingdom for him too. This is interesting: it is the only time that the word "Paradise" appears in the gospels. Jesus promises it to a "poor devil" who, on the wood of the cross, had the courage to proffer him the most humble of requests: "Remember me when you come into your kingdom" (cf. Luke 23:42). He could point to no good works. He had nothing; but he entrusted himself to Jesus, whom he recognized as innocent, good, so different from himself (v. 41). Those words of humble remorse were enough to touch Jesus's heart.

The good thief reminds us of our true condition before God, that we are his children, that he feels compassion for us, that he is defenseless each time we show our nostalgia for his love. In many hospital wards and prison cells this miracle is repeated countless times: there is no person, as bad a life as he may have lived, who, faced with despair, is without recourse to grace. We all appear before God empty-handed, somewhat like the tax collector in the parable who had stopped to pray at the back of the temple (cf. Luke 18:13). Each time a person, performing the last examination of conscience of his life, discovers that his shortcomings far exceed his good deeds, he must not feel discouraged, but must entrust himself to God's mercy. And this gives us hope; it opens our heart!

God is Father, and he awaits our return to the very end. And when the prodigal son returns and begins to confess his sins, the father silences his words with an embrace. (cf. Luke 15:20). This is God: this is how he loves us!

Paradise is not a fairytale place, much less an enchanted garden. Paradise is the embrace of God, infinite Love, and we enter there thanks to Jesus, who died on the cross for us. Where there is Jesus there is mercy and happiness; without him there is cold and darkness. At the hour of death, a Christian says to Jesus: "Remember me." And even if there may no longer be anyone who remembers us, Jesus is there, beside us. He wants to take us to the most beautiful place that exists. He wants to take us there with the small or great deal of good that we have done in our life, so that nothing of what he has already redeemed may be lost. And into the Father's house he will also bring everything in us that still needs redemption: the shortcomings and mistakes of an entire life. This is the aim of our existence: that all may be fulfilled and be transformed into love.

If we believe this, death ceases to frighten us, and we can also hope to depart from this world in a peaceful way, with so much confidence. Those who have met Jesus no longer fear anything. We too can repeat the words of the elderly Simeon. He too was blessed by the encounter with Christ after a lifetime spent in anticipation of this event: "Master, now you are dismissing your servant in peace, according to your word; for my eyes have seen your salvation" (Luke 2:29–30). At that instant, at last, we will no longer need anything; we will no longer see in a confused way. We will no longer weep in vain, because all has passed—even the prophecies, even consciousness. But not love. This endures, because "love never ends" (1 Cor 13:8).

JESUS, THE CENTER OF HISTORY (23:42)[5]

Christ is the center of the history of humanity and also the center of the history of every individual. To him we can bring the joys and the hopes, the sorrows and troubles which are part of our lives. When Jesus is the center, light shines even amid the darkest times of our lives; he gives us hope, as he does to the good thief in today's gospel.

Whereas all the others treat Jesus with disdain—"If you are the Christ, the Messiah King, save yourself by coming down from the cross!"—the thief, the one who went astray in his life but now repents, clings to the crucified Jesus and begs him: "Remember me, when you come into your kingdom" (v. 42). Jesus promises

him: "Today you will be with me in Paradise" (v. 43), in his kingdom. Jesus speaks only a word of forgiveness, not of condemnation. Whenever anyone finds the courage to ask for this
forgiveness, the Lord does not let such a petition go unheard.
Today we can all think of our own history, our own journey. Each
of us has his or her own history: we think of our mistakes, our
sins, our good times and our bleak times. We would do well, each
one of us, on this day, to think about our own personal history,
to look at Jesus and to keep telling him, sincerely and quietly:
"Remember me, Lord, now that you are in your kingdom! Jesus,
remember me, because I want to be good, but I just don't have
the strength. I am a sinner, I am a sinner. But remember me,
Jesus! You can remember me because you are at the center, you
are truly in your kingdom!" How beautiful this is! Let us all do
this today, each one of us in his or her own heart, again and
again. "Remember me, Lord, you who are at the center, you who
are in your kingdom."

Jesus's promise to the good thief gives us great hope: it tells
us that God's grace is always greater than the prayer which
sought it. The Lord always grants more. He is so generous that
he always gives more than what he has been asked. You ask him
to remember you, and he brings you into his kingdom!

Let us ask the Lord to remember us, in the certainty that by
his mercy we will be able to share his glory in paradise. Let us
go forward together on this road!

THE FREEDOM OF JESUS (23:42)[6]

On this last Sunday of the liturgical year, we celebrate the solemnity of Christ the King. And today's gospel leads us to contemplate Jesus as he introduces himself to Pilate as king of a kingdom
that "is not of this world" (John 18:36). This doesn't mean that
Christ is the king of another world. As king in another manner,
he is king in this world. It is a contrast between two types of logic.
On the one hand, worldly logic is based on ambition, competi-

tion. It fights using the weapons of fear, extortion, and the manipulation of conscience. On the other hand, the logic of the gospel, that is, the logic of Jesus, is expressed in humility and gratuitousness. It is silently but effectively affirmed with the strength of truth. The kingdoms of this world at times are sustained by arrogance, rivalries, and oppression; the reign of Christ is a "kingdom of justice, love, and peace" (preface of the day).

When did Jesus reveal himself as king? In the event of the cross! Those who look at the cross cannot but see the astonishing gratuitousness of love. You could say: "Father, that was a failure!" It is precisely the failure of sin—sin is a failure—the failure of human ambitions: the triumph of the cross is there; the gratuitousness of love is there. In the failure of the cross, love is seen, a love that is gratuitous, a love that Jesus gives us. For a Christian, speaking of power and strength means referring to the power of the cross and the strength of Jesus's love: a love which remains steadfast and complete, even when faced with rejection, and it is shown as the fulfillment of a life expended in total surrender of oneself for the benefit of humanity. On Calvary, the passers-by and the leaders derided Jesus nailed to the cross, and they challenged him: "Save yourself, and come down from the cross!" (Mark 15:30). "Save yourself!" But paradoxically, the truth of Jesus is precisely what is hurled at him in a mocking tone by his adversaries: "He cannot save himself!" (v. 31). Had Jesus come down from the cross, he would have given in to the temptations of the prince of this world. Instead, he cannot save himself precisely so as to be able to save others, precisely because he has given his life for us, for each one of us. To say: "Jesus gave his life for the world" is true. But it is more beautiful to say: "Jesus gave his life for me." And today, in this place, let each one of us say our heart: "He gave his life for me, in order to save each one of us from our sins."

Who understood this? One of the criminals who was crucified with him understood it. It was the so-called "good thief," who implored him, "Jesus remember me when you come into your kingdom" (v. 42). But this was a criminal, a corrupt person, and he was there, in fact, because he had been condemned to death for all of the brutalities he had committed in his life. But he saw love in Jesus's manner, in Jesus's meekness. The kingship of Jesus doesn't oppress us but rather frees us from our weaknesses and miseries, encouraging us to walk the path of the good, of reconciliation, and of forgiveness. Let us look at the cross of Jesus, let us look at the "good thief," and let us all say together what the good thief said: "Jesus, remember me when you come into your kingdom." We must ask Jesus, when we feel that we are weak, that we are sinners, defeated, to look at us, and say to him: "You are there. Don't forget me."

Faced with so many lacerations in the world and too many wounds in the flesh of humankind, let us ask the Virgin Mary to sustain us in our commitment to emulate Jesus, our king, by making his kingdom present with gestures of tenderness, understanding, and mercy.

History Begins Today (23:43)[7]

We know that in God's eyes no one can consider himself just (cf. Rom 2:1–11). But no one can live without the certainty of finding forgiveness! The repentant thief, crucified at Jesus's side, accompanied him into paradise (cf. Luke 23:43). So too may none of you allow yourselves to be held captive by the past! True enough, even if we wanted to, we could never rewrite the past. But the history that starts today and looks to the future has yet to be written, by the grace of God and your personal responsibility. By learning from past mistakes, you can open a new chapter of your life. Let us never yield to the temptation of thinking that we cannot be forgiven. Whatever our hearts may accuse us of, small or great, "God is greater than our hearts" (1 John 3:20). We need only entrust ourselves to his mercy.

Faith, even when it is as tiny as a grain of mustard seed, can move mountains (cf. Matt 17:20). How many times has the power of faith enabled us to utter the word of pardon in humanly impossible situations? People who have suffered violence and abuse, either themselves, or in the person of their loved ones, or their property.... There are some wounds that only God's power, his mercy, can heal. But when violence is met with forgiveness, even the hearts of those who have done wrong can be conquered by the love that triumphs over every form of evil. In this way, among the victims and among those who wronged them, God raises up true witnesses and workers of mercy.

THE INVITATION TO JOY (23:43)[8]

The gospel is a constant invitation to joy. From the outset, the angel says to Mary: "Rejoice!" (Luke 1:28). Rejoice, he says to the shepherds. Rejoice, he says to Elizabeth, an elderly and barren woman.... Rejoice, Jesus says to the thief, for this day you will be with me in paradise (cf. Luke 23:43).

The gospel message is a wellspring of joy: "I have said these things to you so that my joy may be in you, and that your joy may be complete" (John 15:11). A joy that is contagious, passing from generation to generation, a joy that we have inherited. Because we are Christians.

THE FINAL "HERE I AM" (23:46)[9]

The journey toward the Father's house begins, for each one of us, on the very day in which we open our eyes to light and, through baptism, to grace. An important stage in this journey, for us priests and bishops, is the moment when we pronounce, "Here I am!" during our priestly ordination. From that moment, we are united in a special way with Christ, associated with his ministerial priesthood. In the hour of death, we will pronounce the last "here I am," together with that of Jesus, who died entrusting his spirit in the hands of the Father (cf. Luke 23:46).

24

Resurrection and Ascension

ON THE MOVE (24:1–8)[1]

Mary Magdalene and the other women who went to the tomb
that morning (cf. Luke 24:1–8) were women "on the move": they
abandoned their "nest" and set out; they took a risk. The Spirit is
calling you too, Brothers of the Resurrection, to be men who set
out, to be an Institute "on the move" toward every human periphery, wherever the light of the gospel needs to be brought. The
Spirit is calling you to be seekers of the face of God wherever it
is to be found: not in the tombs—"Why do you look for the living
among the dead?" (v. 5)—but where it lives: in the community
and in mission.

MONDAY OF THE ANGEL (24:1–12)[2]

The Monday after Easter is called "Monday of the Angel," according to a very beautiful tradition that corresponds to biblical
sources on the Resurrection. The gospels (cf. Matt 28:1–10; Mark
16:1–7; Luke 24:1–12), in fact, recount that when the women went
to the tomb, they found it open. They feared they would not be

able to enter because the tomb had been sealed with a large rock. Instead, it was open, and a voice from within told them that Jesus was not there but that he had risen (cf. v. 5).

The words: "he has risen" are uttered for the first time. The evangelists tell us that this first announcement was made by angels, that is, by God's messengers. This angelic presence is significant: just as the angel Gabriel announced the Incarnation of the Word, so too a human word was not adequate to announce the Resurrection for the first time. A higher being was needed to communicate a reality that was so awe-inspiring, so incredible, that perhaps no human being would have dared utter it. After this first announcement, the community of disciples begins to repeat: "The Lord has risen indeed, and he has appeared to Simon!" (Luke 24:34). This is a beautiful announcement. We can all say it together now: "The Lord has risen indeed." This first announcement—"The Lord has risen indeed!"—required an intelligence that was superior to that of human beings.

Today is a festive and joyful day customarily spent with family. It is a family day. After celebrating Easter, one feels the need to gather again with one's loved ones and with friends to celebrate, because fraternity is the fruit of the Easter of Christ who, with his death and resurrection, conquered sin that separated man from God, man from himself, man from his brothers. But we know that sin always separates, always creates hostility. Jesus broke down the wall that divides people and restored peace, beginning to weave the fabric of a new fraternity. It is so important in our time to rediscover brotherhood as it was experienced by the early Christian communities; to rediscover how to make room for Jesus who never divides and always unites. There cannot be true communion and commitment to the common good and social justice without fraternity and sharing. Without fraternal sharing, no ecclesial or civil community can be formed: there is only an ensemble of individuals moved or grouped together, according to common interests. But brotherhood is a grace that Jesus creates.

The Easter of Christ has caused another thing to erupt into the world: the novelty of dialogue and relationship, a novelty which has become a responsibility for Christians. In fact, Jesus said: "By this everyone will know that you are my disciples, if you have love for one another" (John 13:35). This is why we cannot close ourselves off in our private world, within our group. Rather, we are called to safeguard the common good and to take care of our brothers and sisters, in particular those who are weakest and most marginalized. Only fraternity can guarantee a lasting peace, overcome poverty, extinguish tension and war, and eradicate corruption and crime. May the angel who tells us, "He has risen," help us to live the fraternity and the novelty of dialogue and relationships and of concern for the common good.

May the Virgin Mary whom, in this time of Easter, we invoke with the title, "Queen of Heaven," support us with her prayers so that the fraternity and communion that we experience in these days of Easter may become our way of life and the spirit of our relationships.

The Road to Emmaus (24:13–14, 17–22)[3]

Before all else, we must not yield to the fear once expressed by Blessed John Henry Newman: "The Christian world is gradually becoming barren and effete, as land which has been worked out and is become sand."[4] We must not yield to disillusionment, discouragement, and complaint. We have labored greatly and, at times, we see what seem to be failures. We feel like those who must tally up a losing season as we consider those who have left us or no longer consider us credible or relevant.

Let us read once again, in this light, the story of Emmaus (cf. Luke 24:13–15). The two disciples have left Jerusalem. They are leaving behind the "nakedness" of God. They are scandalized by the failure of the Messiah in whom they had hoped, and who now appeared utterly vanquished, humiliated—even after the third day (vv. 17–21). Here we have to face the difficult mystery of those people who leave the Church, who, under the illusion of alternative ideas, now think that the Church—their Jerusalem—can no longer offer them anything meaningful and important. So they set off on the road alone, with their disappointment. Perhaps the Church appeared too weak, perhaps too distant from their needs, perhaps too poor to respond to their concerns, perhaps too cold, perhaps too caught up with itself, perhaps a prisoner of its own rigid formulas; perhaps the world seems to have made the Church a relic of the past, unfit for new questions; perhaps the Church could speak to people in their infancy but not to those come of age.[5] It is a fact that nowadays there are many people like the two disciples of Emmaus, not only those looking for answers in the new religious groups that are sprouting up but also those who already seem godless, both in theory and in practice.

Faced with this situation, what are we to do?

We need a Church unafraid of going forth into their night. We need a Church capable of meeting them on their way. We need a Church capable of entering into their conversation. We need a Church able to dialogue with those disciples who, having left Jerusalem behind, are wandering aimlessly, alone, with their own disappointment, disillusioned by a Christianity now considered barren, fruitless soil, incapable of generating meaning.

A relentless process of globalization, an often uncontrolled process of intense urbanization, has promised great things. Many people, on the one hand, have been captivated by the potential of these developments, which of course contain positive elements as, for example, the shortening of distance, the drawing closer of peoples and cultures, the diffusion of information and of services. On the other hand, however, many are living the negative effects of these realities without realizing how they affect a proper vision of humanity and of the world. This generates enormous confusion and an emptiness, which people are unable to explain, regarding the purpose of life, personal disintegration, the loss of the experience of belonging to a "home" and the absence of personal space and strong personal ties.

And since there is no one to accompany them or to show them with his or her own life the true way, many have sought shortcuts, because the standards set by Mother Church seem to be asking too much. There are also those who recognize the ideal of humanity and of life as proposed by the Church, but they do not have the audacity to embrace it. They think that this ideal is too lofty for them, that it is beyond their abilities, and that the goal the Church sets is unattainable. Nonetheless they cannot live without having at least something, even a poor imitation of what seems too grand and distant. With disappointed hearts, they then go off in search of something that will lead them even further astray, or which will bring them to a partial belonging that, ultimately, will not fulfill their lives.

The great sense of abandonment and solitude, of not even belonging to oneself, which often results from this situation, is too painful to hide. Some kind of release is necessary. There is always the option of complaining. But even complaint acts like a boomerang; it comes back and ends up increasing one's unhappiness. Few people are still capable of hearing the voice of pain; the best we can do is to anaesthetize it.

From this perspective, we need a Church capable of walking at people's side, of doing more than simply listening to them; a Church that accompanies them on their journey; a Church able to make sense of the "night" contained in the flight of so many of our brothers and sisters from Jerusalem; a Church that realizes that the reasons why people leave also contain reasons why they can eventually return. But we need to know how to interpret, with courage, the larger picture. Jesus warmed the hearts of the disciples of Emmaus.

Let us ask ourselves today: Are we still a Church capable of warming hearts? A Church capable of leading people back to Jerusalem? Of bringing them home? Jerusalem is where our roots are: scripture, catechesis, sacraments, community, friendship with the Lord, Mary, and the apostles.... Are we still able to speak of these roots in a way that will revive a sense of wonder at their beauty?

Many people have left because they were promised something more *lofty*, more powerful, and faster.

But what is more *lofty* than the love revealed in Jerusalem? Nothing is more lofty than the abasement of the cross, since there we truly approach the height of love! Are we still capable of demonstrating this truth to those who think that the apex of life is to be found elsewhere?

Do we know anything *more powerful* than the strength hidden within the weakness of love, goodness, truth, and beauty?

People today are attracted by things that are *faster and faster*: rapid internet connections, speedy cars and planes, instant relationships. But at the same time, we see a desperate need for calmness, I would even say slowness. Is the Church still able to move slowly, to take the time to listen, to have the patience to mend and reassemble? Or is the Church herself caught up in the frantic pursuit of efficiency? Let us recover the calm to be able to walk at the same pace as our pilgrims, keeping alongside them, remaining close to them, enabling them to speak of the disappointments present in their hearts and to let us address them. They want to forget Jerusalem, where they have their source, but eventually they will experience thirst. We need a Church capable of accompanying them on the road back to Jerusalem! A Church capable of helping them to rediscover the glorious and joyful things that are spoken of Jerusalem, and to understand that she is my Mother, our Mother, and that we are not orphans! We were born in her. Where is our Jerusalem, where were we born? In Baptism, in the first encounter of love, in our calling, in vocation.[6] We need a Church that kindles hearts and warms them.

We need a Church capable of restoring citizenship to her many children who are journeying, as it were, in an exodus.

Jesus Is at Our Side (24:13–15)[7]

The questions lurking in human hearts and the real challenges of life can make us feel bewildered, inadequate, and hopeless. The

Christian mission might appear to be a mere utopian illusion or at least something beyond our reach. Yet, if we contemplate the risen Jesus walking alongside the disciples of Emmaus (cf. Luke 24:13–15), we can be filled with new confidence. In that gospel scene, we have a true "liturgy of the street," preceding that of the word and the breaking of the bread. We see that, at every step of the way, Jesus is at our side! The two disciples, overwhelmed by the scandal of the cross, return home on the path of defeat. Their hearts are broken, their hopes dashed, and their dreams shattered. The joy of the gospel has yielded to sadness. What does Jesus do? He does not judge them but walks with them. Instead of raising a wall, he opens a space. Gradually he transforms their discouragement. He makes their hearts burn within them, and he opens their eyes by proclaiming the word and breaking the bread. In the same way, a Christian does not bear the burden of mission alone but realizes, even amid weariness and misunderstanding, that "Jesus walks with him, speaks to him, breathes with him, works with him. He senses Jesus alive with him in the midst of the missionary enterprise."[8]

CHRISTIANITY IS CHRIST (24:15)[9]

With a friend, we can speak and share our deepest secrets. With Jesus too, we can always have a conversation. Prayer is both a challenge and an adventure. And what an adventure it is! Gradually Jesus makes us appreciate his grandeur and draw nearer to him. Prayer enables us to share with him every aspect of our lives and to rest confidently in his embrace. At the same time, it gives us a share in his own life and love. When we pray, "we open everything we do" to him, and we give him room "so that he can act, enter, and claim victory."[10]

In this way, we can experience a constant closeness to him, greater than anything we can experience with another person: "It is no longer I who live, but it is Christ who lives in me" (Gal 2:20). Do not deprive your youth of this friendship. You will be able to feel him at your side not only when you pray but at every moment. Try to look for him, and you will have the beautiful experience of seeing that he is always at your side. That is what the disciples of Emmaus experienced when, as they walked along dejectedly, Jesus "drew near and walked with them" (Luke 24:15). In the words of a saint, "Christianity is not a collection of truths to be believed, rules to be followed, or prohibitions. Seen that way, it puts us off. Christianity is a person who loved me immensely, who demands and claims my love. Christianity is Christ."[11]

Jesus can bring all the young people of the Church together in a single dream, a great dream, a dream with a place for everyone. The dream for which Jesus gave his life on the cross, for which the Holy Spirit was poured out on the day of Pentecost and brought fire to the heart of every man and woman, to your heart and mine. To your heart too, he brought that fire, in the hope of finding room for it to grow and flourish. A dream whose name is Jesus, planted by the Father in the confidence that it would grow and live in every heart. A tangible dream who is a person, running through our veins, thrilling our hearts and making them dance."[12]

THE PATH OF HOPE (24:13–35)[13]

I would like to reflect on the experience of the two disciples of Emmaus, narrated in the Gospel of Luke. Let us imagine the scene: two men are walking—disappointed, sad, convinced that they are leaving behind them the bitterness of an event that ended badly. Before that Easter, they had been full of enthusiasm, convinced that those days would be decisive. Their expectations were the hopes of all the people. Jesus, to whom they had entrusted their lives, had seemed to arrive at the final battle. After a long period of preparation and concealment, he would now manifest his power. This is what they were expecting. And it was not to be.

The two pilgrims had been nurturing a uniquely human hope which was now falling to pieces. That cross raised on Calvary was the most eloquent sign of a defeat which they had not foreseen. If that Jesus was truly in accordance with God's heart, then they had to conclude that God was unarmed, defenseless in the hands of violent people, unable to offer any resistance to evil.

So on that Sunday morning, these two men flee from Jerusalem. They still envision the events of the Passion and death of Jesus unfold, and their souls bear the painful torment of those events during Saturday's forced repose. That Easter, which should have inspired a song of liberation, has instead been transformed into the most painful day of their lives. They leave Jerusalem to go elsewhere, to a tranquil village. They look like people who are intent on removing a burning memory. They are thus on the road, walking in sadness. This scenario—the road—had already been important in the gospel narratives. It will now become increasingly more important as the moment in which the history of the Church begins to be told.

Jesus's encounter with those two disciples appears to be completely fortuitous. It seems to be one of those chance meetings that happen in life. The two disciples are walking, deep in thought, and a stranger comes up alongside them. It is Jesus, but their eyes are not able to recognize him. And therefore, Jesus begins his "therapy of hope." What takes place on this road is a therapy of hope. Who administers it? Jesus.

First, he asks and he listens. Our God is not an intrusive God. Even though he knows the reason for the disappointment of those two men, he gives them time to fathom the bitterness that has overcome them. Out of this comes a confession that is a refrain in human existence. "We had hoped, but.... We had hoped, but..." (v. 21). How much sadness, how many defeats, how many failures there are in the lives of every person! Deep down, we are all a little like those two disciples. How many times we have hoped in our lives? How many times we have felt like we were one step away from happiness only to find ourselves knocked to the ground, disappointed? But Jesus walks with all people who, discouraged, walk with their heads hung low. And walking with them in a discreet manner, he is able to restore hope.

Jesus speaks to them, above all through the scriptures. Those who take up God's Book will not encounter easy heroism or fierce campaigns of conquest. True hope never comes cheaply. It always undergoes defeat. The hope of those who do not suffer is perhaps not even hope. God does not like to be loved as one would love a ruler who leads his people to victory, annihilating his enemies in a bloodbath. Our God is a faint light burning on a cold and windy day, and as fragile as his presence in this world may appear, he has chosen the place that we all disdain.

Jesus then repeats for the disciples the fundamental gesture of every Eucharist. He takes bread, blesses it, breaks it, and gives it. Does not Jesus's entire history perhaps lie in this series of gestures? And is there not in every Eucharist also the symbol of what the Church should be? Jesus takes us, blesses us, "breaks" our life—because there is no love without sacrifice—and offers it to others; he offers it to everyone.

Jesus's encounter with the two disciples of Emmaus is a fleeting one. But the entire destiny of the Church is contained within it. It tells us that the Christian community is not enclosed within a fortified citadel, but rather journeys along in its most essential environment, which is the road. And there it encounters people with their hopes and disappointments, burdensome at times. The Church listens to everyone's stories as they emerge from the treasure chest of personal conscience, in order to then offer the Word of Life, the witness of love, a love that is faithful until the end. And thus, the hearts of people reignite with hope.

We have all had difficult moments in life, dark moments in which we walked in sadness: pensive, without horizons, with only a wall before us. And Jesus is always beside us to give us hope, to warm our hearts and to say: "Go ahead, I am with you. Go ahead." The secret of the road that leads to Emmaus is simply this: despite appearances to the contrary, we continue to be loved and God will never stop loving us. God will walk with us always, always, even in the most painful moments, even in the worst moments, and even in moments of defeat. That is where the Lord is. And this is our hope. Let us go forward with this hope! Because he is beside us and walks with us. Always!

No Fear of Joy (24:36–49)[14]

On the evening of the resurrection, the disciples were talking about what they had seen. The two disciples from Emmaus spoke about their encounter with Jesus on the road, and how he had also appeared to Peter. They were all happy because the Lord had risen; they were sure that the Lord had risen. However, as they were speaking, the gospel says, "Jesus himself stood among them" and greeted them saying: "Peace be with you" (v. 36).

At that moment, the completely unexpected happened — something other than peace. In fact, the gospel describes the apostles as "startled and frightened." They didn't know what to do, thinking that they were seeing a spirit. Thus, Jesus sought most of all to reassure them: "Look, I am not a spirit. Touch me. Look at my wounds!"

There is a word in this gospel passage that explains well for us what happened at that moment. We read in the text: "While in their joy they were disbelieving...." This is the focal point: the disciples could not believe because they were afraid of joy. Jesus leads them to joy, the joy of the resurrection, the joy of his presence among them. However, for them this joy posed a problem for belief: they disbelieved for joy and they were full of amazement.

Essentially, the disciples "preferred to think that Jesus was an idea, a spirit, but not a reality. Therefore, Jesus's whole task was to make them understand that he was real: "Have you anything here to eat?" "Touch me, it is I! A spirit does not have flesh, does not have a body, it is I!" Furthermore, let's remember that this occurred after several of them had seen him during the day: they were sure he was alive. Then we don't know what happened.

The gospel passage suggests that the fear of joy is a Christian illness. We too are afraid of joy, and we tell ourselves that it is better to think: "Yes, God exists, but he is out there. Jesus is risen, he is out there!" We tell ourselves: "Let's keep a little distance...." We are afraid of Jesus's closeness because this brings us joy.

This attitude also explains why there are so many "funeral Christians" for whom life seems like a continual funeral, Christians who prefer sadness and not joy. They move better not in the light of joy but in the shadows, just like those animals that manage to go out at night but don't see anything in the light of day. Like bats! And with a little bit of humor we can say that they are "bat Christians" who prefer the shadows to the light of the presence of the Lord.

We are afraid of joy, and Jesus, by his resurrection, gives us joy: the joy of being Christians, the joy of following him closely, the joy of taking the road of the Beatitudes, the joy of being with him. Many times we are either startled when this joy comes to meet us or we are full of fear; either we believe we are seeing a ghost or we think that Jesus is a way of acting— indeed, we say, "We are Christians, and we have to do it this way!" Rather, we should ask ourselves: "Do you speak with Jesus? Do you tell him: Jesus, I believe that you are alive, that you are risen, that you are close to me, that you will not abandon me"? This is the dialogue with Jesus that is proper to the Christian life and is enlivened by the knowledge that Jesus is always with us; he is always with our problems, with our struggles and with our good works.

Therefore, we need to overcome "the fear of joy." We need to think of the many times that we are not joyful because we are afraid, like the disciples who were startled and frightened by the mystery of the cross. This was the cause of their fear. In my homeland, there is a saying that goes like this: "When someone gets burned by boiling milk, he cries when he sees a cow." The disciples, who were burned by the drama of the cross, said: "No, let's stop here! He is in heaven, that's excellent. He is risen, but may he not come back again because we can't handle it!"

May the Lord do for us all what he did for the disciples who were afraid of joy: open our minds. Indeed, in the gospel we read: "He opened their minds to understand the scriptures" (v. 45). Let the Lord open our minds and make us understand that he is a living reality, that he has a body, that he is with, and that he accompanies us, and that he has conquered. Let us ask the Lord for the grace not to be afraid of joy.

MERCY AND CONVERSION (24:45–48)[15]

After his resurrection, Jesus appeared several times to his disciples before ascending to the glory of the Father. This gospel passage (Luke 24:45–48) recounts one of the manifestations in which the Lord indicates the fundamental content of the preaching that they must offer the world. We can synthesize it in two words: "conversion" and "forgiveness of sins." These are the two qualifying aspects of the mercy of God who lovingly cares for us. Today let us consider conversion.

What is conversion? It is present throughout the Bible, and particularly in the preaching of the prophets who continually urge the people to "return to the Lord" by asking him for forgiveness and changing their ways. Conversion, according to the prophets, means changing direction and turning to the Lord anew, relying on the certainty that he loves us and that his love is ever steadfast. Returning to the Lord.

OUR ADVOCATE (24:50–53)[16]

In the Creed we say that Jesus "ascended into heaven and is seated at the right hand of the Father." Jesus's earthly life culminated with the Ascension, when he passed from this world to the

Father and was raised to sit on his right. What does this event mean? How does it affect our life? What does contemplating Jesus seated at the right hand of the Father mean? Let us let the evangelist Luke guide us in this.

Let us start from the moment when Jesus decided to make his last pilgrimage to Jerusalem. Saint Luke notes: "When the days drew near for him to be taken up, he set his face to go to Jerusalem" (Luke 9:51). While he was "going up" to the Holy City, where his own "exodus" from this life was to occur, Jesus already saw the destination, heaven, but he knew well that the way which would lead him to the glory of the Father passed through the cross, through obedience to the divine design of love for mankind. The *Catechism of the Catholic Church* states that: "The lifting up of Jesus on the cross signifies and announces his lifting up by his Ascension into heaven" (n. 662).

We too should be clear in our Christian life that entering the glory of God demands daily fidelity to his will, even when it involves sacrifice and sometimes requires us to change our plans. The Ascension of Jesus actually happened on the Mount of Olives, close to the place where he had withdrawn to pray before the Passion in order to remain in deep union with the Father: once again we see that prayer gives us the grace to be faithful to God's plan.

At the end of his Gospel, Saint Luke gives a very concise account of the event of the Ascension. Jesus led his disciples "out as far as Bethany, and, lifting up his hands, he blessed them. While he was blessing them, he withdrew from them and was carried up into heaven. And they worshipped him and returned to Jerusalem with great joy; and they were continually in the temple blessing God" (Luke 24:50–53). This is what Saint Luke says.

I would like to note two elements in the account. First, during the Ascension, Jesus made the priestly gesture of blessing, and the disciples certainly expressed their faith with prostration; they knelt with bowed heads. This is a first important point: Jesus is the one eternal High Priest who with his Passion passed through death and the tomb and ascended into heaven. He is with God the Father where he intercedes forever in our favor (cf. Heb 9:24). As Saint John says in his First Letter, he is our Advocate: How beautiful it is to hear this! When someone is summoned by a judge or is involved in legal proceedings, the first thing he does is to seek a lawyer to defend him. We have One who always defends us, who defends us from the snares of the devil, who defends us from ourselves and from our sins!

We have this Advocate. Let us not be afraid to turn to him to ask forgiveness, to ask for a blessing, to ask for mercy! He always pardons us. He is our Advocate: he always defends us! Don't forget this! The Ascension of Jesus into heaven acquaints us with this deeply consoling reality on our journey: in Christ, true God and true man, our humanity was taken to God. Christ opened the path to us. He is like a guide to whom we are roped as we climb a mountain who, on reaching the summit, pulls us up to him and leads us to God. If we entrust our life to him, if we let ourselves be guided by him, we are certain to be in safe hands, in the hands of our Savior, of our Advocate.

Second, Saint Luke says that having seen Jesus ascending into heaven, the apostles returned to Jerusalem "with great joy." This seems to us a little odd. When we are separated from our relatives, from our friends, because of a definitive departure and, especially, death, there is usually a natural sadness in us, since we will no longer see their face, no longer hear their voice, or enjoy their love, their presence. The evangelist instead emphasizes the profound joy of the apostles.

But how could this be? Precisely because, with the gaze of faith they understand that although he has been removed from their sight, Jesus stays with them forever. He does not abandon them and in the glory of the Father supports them, guides them, and intercedes for them.

Saint Luke recounts the event of the Ascension also at the beginning of the Acts of the Apostles—to emphasize that this event is like a link in the chain that connects Jesus's earthly life to the life of the Church. Here Saint Luke speaks of the cloud that hid Jesus from the sight of the disciples, who stood gazing at him ascending to God (cf. Acts 1:9–10). Then two men in white robes appeared and asked them not to stand there looking up to heaven but to nourish their lives and their witness with the certainty that Jesus will come again in the same way in which they saw him ascending into heaven (cf. Acts 1:10–11). This is an invitation to base our contemplation on Christ's lordship, to find in him the strength to spread the gospel and to witness to it in everyday life: contemplation and action, *ora et labora*, as Saint Benedict taught, are both necessary in our life as Christians.

Dear brothers and sisters, the Ascension does not point to Jesus's absence but tells us that he is alive among us in a new way. He is no longer in a specific place in the world as he was before the Ascension. He is now in the lordship of God, present in every space and time, close to each one of us. In our life, we are never alone: we have this Advocate who awaits us, who defends us. We are never alone: the crucified and Risen Lord guides us. We have with us a multitude of brothers and sisters who, in silence and solitude, in their family life and at work, in their problems and hardships, in their joys and hopes, live faith daily and together with us bring the world the lordship of God's love, in the Risen Jesus Christ, ascended into heaven, our own Advocate.

Notes

1: *Annunciation*

1. Pope Francis, Angelus, December 24, 2017.

2. Pope Francis, Angelus, December 8, 2017.

3. Georges Bernanos, *The Diary of a Country Priest: A Novel* (Cambridge, MA: Da Capo Press, 2002), 212.

4. Pope Francis, Message on the Occasion of the Thirty-third World Youth Day 2018, February 11, 2018.

5. Pope Francis, Address to the Camaldolese Benedictine Nuns at the Celebration of Vespers, November 21, 2013.

6. Pope Francis, Address to Members of St. Peter's Circle, May 9, 2016.

7. Francis, Address on the Occasion of the Thirty-first World Youth Day Meeting with the Volunteers and the Organizing Committee and Benefactors, July 31, 2016.

8. Pope Francis, Angelus, August 15, 2017.

9. Pope Francis, Angelus, December 20, 2015.

10. Pope Francis, Homily on the Occasion of the Feast of Our Lady of Guadalupe, December 12, 2016.

11. Romano Guardini, *The Lord: Meditations on the Life of Christ* (Washington, DC: Regnery Publishing, 1954), 216.

12. Pope Francis, apostolic exhortation *Evangelii Gaudium*, 288.

13. Pope Francis, Homily on the Apostolic Journey to Armenia, June 25, 2016.

2: *The Birth of Jesus*

1. Pope Francis, Homily, Midnight Mass, Solemnity of the Nativity of the Lord, December 24, 2013.

2. Pope Francis, Homily, Midnight Mass, Solemnity of the Nativity of the Lord, December 24, 2016.

3. Pope Francis, Angelus, January 1, 2020.

4. Pope Francis, Angelus, January 1, 2018.

5. Pope Francis, Homily, January 1, 2017.

6. Pope Francis, General Audience, May 1, 2013.

7. Pope Francis, General Audience, December 30, 2015.

8. Pope Francis, Homily on the Occasion of the Twenty-fifth Anniversary of the Holy Father's Episcopal Ordination, June 27, 2017.

9. Pope Francis, Homily, Feast of the Presentation of the Lord and the Twenty-second World Day of Consecrated Life, February 2, 2018.

10. Pope Francis, *Christus Vivit*, 26–29.

11. Pope John Paul II, Catechesis (June 27, 1990), 2–3: *Insegnamenti* 13, 1 (1990), 1680–1681.

12. Pope Francis, apostolic exhortation *Amoris Laetitia*, 384.

13. Pope Francis, apostolic exhortation *Amoris Laetitia*, 18.

14. Pope Francis, Address in the Mall of Asia Arena, Manila, January 16, 2015.

3: Preparing for Public Ministry

1. Pope Francis, Angelus, December 6, 2015.

2. Pope Francis, Angelus, December 13, 2015.

3. Pope Francis, Homily, Holy Mass and Opening of the Holy Door of the Basilica of St. John Lateran, December 13, 2015.

4. Pope Francis, Angelus, January 10, 2016.

4. The Good News

1. Pope Francis, Angelus, December 17, 2017.

2. Pope Francis, Message for the Fifty-fifth World Day of Prayer for Vocations, December 3, 2018.

3. Pope Francis, Synod of Bishops, Fifteenth Ordinary General Assembly, *Youth, Faith and Vocational Discernment*, II, 2.

4. Pope Francis, Homily, Holy Chrism Mass, April 13, 2017.

5. Pope Francis, Angelus, January 24, 2016.

6. Pope Francis, Homily, February 2, 2017.

7. Pope Francis, Angelus, January 31, 2016.

8. Pope Francis, Morning Meditation, September 2, 2014.

9. Pope Francis, apostolic exhortation *Evangelii Gaudium*, 180.

5. The Mission of the Disciples

1. Pope Francis, Angelus, February 10, 2019.

2. Pope Francis, Homily, Simón Bolívar Park, Bogotá, Colombia, September 7, 2017.

3. Pope Francis, apostolic exhortation *Amoris Laetitia*, 322.

4. Gabriel Marcel, *Homo Viator: An Introduction to a Metaphysics of Hope* (London: Victor Gollancz, Ltd., 1951), 49.

5. Pope Francis, Homily, Holy Mass with Priests, Men and Women Religious, Consecrated People and Polish Seminarians, Kraków, Poland, July 30, 2016.

6. Pope Francis, General Audience, June 22, 2016.

7. Pope Francis, Morning Meditation, December 5, 2016.

8. Pope Francis, Address to Participants in the International Conference on Pastoral Work for Vocations, October 21, 2016.

9. Pope Francis, apostolic exhortation *Evangelii Gaudium*, 33.

10. Pope Francis, Morning Meditation, September 5, 2014.

11. Pope Francis, Address to the Participants in the General Chapter of the Order of Clerics Regular of Somasca, March 30, 2017.

6. The Way of Jesus

1. Pope Francis, Morning Meditation, September 7, 2015.

2. Pope Francis, Morning Meditation, October 28, 2014.

3. Pope Francis, apostolic exhortation *Evangelii Gaudium*, 197.

4. Pope Francis, Morning Meditation, June 6, 2016.

5. Pope Francis, Address to Participants in the Pilgrimage of Poor from the Diocese of the French Province of Lyons, July 6, 2016.

6. Pope Francis, Morning Meditation, September 10, 2015.

7. Pope Francis, apostolic exhortation *Amoris Laetitia*, 102.

8. Thomas Aquinas, *Summa Theologiae*, II-II, q. 27, art. 1, ad 2.

9. Thomas Aquinas, *Summa Theologiae*, II-II, q. 27, art. 1.

10. Pope Francis, Morning Mediation, February 26, 2018.

11. Pope Francis, Address at the Opening of the Pastoral Congress of the Diocese of Rome, June 16, 2016.

12. Pope Francis, apostolic exhortation *Amoris Laetitia*, 308.

13. Pope Francis, Morning Meditation, September 12, 2014.

14. Pope Francis, General Audience, November 16, 2016.

7. *The Way of Mercy*

1. Pope Francis, Morning Meditation, September 16, 2013.

2. Pope Francis, General Audience, June 17, 2015.

3. Pope Francis, Morning Meditation, September 13, 2016.

4. Pope Francis, Morning Meditation, September 19, 2017.

5. Pope Francis, Twenty-fourth World Day of the Sick 2016, September 15, 2015.

6. Pope Francis, Morning Meditation, December 15, 2016.

7. Pope Francis, Morning Meditation, March 24, 2015.

8. Pope Francis, General Audience, April 20, 2016.

9. Pope Francis, Homily, Holy Mass for "*Evangelium Vitae*" Day, June 16, 2013.

10. Pope Francis, General Audience, August 9, 2017.

11. Pope Francis, apostolic exhortation *Amoris Laetitia*, 100.

8. *Parables and Miracles*

1. Pope Francis, General Audience, May 14, 2014.

2. Pope Francis, Address to the Educators at the Pontifical Catholic University of Ecuador, Quito, July 7, 2017.

3. Pope Francis, encyclical *Lumen Fidei*, 58.

4. Pope Francis, Morning Meditation, September 19, 2016.

5. Pope Francis, Morning Meditation, September 26, 2017.

6. Pope Francis, General Audience, December 2, 2015.

7. Pope Francis, encyclical *Lumen Fidei*, 31.

8. St. Augustine, *Sermo* 229/L (Guelf. 14), 2 (*Miscellanea Augustiniana* 1, 487/488): "*Tangere autem corde, hoc est credere.*"

9. *Discipleship*

1. Pope Francis, Morning Meditation, September 28, 2017.

2. Pope Francis, Angelus, June 2, 2013.

3. Pope Francis, General Audience, June 5, 2013.

4. Pope Francis, Meditation, March 2, 2017.

5. Pope Francis, Address at the Twenty-fourth World Day of the Sick 2016, September 15, 2016.

6. Pope Francis, Angelus, June 23, 2013.

7. Pope Francis, Address to the Bishops Appointed over the Past Year, September 10, 2015.

8. Pope Francis, Greeting at the Welcoming Ceremony for the Twenty-eighth World Youth Day, Copacabana, Rio de Janeiro, Brazil, July 25, 2013.

9. Pope Francis, General Audience, October 8, 2014.

10. Pope Francis, Morning Meditation, October 3, 2017.

11. Pope Francis, Angelus, June 30, 2013.

12. Pope Francis, Address to the Bishops Ordained over the Past Year, September 14, 2017.

13. Pope Francis, Address to the Participants of the General Chapter of the Congregation of the Sacred Stigmata (Stigmatines), February 10, 2018.

10. The Christian Life

1. Pope Francis, Morning Meditation, February 14, 2017.

2. Pope Francis, Message for the Fifty-second World Day of Prayer for Vocations, April 26, 2015.

3. Second Vatican Council, *Ad Gentes*, 2.

4. Pope Benedict XVI, encyclical *Deus Caritas Est*, 6.

5. Pope Francis, apostolic exhortation *Evangelii Gaudium*, 21.

6. Pope Francis, Morning Meditation, November 29, 2016.

7. Pope Francis, encyclical *Fratelli Tutti*, nos. 57, 59–60.

8. *Talmud Bavli* (Babylonian Talmud), *Shabbat*, 31a.

9. Pope Francis, Address to All Workers of Mercy in the Jubilee Year, September 3, 2016.

10. Pope Francis, Angelus, July 10, 2016.

11. Pope Francis, Message on the Occasion of the World Meetings of Popular Movements in Modesto, California, February 10, 2017.

12. Pope Francis, Message on the Forty-ninth World Day of Peace, 2016, December 8, 2015.

13. Pope Francis, encyclical *Fratelli Tutti*, nos. 80–82.

14. Pope Francis, Address on the 50th Anniversary of the Foundation of the St. Egidio Community, March 11, 2018.

15. Pope Francis, Angelus, July 17, 2016.

11. Prayer

1. Pope Francis, General Audience, November 15, 2017.
2. Pope Francis, Angelus, July 24, 2016.
3. Pope Francis, Address at the Celebration of Vespers, Tirana, September 21, 2014.
4. Pope Francis, Morning Meditation, March 12, 2015.
5. Pope Francis, Morning Meditation, October 13, 2017.
6. Pope Francis, Morning Meditation, October 13, 2014.
7. Pope Francis, Morning Meditation, October 17, 2017.
8. Pope Francis, Morning Meditation, October 19, 2017.

12. The Challenges

1. Pope Francis, Morning Meditation, October 14, 2016.
2. Pope Francis, encyclical *Laudato Si'*, 96.
3. Pope Francis, apostolic exhortation *Querida Amazonia*, 57.
4. Pope Francis, encyclical *Laudato Si'*, 887.
5. Pope Francis, Morning Meditation, October 19, 2015.
6. Pope Francis, apostolic exhortation *Evangelii Gaudium*, 141.
7. Pope Francis, Angelus, August 7, 2016.
8. Pope Francis, General Audience, October 11, 2017.
9. Pope Francis, Morning Meditation, October 26, 2017.
10. Pope Francis, Angelus, August 18, 2013.
11. Pope Francis, Address to the Bishops Ordained over the Last Year, September 14, 2017.
12. cf. Saint Augustine, *Confessions* vii, 10:16.

13. Conversion

1. Pope Francis, Angelus, February 28, 2016.
2. Pope Francis, Address to Priests, Men and Women Religious, and Seminarians of the Ecclesiastical Provinces of Northern Peru, Saints Carlos and Marcelo Seminary College Trujillo, January 20, 2018.
3. Pope Francis, Message for World Mission Day, 2016, May 15, 2016.
4. Pope Francis, Morning Meditation, October, 24, 2016.
5. Pope Francis, Morning Meditation, October 30, 2017.
6. Pope Francis, Morning Meditation, October 31, 2017.

7. Pope Francis, Angelus, August 21, 2016.

8. Pope Francis, Angelus, August 25, 2013.

9. Pope Francis, Morning Meditation, October 27, 2016.

10. Pope Francis, Morning Meditation, October 29, 2015.

14. *The Kingdom of God*

1. Pope Francis, Morning Meditation, October 30, 2015.

2. Pope Francis, Angelus, August 28, 2016.

3. Pope Francis, apostolic exhortation *Amoris Laetitia*, 183.

4. Pope Francis, Address on World Missionary Day 2015, May 24, 2015.

5. Pope Francis, apostolic exhortation *Evangelii Gaudium*, 48.

6. Pope Francis, apostolic exhortation *Evangelii Gaudium*, 48.

7. Pope Benedict XVI, Address to the Brazilian Bishops in the Cathedral of São Paulo, Brazil, May 11, 2007, 3: *AAS* 99 (2007), 428.

8. Pope Francis, Morning Meditation, November 4, 2014.

9. Pope Francis, Morning Meditation, November 7, 2017.

10. Pope Francis, Homily at the Holy Mass and Canonization of Blessed Mother Teresa of Calcutta, Jubilee for Workers of Mercy and Volunteers, September 4, 2016.

11. Pope Francis, Angelus, September 8, 2013.

15. *Parables of Mercy*

1. Pope Francis, Angelus, September 11, 2016.

2. Pope Francis, General Audience, May 4, 2016.

3. Pope Francis, Homily, Holy Mass, Third Worldwide Priests' Retreat, June 12, 2015.

4. Pope Francis, Homily for the Jubilee of Mercy for Priests, June 3, 2016.

5. Pope Francis, General Audience, April 30, 2016.

6. Pope Francis, Homily, Extraordinary Jubilee of Mercy, Jubilee of Priests, June 3, 2016.

7. Pope Francis, apostolic exhortation *Evangelii Gaudium*, 16.

8. Fifth General Conference of the Latin American and Caribbean Bishops, Aparecida Document, June 29, 2007, no. 548.

9. Fifth General Conference of the Latin American and Caribbean Bishops, Aparecida Document, June 29, 2007, no. 370.

10. Pope Francis, encyclical *Lumen Fidei*, 19.

11. Pope Francis, Message at the Fiftieth World Day of Social Communication, January 24, 2016.

12. Pope Francis, General Audience, May 11, 2016.

16. Parables of Living

1. Pope Francis, Homily on the Occasion of the Two-hundredth Anniversary of the Gendarmeria, September 18, 2016.

2. Pope Francis, Angelus, September 18, 2016.

3. Pope Francis, apostolic exhortation *Amoris Laetitia*, 26.

4. Pope Francis, Address to Participants in the International Conference of the Christian Union of the Business Executives (UNIAPAC), November 17, 2016.

5. Cf. St. Thomas Aquinas, *Catena Aurea: Commentary on the Four Gospels*, vol. 1, Luke 16:8–13.

6. Pope Francis, Morning Meditation, March 16, 2017.

7. Pope Francis, General Audience, May, 18, 2016.

8. Pope Francis, Extraordinary Jubilee of Mercy, Jubilee for Catechists, September 25, 2016.

9. Pope Francis, Message for Lent 2017, October 18, 2016.

10. Pope Francis, apostolic exhortation *Evangelii Gaudium*, 55.

11. Pope Francis, apostolic exhortation *Evangelii Gaudium*, 62.

17. Faith

1. Pope Francis, Message for the World Day of Migrants and Refugees 2017, September 8, 2016.

2. Pope Francis, Address to the Parish Priests of the Diocese of Rome, March 2, 2017.

3. *Catechism of the Catholic Church*, §162.

4. Pope Francis, apostolic exhortation *Evangelii Gaudium*, 160.

5. Pope Francis, apostolic exhortation *Evangelii Gaudium*, 161.

6. Pope Francis, Angelus, October 6, 2013.

7. Pope Francis, Homily, Holy Mass at the Church of the Immaculate Conception, Baku, Azerbaijan, October 2, 2016.

8. Pope Francis, Morning Meditation, November 8, 2016.

9. Pope Francis, Homily, Holy Mass for the Marian Jubilee, October 9, 2016.

10. Pope Francis, General Audience, May 13, 2015.

11. Pope Francis, Homily, Holy Mass on the Occasion of the Thirty-first World Youth Day at Częstochowa, July 28, 2016.

12. Pope Francis, Morning Meditation, November 10, 2016.

13. Pope Francis, Message on the LV World Day of Prayer for Vocations, December 3, 2017.

14. Pope Francis, Morning Meditation, November 17, 2017.

18. The Treasure

1. Pope Francis, Angelus, October 20, 2013.

2. Pope Francis, General Audience, May 25, 2016.

3. Pope Francis, General Audience, June 1, 2016.

4. Pope Francis, General Audience, January 3, 2018.

5. Pope Francis, Address at the Opening of the Pastoral Congress of the Diocese of Rome, June 16, 2016.

6. Cf. Pope Francis, apostolic exhortation *Amoris Laetitia*, 229.

7. Pope Francis, Message for the Thirtieth World Youth Day 2015, January 31, 2015.

8. Cf. Pope Francis, Interview with Young People from Belgium, March 31, 2014.

9. Pope Francis, Message for the Eght-hundredth Anniversary of the Order of the Blessed Virgin Mary of Mercy, December 6, 2017.

10. Cf. Pope Francis, apostolic exhortation *Evangelii Gaudium*, 20.

11. Pope Francis, Morning Meditation, November 17, 2014.

19. Jerusalem

1. Pope Francis, Angelus, November 3, 2013.

2. Pope Francis, Morning Meditation, November 15, 2016.

3. Pope Francis, General Audience, June 18, 2016.

4. Pope Francis, Homily, Holy Mass at the Thirty-third World Youth Day, Palm Sunday, March 25, 2018.

5. Cf. R. Guardini, *The Lord* (Chicago: Henry Regnery Co., 1959), 365.

6. Cf. Pope Francis, apostolic exhortation *Evangelii Gaudium*, 94.

7. Pope Francis, Homily, Holy Saturday, March 31, 2018.

8. Pope Francis, apostolic exhortation *Amoris Laetitia*, 144.

9. Pope Francis, Morning Meditation, November 19, 2015.

10. Pope Francis, Morning Meditation, November 20, 2015.

20. The Authority of Jesus

1. Pope Francis, Angelus, October 22, 2017.

2. Pope Francis, Angelus, November 6, 2016.

3. Pope Francis, Angelus, November 10, 2013.

4. Pope Francis, Homily, Jubilee of Mercy, Jubilee for Prisoners, November 6, 2016.

21. Signs of the Times

1. Pope Francis, Homily, Mikheil Meskhi Stadium, Tbilisi, Georgia, October 1, 2016.

2. Pope Francis, Morning Meditation, November 23, 2015.

3. Pope Francis, Message, Twenty-ninth World Youth Day 2014, January 21, 2014.

4. Pope Francis, Homily, Jubilee of Mercy, Jubilee for Socially Excluded People, November 13, 2016.

5. Pope Francis, Morning Meditation, November 22, 2016.

6. Pope Francis, Homily, Kyaikkasan Ground, Yangon, Myanmar, November 29, 2017.

7. Pope Francis, Morning Meditation, November 24, 2016.

8. Pope Francis, Morning Meditation, November 25, 2016.

22. The Passion of Jesus

1. Pope Francis, apostolic exhortation *Evangelii Gaudium*, 13.

2. Pope Francis, Homily, Holy Mass in Christ the Redeemer Square, Santa Cruz de la Sierra, Bolivia, July 9, 2015.

3. Pope Francis, *Christus Vivit*, 14.

4. Pope Francis, Message for the Forty-seventh World Day of Peace 2014, December 8, 2013.

5. Pope Francis, Message for the Twenty-third World Day of the Sick 2015, December 3, 2014.

6. Pope Francis, encyclical *Lumen Fidei,* 5.

7. *Acta Sanctorum,* Junii, I, 21.

8. Pope Francis, Address to the Parish Priests of the Diocese of Rome, January 16, 2018.

9. Pope Francis, Address to Priests, Religious, and Seminarians, Church of Gethsemane at the foot of the Mount of Olives, Jerusalem, May 26, 2014.

10. Pope Francis, Address to the Bishops of Mexico, Metropolitan Cathedral of the Assumption, Mexico City, February 13, 2016.

23. The Death of Jesus

1. Pope Francis, General Audience, April 6, 2016.

2. Pope Francis, Homily and Opening of the Holy Doors of the Basilica of Santa Maria Major, January 1, 2016.

3. Pope Francis, Homily for the Solemnity of Our Lord Jesus Christ, King of the Universe, November 20, 2016.

4. Pope Francis, General Audience, October 25, 2017.

5. Pope Francis, Homily, Mass at the Conclusion of the Year of Faith, November 24, 2013.

6. Pope Francis, Angelus, November 22, 2015.

7. Pope Francis, Homily, Jubilee for Prisoners, Vatican Basilica, November 6, 2016.

8. Pope Francis, Homily, Mass of Our Lady of Mount Carmel, Lobito Campus, Iquique, January 18, 2018.

9. Pope Francis, Homily, Papal Mass for the Repose of the Souls of the Cardinals and Bishops Who Died Over the Course of the Year, Papal Chapel, November 4, 2016.

24. Resurrection and Ascension

1. Pope Francis, Address to Participants in the General Chapter of the Congregation of the Resurrection of Our Lord Jesus Christ, June 24, 2017.

2. Pope Francis, Angelus, April 2, 2018.

3. Pope Francis, Address at the Meeting with the Bishops of Brazil, Archbishop's House, Rio de Janeiro, July 27, 2013.

4. John Henry Newman, "Letter of January 26, 1833 to his mother," *The Letters and Diaries of John Henry Newman*, vol. III (Oxford: Oxford University Press, 1979), 204.

5. The Aparecida Document provides a synthetic presentation of the deeper reasons behind this phenomenon (cf. no. 225).

6. Cf. also the four points mentioned by Aparecida, no. 226.

7. Pope Francis, Message for the World Day of Vocations 2017, November 27, 2016.

8. Pope Francis, apostolic exhortation *Evangelii Gaudium*, 266.

9. Pope Francis, apostolic exhortation *Christus Vivit*, 155–157.

10. Pope Francis, Address to the Volunteers of the Thirty-fourth World Youth Day in Panama, January 27, 2019.

11. Saint Oscar Romero, Homily, November 6, 1977, in *Monseñor Óscar A. Romero: Su pensamiento*, I-II (San Salvador: Publicaciones Pastorales del Arzobispado, 2000), 312.

12. Pope Francis, Address at the Opening of the Thirty-fourth World Youth Day in Panama, January 24, 2019.

13. Pope Francis, General Audience, May 24, 2017.

14. Pope Francis, Morning Meditation, April 24, 2014.

15. Pope Francis, General Audience, June 18, 2016.

16. Pope Francis, General Audience, April 17, 2013.

Bibliography

VATICAN DOCUMENTS

The texts (homilies, meditations, speeches, adresses, etc.) after the beginning of Pope Francis's pontificate are adapted from:
  http://w2.vatican.va/content/vatican/en.html.

Francis. *Evangelii Gaudium*, apostolic exhortation on the proclamation of the Gospel in today's world (November 24, 2013).

Francis. *Lumen Fidei*, encyclical letter on the faith (June 29, 2013).

Francis. *Laudato Si'*, encyclical letter on care for our common home (May 24, 2015).

Francis. *Amoris Laetitia*, post-synodal apostolic exhortation on love in the family (March 19, 2016).

Francis. *Misericordia et Misera*, apostolic letter at the conclusion of the Extraordinary Jubilee of Mercy (November 20, 2016).

Francis. *Gaudete et Exsultate*, apostolic exhortation on the call to holiness in today's world (March 19, 2018).

Francis. "*Querida Amazonia*," post-synodal exhortation to the People of God and to all persons of good will (February 2, 2020).

Francis. "*Christus Vivit*," post-synodal exhortation to young people and to the entire People of God (March 25, 2019).

Francis. *Fratelli Tutti*, encyclical letter on fraternity and social friendship (October 3, 2020).

John Paul II. *Pastores Dabo Vobis*, post-synodal apostolic exhortation (March 25, 1992).

OTHER SOURCES

Catechism of the Catholic Church. Vatican City, Libreria Editrice Vaticana, 1993. www.vatican.va.

Ignatius of Loyola, *Spiritual Exercises: A Translation and Commentary* by George E. Ganss, SJ. Chicago, IL: Loyola Press, 1992.